Nomadic Theatre

Thinking through Theatre seeks to advance knowledge and understanding of theatre by exploring the questions performance itself is uniquely capable of asking, and by interrogating the ways in which it asks them. The series seeks to problematize the distinction between "making" and "thinking" by stressing their interrelation and by identifying in theatre and performance practices aesthetic and political forms of thought and action.

Thinking through Theatre examines the ways in which theatre is continually rethinking the possibilities of movement, space, action, image, or voice, exploring the logics of creative invention and critical investigation that enable performance to operate as a mode of thought *sui generis*.

Series Editors
Maaike Bleeker (Utrecht University, Netherlands), Adrian Kear (Wimbledon College of Arts, University of the Arts London, UK), Joe Kelleher (University of Roehampton, London, UK) and Heike Roms (University of Exeter, UK)

Thinking Through Theatre
edited by Maaike Bleeker, Adrian Kear, Joe Kelleher and Heike Roms

Forthcoming Titles
In Solitude: The Philosophy of Digital Performance Encounters
Eirini Nedelkopoulou

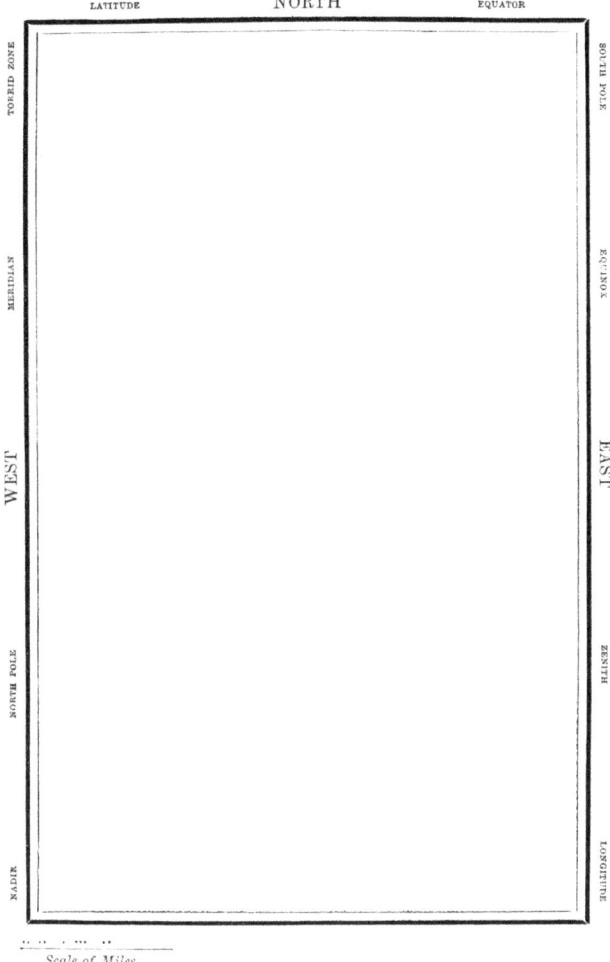

*He had bought a large map
representing the sea,
Without the least vestige of land:
And the crew were much pleased
when they found it to be
A map they could all understand.*

Figure 0.1 Ocean-Chart (The Bellman's Map). Creator unknown, 1874. Source: Lewis Carroll, *The Hunting of the Snark: an Agony in Eight Fits*. New York: Macmillan and Co, 1891.

Nomadic Theatre

Mobilizing Theory and Practice on the European Stage

Liesbeth Groot Nibbelink

methuen | drama
LONDON • NEW YORK • OXFORD • NEW DELHI • SYDNEY

METHUEN DRAMA
Bloomsbury Publishing Plc
50 Bedford Square, London, WC1B 3DP, UK
1385 Broadway, New York, NY 10018, USA

BLOOMSBURY, METHUEN DRAMA and the Methuen Drama logo
are trademarks of Bloomsbury Publishing Plc

First published in Great Britain 2019
This paperback edition published 2020

Copyright © Liesbeth Groot Nibbelink, 2019, 2020

Liesbeth Groot Nibbelink has asserted her right under the Copyright,
Designs and Patents Act, 1988, to be identified as the author of this work.

For legal purposes the Acknowledgments on pp. xi–xii
constitute an extension of this copyright page.

Cover image: *No Man's Land* © Maarten van Haaff

All rights reserved. No part of this publication may be reproduced or transmitted in any form or by any means, electronic or mechanical, including photocopying, recording, or any information storage or retrieval system, without prior permission in writing from the publishers.

Bloomsbury Publishing Plc does not have any control over, or responsibility for, any third-party websites referred to or in this book. All internet addresses given in this book were correct at the time of going to press. The author and publisher regret any inconvenience caused if addresses have changed or sites have ceased to exist, but can accept no responsibility for any such changes.

A catalogue record for this book is available from the British Library.

Library of Congress Control Number: 2019938695

ISBN:	HB:	978-1-350-05103-4
	PB:	978-1-350-17508-2
	ePDF:	978-1-350-05105-8
	eBook:	978-1-350-05104-1

Series: Thinking through Theatre

Typeset by Integra Software Services Pvt. Ltd.,

To find out more about our authors and books visit www.bloomsbury.com
and sign up for our newsletters.

Contents

	List of Figures	x
	Acknowledgments	xi
1	Introduction: Deterritorializing the Stage	1
	Primary Coordinates	1
	On the Move	4
	Theatre, Technology, Mobility	5
	A Note on Participation	7
	Theatre, Performance, Movement	9
	Deterritorialization	11
	Pause	12
	Deleuze's Nomads	13
	Nomadic Theatre: A Concept, a Toolbox	15
	Theory as Tool: How to Do Things with Deleuze?	19
	Spatial Dramaturgy	21
	Points Are Relays on a Trajectory: Chapter Overview	24
	Playgrounding	28
2	Encounter: Meeting Multiplicity in Dries Verhoeven's *No Man's Land*	31
	Of Horses and Wasps	31
	The Rhythms of a Smooth Stage	33
	Mind the Gap	36
	Performance Installations	37
	Staging the Spectator	39
	Walking with Abderraghman	41
	Triads and Constellations	44
	A Problem of Referentiality	46
	This Is Not My Voice: A Problem of Referentiality, Part 2	47
	Fractured Reciprocity	51
	Building Performance	53
	Expanding Spectatorship	56

3	Displacement: The Situated Pathways of Rimini Protokoll	59
	Urban Moves	59
	The City as Stage	62
	Theatre Goes Global	67
	The Production of Space	68
	Performing Locality	70
	Navigating Representation	73
	Outsourced Performance	77
	Parallax	80
4	Cartographies: *Trail Tracking* and Map-Making as Staging Strategy	85
	You Are Here	85
	Cartography: Fifth Principle of the Rhizome	87
	The Theatre of Cartography	90
	Performing Cartography	92
	Charting the Virtual	97
	Navigational Spaces	99
	Personal Velocity	101
	Material Maps	105
	Thinking Subjectivity Through Space: Politics of Location	107
	Witnessed Presence	109
	The Cartography of Theatre	112
5	Diagrams: Staging Proximity in Ontroerend Goed's *The Smile Off Your Face*	115
	A Nomad Does Not Necessarily Move	115
	A Wheelchair's Thresholds	118
	Pleats of Proximity	120
	Event/Situation	122
	Into the Laboratory	125
	Thinking Through the Diagram	126
	The Grid of Capital	128
	Distributions of the Sensible	132
	A Spectator in the Dark	135
	The Dramaturgy of Proximity	137
	A Theatre of Folds	139

6	Architextures: The Rhizomatic Gameboards of Signa's	
	The Ruby Town Oracle	141
	Drifting/Dwelling	141
	Borderzones	144
	Narrative Architecture and Environmental Storytelling	148
	Architectural Performances	151
	Evocative Spaces	153
	Procedural Passageways	157
	Playing at the Limits	159
	The Entirety of the Map	161
	Tissue, Traces, Tracks	164
7	Distributed Performance: Epilogue	167
	Pop-up Stores	167
	Trajectories of the Stage	168
	Folds of Spectating	170
	Lived Space and Diffractive Reading	173
	Staging Connections	175
	Procedural Dramaturgy/When Attitude Becomes Form	176
	Thinking Through Practice	178
	Thresholds of the Imagination	181
Notes		183
Bibliography		193
Index		206

List of Figures

0.1 Ocean-Chart (The Bellman's Map). Creator unknown, 1874.	iii
2.1 Opening scene of Dries Verhoeven's *No Man's Land* in Athens, 2014.	36
2.2 Leaving the station, in *No Man's Land* by Dries Verhoeven, Utrecht 2013.	41
2.3 Closing scene of *No Man's Land* by Dries Verhoeven, Utrecht 2013.	53
3.1 The call-center in Calcutta, in Rimini Protokoll's *Call Cutta*.	63
3.2 On the road in Berlin, in *Call Cutta* by Rimini Protokoll.	64
4.1 A spectator wandering around in the railway museum in Utrecht, in Dries Verhoeven's *Trail Tracking*, 2005.	93
4.2 Closing scene of *Trail Tracking* by Dries Verhoeven, Utrecht 2005.	111
5.1 Closing scene in Ontroerend Goed's *The Smile Off Your Face*.	139
6.1 A military officer guarding the Temporary Autonomous Zone, in Signa's *Die Erscheinungen der Martha Rubin—The Ruby Town Oracle*.	142
6.2 Signa Köstler, as the oracle Martha Rubin, in Signa's *Die Erscheinungen der Martha Rubin—The Ruby Town Oracle*.	156
6.3 Peepshow scene in *Die Erscheinungen der Martha Rubin – The Ruby Town Oracle* by Signa.	157

Acknowledgments

There are many things that I like in the work of Gilles Deleuze, but my number one favorite is his stance that thinking is a creative act. This is why I am deeply grateful to the series editors Maaike Bleeker, Adrian Kear, Joe Kelleher, and Heike Roms, for inviting *Nomadic Theatre* into their series *Thinking Through Theatre*. I could not have envisioned a better context for this book. Even though thinking may be an act of creation, it does not mean, of course, that thoughts are tame creatures. Over the years of undertaking this research, a small note was pinned next to my desk, with a quote by Christopher Bollas: "I often find that although I am working on an idea without knowing exactly what it is I think, I am engaged in thinking an idea struggling to have me think it" (found in Bal 2002, 97). I feel I have been tremendously lucky to have encountered two people who seemed to understand what I was doing, even if I was thoroughly entangled in ideas and intuitive thoughts struggling to have me think them. Therefore I thank Maaike Bleeker and Nanna Verhoeff, for their confidence and support. Inspired by their critical and creative inquiries and suggestions, I have had the wonderful opportunity to forge my own personal bond between thinking and creation, between theory and practice. I never could have envisioned this project, had I not encountered Maaike, in person and in her work, who opened my eyes to other ways of academic writing and thinking than I was familiar with. And it would have turned into a mess, had not Nanna sharpened my pen both conceptually and methodologically.

There are many people and organizations who made this project possible. I would like to thank the theatre-makers, whose work inspired this book in the first place: Rimini Protokoll, Ontroerend Goed, Studio Dries Verhoeven and Signa. I thank in particular Dries Verhoeven, Alexander Devriendt, and Signa and Arthur Köstler for taking time to discuss their work with me. I thank you and the photographers who documented your work for the kind permission to reproduce some of these photographs in this book. I am also grateful to those who gave me the opportunity to share some parts of my work-in-progress with a wider audience. Smaller parts of Chapter 4 have appeared in "Sporen zoeken. Over de 'politics of location' in Sporenonderzoek van Dries Verhoeven," in *Theater Topics 4: Concepten en objecten*, edited by Maaike Bleeker, Lucia van Heteren, Chiel Kattenbelt, and Rob van der Zalm (Amsterdam: Amsterdam University Press 2009, 26–37). I published an article on an earlier phase of my thinking about *The Smile Off Your Face* in "Radical Intimacy: Ontroerend Goed meets The Emancipated Spectator," *Contemporary Theatre Review* 22 (3) (2012): 412–20. First reflections on Signa's performance appeared in "The Signa Store: Nomadic Manoeuvres in Ruby Town," *Performance Research* 17 (3) (2012): 63–7.

I am grateful to the Media and Culture Studies Department and the ICON Media and Performance research group of Utrecht University for supporting and facilitating part of this research. Furthermore, I tremendously appreciated the possibility to test and exchange ideas in the very open atmosphere of the IFTR research group on Intermediality in Theatre and Performance, and at the media and performance seminars at Utrecht University. I have been inspired by many talks with close colleagues at the Media and Culture Studies Department and with my cherished co-travelers of Platform-Scenography. I would like to mention specifically a few fellow scholars, aka friends, aka "partners in crime." Although we all take individual pathways, it gives me much pleasure and strength to know we are on the same track: Sigrid Merx, Marijn de Langen, Laura Karreman, Isis Germano, and Konstantina Georgelou. Lastly I thank my close friends and family, without whose loving support I could not have written this book.

1

Introduction

Deterritorializing the Stage

Primary Coordinates

In 2005, the German performers' collective Rimini Protokoll presented *Call Cutta*, a remarkable example of mobile phone theatre. In this ambulatory performance, a single spectator navigates the streets of Berlin's Kreuzberg district, guided by a call-center employee in Calcutta, India, who provides directions over the phone. The mobile phone connects the two places of performance, and interactively engages a single performer and a single spectator in a conversation about the local particularities at both ends of the line. *Call Cutta* is presented as theatre, it surely can be considered as such—as both the performer and the spectator are joined in a situation that is distinctively staged—yet it radically plays with the conventions of theatre. In *Call Cutta*, spectators have become *mobile*; they have left their traditional seat in the (darkened) auditorium and instead traverse the city. They are also mobilized out of the larger audience: they are singled out and start and finish the performance one by one. Subsequently, not only the spectators have become mobile; the theatre space is in motion as well. The theatre space loses the architectural coherence usually conferred by physical buildings or clearly designated areas, and, seen from the perspective of the spectator in Berlin, starts to *move along* with the spectator. Finally, the stage is also in motion. Instead of spectators looking at a stage, one may wonder: where exactly *is* this stage? The stage seems to be smashed to pieces—split up between a "here," an "over there," and a "Hertzian space" in-between.[1] In an essay on *Call Cutta*, theatre scholar and director Heiner Goebbels observes that, actually, one did not *see* this performance: there were no performers on a stage, no protagonists to identify with; actually there was no one to be seen (2007, 118). This is rather remarkable, given the etymology of the word "theatre": a place for seeing or viewing (Freshwater 2009, 5). The performer has left the center, Goebbels observes; in fact the center of the stage is empty, which makes room for the spectator as a subject of communication. Rimini

Protokoll removes the focus on (the presence of) the actor, without occupying the center with something else—for instance, the ego of the artist—and redirects attention to how the spectator is perceptively engaged with this performance (2007, 123–4). All in all, an ambulatory performance like *Call Cutta* mobilizes the codes, conventions, and boundaries of the stage, and therefore *deterritorializes* the stage.

Call Cutta is not the only performance in which this disruption of conventional territories in the theatre can be seen at work. Over the last decade, there seems to have been an increasing number of performances that literally attempt to mobilize the spectator and rethink the conditions of the stage.[2] Whether the urban games of Blast Theory or Gob Squad, the video walks by Janet Cardiff and George Bures Miller, promenade performances by Lone Twin, Benjamin Vandewalle or Wrights & Sites, Ligna's radio ballets, Lundahl & Seitl's headphone theatre, Christine de Smedt's social choreographies, or Female Economy's urban safaris, to name but a few, they all twist the relationships between performers, spectators, and space.[3] Spectators traverse the city by bike; they are driven around in wheelchairs or cars, travel by motorbikes or in mini-vans, or drift across labyrinthine performance installations. Performers forsake their usual center-stage position and turn into guides, tour operators, or voices on an audiotape. Theatre spaces are produced in the appointment of temporary and changing coordinates; contrary to the usual conflation with a theatre building, they emerge in and as the *process* of performance and as temporary *situations*.

In this book, I examine how ambulatory performances and performative installations stage such movements and in turn mobilize the stage. Through a detailed analysis of theatre performances by leading European artists and companies such as Rimini Protokoll, Dries Verhoeven, Ontroerend Goed, and Signa, this books demonstrates how mobile performances radically rethink the conditions of the stage and alter our understanding of spectatorship. These artists create new and exciting dramaturgical strategies, by playing with the (dis)placement of performers, the mobilization of spectators, and the movements of theatre spaces. This way of theatre-making profoundly impacts our modes of theorizing and analyzing performance. Such work has been studied in terms of participatory, interactive, or immersive theatre (Frieze 2016; Alston 2016; Hill and Paris 2014; Machon 2013; White 2013; Deck and Sieburg 2008), but these terms are not central to my analysis. *Nomadic Theatre* instead focuses on how we might look at ambulatory performances and performative installations from a process-based perspective, and with a genuine commitment to movement, mobility, and changeability. Mobile theatre performances, on the one hand, play with conventions and solidified forms of theatre, while on the other they self-reflexively point to the very thing theatre is made of, as they continuously reveal the theatre as a live and transitory event. On top of this, that which initially appears as physical movement only, on closer inspection involves theoretical movement as well. Mobile theatre puts our thoughts in motion, inviting us to examine how movement and mobility effect and implicate the theatre, how these forms address and position spectators in performance, how mobility is staged and effects the stage, and why some theatre practitioners prefer these mobile forms of theatre-making.

Both these physical and theoretical movements are examined through a specific, newly invented concept: *nomadic theatre*. From the outset, I wish to emphasize that I do not use the term to designate a genre. I do not seek to label or categorize a set of performances—this would create a form of arrest that does not do justice to either the process-character of these events, or to the movements that precisely mobilize thought. Instead, I use this concept to deploy a mode of thinking that attempts to be as mobile and flexible as the phenomena it wishes to describe. By exploring the potential of nomadic theatre as an analytical concept, I navigate through a field without demarcating that field. While analyzing performances and their dramaturgical strategies, I traverse a field that refuses to become territory, with three flexible coordinates as my guides: performer, spectator, and space. I follow the movements and temporary occupations of this threefold constellation, which is also a way of thinking through practice and of mobilizing theory.

The term "nomadic theatre" is occasionally used to identify travelling theatre troupes or street theatre events, yet as an analytical concept it does not yet exist. Nomadic theatre is a product of invention and creation, through which I stage an encounter between the theatre and the nomadic, mainly as has been theorized by Gilles Deleuze, partly in collaboration with Félix Guattari. This study explores the potential of nomadic theatre, by putting the concept to work in a milieu of European theatre performances, Deleuze and Guattari's nomadology, and related insights derived from disciplines as diverse as media theory, urban theory, cartography, architecture, and game theory. Following Deleuze and Guattari's take on philosophical concepts, concepts themselves are creative, in the sense that they produce events. Events cannot be captured; they can only be neared. Similarly, a quasi-philosophical concept like nomadic theatre, which at some points fundamentally differs from a philosophical concept, can only be approached by a process of bordering and encircling. This is precisely what this introduction does: it borders and circles around the concept of nomadic theatre, in relation to its object, and through these approximations both object and concept grow in force and volume.

The introduction is a rather lengthy one, since nomadic theatre cuts across a wide range of domains, debates, and disciplines. Firstly, I connect mobile theatre and performance to larger developments in society and to specific debates in theatre and performance studies—contexts that are relevant to the analysis of dramaturgical strategies later on in this book. Secondly, I provide an introduction to (Deleuzian) nomadology, and to the concept of nomadic theatre. Finally, I describe and reflect on the methodology of concept-based performance analysis and, closely connected to this, briefly elaborate on the topic of spatial dramaturgy. Dispersed through this trajectory are some considerations regarding central choices and arguments made in this book.

On the Move

Life in the twenty-first century is increasingly marked by the mobility of people, information, technologies, goods, and services. We live in a world that seems constantly on the move, which also creates tensions between the global and the local, or between the sedentary and those who (are forced to) move (Hopkins and Solga 2015). In Europe, migration is one of the most decisive and dividing issues on the political agenda of nation states. Contemporary theatre and performance, evolving in close parallel to societal developments, expose and respond to this "mobile turn" in society (Cresswell and Merriman 2011).[4] Many European theatre-makers have critically addressed issues as diverse as political or economic migration, border politics and surveillance tactics, fluid citizenship and the globalization of labor, the increasing numbers of refugees and the hardening of asylum procedures, or the significant role that mobile communication technologies play in all this.

In *Mobilities* (2007), sociologist John Urry argues that during the last decades, the concept of mobility began to move beyond referring purely to physical or vehicular mobility, and now equally involves other mobility systems that deal with the transport and distribution of information, services, money, goods, technologies, and with virtual and imaginary travels. Taking theatre's capacity to actively mirror and respond to developments in society into account, it is not a surprise that theatre increasingly incorporates such hybrid mobility systems *and* reflects on how these systems change and impact societal processes and cultural experience. This is also observed by Fiona Wilkie, in *Performance, Transport and Mobility: Making Passage* (2015a). Whereas Wilkie focuses on states of transit and various types of travel and transport (on foot, by train, or by boat, for instance), I am interested instead in movement, mobility, flexibility, and changeability as recurring tropes in theatre and performance, in parallel to societal developments. Our lifeworld changes rapidly: we are witness to shifting centers of power, both politically and economically; to large-scale environmental crises and climate change; to societies struggling with an increasing heterogeneity of ethnic identities. In response to these shifts and changes, one can observe another "movement," that is, the rise of nationalism, populism, and post-secularism, and, often connected to this, stringent border politics, the re-entrance of dualistic thinking (us vs. them), and the (over)articulation of difference. These are wide-spread, world-spanning developments, yet they certainly characterize the current political and societal climate in Europe as well. How to cope with such complex issues is a concern of many contemporary theatre artists. The works discussed in this book also relate to these questions, either directly or indirectly. These performances certainly do not attempt to change the world directly, nor do they naively try "to make the world a better place." Instead they do what theatre is good at, in my view fulfilling a pivotal role in contemporary society: they provide a "thinking arena" or *denkpiste*, as the Flemish say it so aptly, a space for reflection and engagement. They carve out time to explore, elaborate, and experiment with these issues and, vitally, they create situations in which we can actually engage with and (physically) experience complex and ambiguous phenomena, allowing us to (re)connect with themes and topics that often seem too large to handle.

Theatre, Technology, Mobility

Next to this large-scale societal context, mobile, digital technologies inflect the ways in which theatre is made, composed, and practiced. What is more, the performances discussed in this book are part of a larger development in which digital equipment such as smart phones, tracking devices, GPS-based software, and other locative media fuse with artistic and cultural practice. Mobile media and pervasive computing not only enter the theatre but are equally put to use in urban games, museums, city tours, Layar-based artworks, heritage walks, biomapping, environmental storytelling, architectural apps, or networked (music) performances (Farman 2014, 2012; Verhoeff 2012; Doruff 2009). These examples can all be understood as cultural expressions of a world "on the move" *and* as practices that profoundly change our concepts of space, time, or reality. These practices work with layered or mixed realities, in which the physical environment is augmented by digital space, or they surpass physical distance by web-based connectivity. Both contemporary theatre and performance then, as well as these twin practices, seem to be invaded by what John Urry terms a "mobilities paradigm," where space is increasingly charged with temporality and time gets infused with spatiality; where distance is countered by simultaneity, synchronicity, or co-presence, and daily life is increasingly spent in "movement-space" (2007, 44–7).

Remarkably, while these space-time reconfigurations define the spatiotemporal identity of the twenty-first-century world, they equally emerge as the distinctive properties of (mobile) theatre performances. Mobility in performance foregrounds the *spatiality* of performer–spectator relationships: performers and spectators start to conjoin with scale, gauged between the extremely close, the far distance, and an occasional disappearance. These configurations similarly emphasize the *temporality* and *situationality* of theatre spaces. We can see this at work in *Call Cutta*, but also in *No Man's Land* (2008–14), a promenade performance by Dutch director Dries Verhoeven, presented in a range of major European cities, each time slightly adapted to local circumstances. *No Man's Land* distributes the spectators over twenty slightly different trajectories; each track exhibits a single spectator following a migrant on a walk through the city. The spectator wears headphones and listens to an audio track that provides a commentary on both the walk and the encounter. Both *Call Cutta* and *No Man's Land* redefine the spatio-temporal conditions of the stage. In *Call Cutta*, the stage is constituted through co-presence, whereas *No Man's Land* operates through simultaneity: the stage is distributed over the urban environment and resurfaces as a series of synchronous trajectories. Both performances reconceptualize the notion of (aesthetic) distance, and challenge the idea that a theatre performance always takes place in a fixed location. They both enquire, each in their own way, into what exactly constitutes the shared space that is so characteristic of theatre—a significant question that becomes dramaturgically active as well (see Chapters 2 and 3).

Not all the cases discussed in this study use mobile or digital technology, but these performances seem equally scripted by digital culture, even if distinctively analogue. They work, for instance, through interactivity, connectivity, changeability, and co-creation, key terms that also define digital and participatory culture (Bay-Cheng et al. 2010; Lister et al. 2009; Van den Boomen et al. 2009). This pertains in particular to some of the one-to-one performances I will discuss, performances in which one spectator encounters one performer. Both Ontroerend Goed's *The Smile Off Your Face* (2006–present[5]) and Dries Verhoeven's *Trail Tracking* (2005) draw on spectators' personal memories and sensorial perceptions. They rely on user-generated content and personal customization, which also characterize digital, participatory technology, social media platforms, and other expressions of algorithmic culture. When theatre and performance start using similar formats and strategies, we might understand this as a form of *cultural transcoding*, referring to situations in which computer-based processes are translated to other realms of cultural experience (Manovich 2001).

One-to-one communication is perhaps hardly noteworthy in relation to city tours or serious games, yet in comparison to the above mentioned twin practices, isolating or singling out the spectator in the theatre is quite a remarkable gesture, as it mobilizes the very notion of audience. The audience, or the *public*, throughout theatre history has been regarded as representative of the society at large; the audience embodies a community that mirrors a wider (political, democratic) community (Lehmann 2006; cf. Rancière 2009). So what remains of the public when spectators no longer sit *next* to each other, in a group, but are singled out, and asked to enter or leave the theatre *after* each other? This question of course not only involves theatre conventions, but further relates the mobility of the spectator to the much larger question of how these theatre performances position relationships between performance and the spectator, and between the theatre and society at large. Taking the mobile spectator as a starting point, then, ultimately leads to questions of theatrical engagement, an issue that is also on Andy Lavender's agenda, in *Performance in the Twenty-First Century: Theatres of Engagement* (2016). It is not a coincidence that he discusses similar theatre-makers and companies and, amongst others, the work of Rimini Protokoll, Dries Verhoeven, and Ontroerend Goed, who are well-known in Europe for their critical inquiries and creative strategies for audience engagement. Lavender explicitly chooses a broad-spectrum approach to societal and political engagement, asking what happened in theatre after postmodernism, whereas this book opts for a much more *spatially* oriented approach to the topic, and above all provides a specific methodology for analyzing mobile forms of theatre-making, and a pathway for thinking through practice.

A Note on Participation

Theatre's embeddedness in mobile, digital culture and the changing qualities of the stage alter the "modes of spectating" through which spectators engage with performance (Oddey and White 2009). The works discussed here can be qualified as participatory or interactive performances but these are not the terms that I am interested in, however strange this may seem, so a few clarifications are to be made. I agree with some game studies scholars that participation is to be preferred above interactivity. The argument here, to put it (too) boldly, is that interactivity promises a mutual two-way stream of influence, which is hardly ever the case—certainly not in my case studies—and "mutated" forms of interactivity are better seen as a subset of participation.[6] I regard the relation between performers and spectators as a co-constructive, yet fundamentally asymmetric relationship: performers carry out or represent a partially pre-designed structure, whereas the spectators "merely" participate in the execution of this design. Due to the fact that spectators are performatively engaged in these structures or compositions, they are often referred to as performers, or actors, or spect-actors—a term coined by Augusto Boal (Babbage 2004, 41–2)—or occasionally as characters. These spectators are adjectively marked as *active* spectators, in order to distinguish this co-creative position from the "passive" onlooker or voyeur in the (darkened) auditorium. I agree with Rancière (2009) that spectators in conventional set-ups are by no means more or less active than the mobile spectators who travel through these pages. However, labeling mobile spectators as participants does not solve the problem of distinguishing active from passive spectators. As soon as one explores such terms more closely, one gets entangled in a feedback-loop, because spectators in whatever theatrical constellation are always participants in the event; they are always actively engaged, by way of observing, meaning-making, memorizing, and as such, they are always co-producers of the performance event (cf. Frieze 2016; Alston 2016). My point of departure here is the mobile spectator, who in my account remains a spectator, despite remarkable shifts and movements in spectatorship. In addition, I value the performances discussed here precisely for setting this feedback-loop to work, as they self-referentially emphasize qualities of theatre that are always there but do not always rise to the surface.

Participation has also been a trending topic in fine arts during recent decades, indicative of a social turn in the arts (Bishop 2012, 2006b), where it appears alongside conversational art (Kester 2004), New Institutionalism in curating, and *relational art*, a term with which curator Nicolas Bourriaud describes art projects that create temporary communities and open environments as set-ups for intersubjective relations (Bourriaud 1998/2002). Both Bishop and Bourriaud connect these art projects to their imbrication within advanced global capitalism, and to the shift from a goods- to a service-based economy. They refer, for example, to do-it-yourself principles (DIY), both as a token of commodification and as an artistic model (Bishop 2004, 54), which comes quite close to my way of positing personal customization as a slightly uncomfortable, yet also intriguing, hybrid of art and contemporary consumer society (see Chapter 3). Interestingly, whereas one-to-one performances explore spectatorial engagement through the deterritorialization of the collective audience, Bourriaud's relational art abandons the traditional one-to-one relationship between the viewer and the artwork, in order to establish a sense of (democratic) community. Rancière (2009) would certainly disagree with these communitarian assumptions, and so does art critic and scholar Claire Bishop, in various essays and in her book *Artificial Hells* (2012). Her main point of critique is that Bourriaud sees all relational art as democratic artworks, yet relational works are not democratic by default. Drawing on Chantal Mouffe and Ernesto Laclau, Bishop grounds democracy in antagonism, and argues that relational artworks should draw on dissensus—definitely a Rancièrian take on the subject—as a way of sincerely investigating the *quality* of relations and the way viewers are addressed by the artwork (2004, 78). Next she argues that social artworks should still be evaluated in terms of art and not (only) valued for their social or ethical accomplishments (2012, 13–26). In line with Bishop, I do not discuss the performances in terms of their social achievements. I am instead interested in how movement and mobility are staged and generate new dramaturgical strategies.

Theatre, Performance, Movement

Next to societal developments, the works discussed in this book also relate to specific developments in theatre and performance studies. Through their focus on process and situation, these performances expose a particular subset of postdramatic theatre, as described by the German theatre scholar Hans-Thies Lehmann, namely the "event/situation" (2006, 104–7). In *Postdramatic Theatre* (1999/2006), Lehmann observes a shift from a dramatic toward a postdramatic aesthetic architecture taking place on the European stage since approximately the 1970s. Dramatic theatre is the storehouse of theatre conventions: it positions theatre as the staging of plays, deals with mimesis and representation, and seeks to create illusionary worlds on the stage; dramatic theatre is based on the primacy of the text and organized through hierarchical principles of *logos* and (goal-centered) *telos*, and hence is grounded in logocentrism. In postdramatic theatre, the text is deterritorialized and becomes equally autonomous as the other constitutive elements of theatre: space, time, bodies. Postdramatic theatre follows the order of a landscape and uses non-hierarchical composition principles such as simultaneity, montage, juxtaposition, seriality, and polyvocality (Lehmann 1997). Postdramatic theatre increasingly incorporates qualities that in the 1960s–1980s were attributed to performance art; Lehmann remarks that in postdramatic theatre, the focus has shifted from representation to presence, from work to process, from internal to external communication, from staged illusionary worlds toward the performance as a live event, which explicitly addresses the relationship between the stage and the audience (cf. Lehmann 2006, 85–107; Carlson 2004). On the postdramatic stage, the terms "theatre" and "performance" are not that distinct anymore. Therefore I use these terms together, often as equivalents, as contemporary practice renders the distinction obsolete.

Lehmann's study points to the need for adequate analytical tools and terms with which theatre-as-process can be studied in more detail, other than through negation.[7] Some theatre and performance scholars do account for the theatre as a transformational process, but their agenda is somewhat different, as they concentrate for instance on the actor (Pavis 2003), on transformations (Fischer-Lichte 2004/2008),[8] or on technological histories (Salter 2010). I focus instead on the mobile, threefold constellation of performers, spectators, *and* spaces, which requires a much more spatially oriented analysis, and a more intense alliance with movement. To these ends, Deleuze provides a fruitful starting point.

Deleuze is no stranger in the field of performance studies; quite a few publications in the field refer to his work. In the introduction to *Deleuze and Performance* (2009), however, editor Laura Cull remarks that while performance (studies) and Deleuze share a profound interest in processes, relations, movement, and variation, the field has been relatively slow to import Deleuze's thoughts (3–4). Deleuze did not write much on theatre; his essay on the Italian avant-gardist director Carmelo Bene is the most explicit exception (Deleuze 1979/1997).[9] Regarding *movement* in/and the arts, Deleuze is much more known for relating movement to film.[10] However, Deleuze occasionally links movement to theatre, when alluding to the perpetual variation inherent in any theatre performance, which in the case of Carmelo Bene becomes a radical staging strategy. Movement, then, is closely aligned with the idea of non-repeatable and non-representational immediacy—which partly echoes the 1960s discourse on performance art, to which postdramatic theatre is also indebted. Remarkably, movement also bridges theatre and the act of thinking. In *Difference and Repetition* (1968/2004a), Deleuze qualifies the work of Nietzsche and Kierkegaard as a "*theatre* within philosophy" (my emphasis), as their writings carry out "immediate acts" that produce "within the work a movement capable of affecting the mind outside of all representation; it is a question of making movement itself a work ... of inventing vibrations, rotations, whirlings, gravitations, dances or leaps which directly touch the mind" (2004a, 9).

Such vibrations and rotations come close to Deleuze's view on the nomadic. It is tempting to equate nomadism with physical movement and displacement. In *Dramaturgy and Performance* (2008), for instance, Cathy Turner and Synne Behrndt shortly mention the "nomadic dramaturgy" of performances that take the form of journeys (197); in his essay "Audio Theatre," Christopher Balme relates nomadism to the use of mobile media in ambulatory performances (in Chapple and Kattenbelt 2006, 119). However, Deleuze's nomadology offers a slightly different orientation. "It is false to define the nomad by movement," write Deleuze and Guattari in *A Thousand Plateaus: Capitalism and Schizophrenia* (1980/2004, 420). According to them, it is not movement that distinguishes the nomad, but speed. In a

Deleuzian universe, speed relates to continuous deferral and differentiation, to intensities and lines of flight—which can be understood as the whirlings and leaps of the mind referred to above—and to *deterritorialization:* the destabilization or undoing of territories. Deterritorialization is a very helpful concept for introducing Deleuze and Guattari's nomadology, and the concept is also key to the concept of nomadic theatre.

Deterritorialization

Deterritorialization concerns the (temporary) occupation, displacement, or disturbance of territories. It engages acts that capture, change, or escape the codes or laws of a system and relates to strategies that render territory into a state of continuous variation (Deleuze 1973/2004b). These processes can also be seen at work in performance, in which the urban environment, for instance, partly occupies the theatre space, and performance in turn nests within and captures the codes of everyday life in the city.

Staging a performance in urban space produces a range of such deterritorializations: the city becomes a stage, where performance and the everyday life constitute mutual interpretative frameworks; the public environment interferes with the private encounter, and so on. We may also say then, that both the stage and the urban environment *re*territorialize each other, as they become functions in each other's system. In their respective essays on these Deleuzian terms, both Ronald Bogue (1997) and Stuart Elden (2006) point out that deterritorialization cannot be separated from reterritorialization, as they are always co-existent. Ronald Bogue describes the process of de- and reterritorialization as respectively "the detachment or unfixing of elements and their reorganization within new assemblages" (1997, 475). Reterritorialization has nothing to do with a return to a previous situation, a going back to "the same." Nor does it involve the establishment of a new territory, although in daily reality, we see only relative forms of de- and reterritorialization. Through deterritorialization, elements are given greater autonomy; through reterritorialization, components acquire new functions within newly created fields (1997). Reterritorialization is, similarly to deterritorialization, involved with acts of (temporary) occupation, but is also related to the distribution or transportation of parts or elements of a system onto another system. In my case studies, similar patterns are active. In *Call Cutta* for instance, the stage is deterritorialized, as it has no center or fixed location: the stage "happens" simultaneously in Berlin, Calcutta, and in-between. Concurrently, global and digital mobility reterritorialize the theatre: through the mobile phone, the stage is distributed over several locations and resurfaces on three different platforms across the globe.

Reviewer Peter Michalzik remarks that "[t]he theatre of Rimini Protokoll does not set up an opposition between the stage and the audience, but integrates the two spheres in ever changing experimental set-ups" (2006). All the works discussed collapse the distinction between the stage and the auditorium; instead these territories become laboratories, caught up in a process of continuous variation. Although employing rather different staging strategies, they all remove the actor from the usual position at center-stage. The performer is no longer the center of attention, and somehow the spectator occupies the stage as well. I write "somehow" because the spectator has a complex relationship with the stage. A stage, in whatever material condition, comes into being because there is someone who notices what is being presented on stage. When this spectator is present on the stage as well, this by definition creates an unstable situation, a multiperspectival cubism, in which the spectator is both participant and reflexive observer at the same time. One could, of course, abandon the notion of the stage altogether, but then we would abandon theatre, in my opinion. Instead, I propose that it is more productive to follow the workings of territory within these patterns of deterritorialization. The spectator on the stage deterritorializes the stage from within, and, in turn, the stage reterritorializes on the spectator, as the stage puts the activities of the spectator in the spotlight, and exposes how spectatorship is always being staged. This is why the mobile spectator is a powerful deterritorializing force and, consequently, often the starting point for my enquiries.

Pause

The nomad goes from point to point, observe Deleuze and Guattari. These points are relays on a trajectory: temporary places of condensation that are "reached only in order to be left behind" (Deleuze and Guattari 2004, 419). So, at *this* relay: what have I assembled so far? We have come across forms of movement and mobility in the theatre, corresponding to a larger mobile turn in society. More concrete: mobile performers and spectators produce mobile theatre spaces, and deterritorialize the stage. More abstract: these movements relate to Deleuze's nomadic thought and to the concept of nomadic theatre. Moving sideways: movement unfolds in space and time. Zooming in on space: theatre requires space, as it always takes place somewhere. Theatre always takes place. It happens, and it "takes a place." Moving sideways again: to take a place involves acts of de- and reterritorialization. My goal is to examine patterns of de- and reterritorialization through the concept of nomadic theatre. In order to flesh out that concept, I will look further into Deleuze and Guattari's nomadology—an encounter that is already on its way.

Deleuze's Nomads

The nomadic intensely allies with processes of de- and reterritorialization, but what exactly defines the nomadic, according to Deleuze? Deleuze is not a philosopher who provides clear-cut descriptions, but rather puts a term or concept to work in a variety of contexts, demonstrating rather than explaining what a concept is. Since in Deleuze's rhizomatic universe we can start anywhere, let's start with a spatial nomad, the stereotypical nomad in fact, the one that is often imagined as randomly roaming the desert. It is worth emphasizing, though, that one of the first nomads to roam Deleuze's work is a philosopher, and nomadic troupes that rove the steppes, which appear in Deleuze and Guattari's extensive chapter on nomadology in *A Thousand Plateaus*, only enter halfway through the chapter.

In daily life, the word "nomad" quite often conjures up associations with a rootless wandering of rambling vagabonds, and is rather easily translated into "city-nomads" when referring to the urban homeless. For Deleuze and Guattari, however, the heart of the matter lies elsewhere. When Deleuze and Guattari refer to nomadic tribes, they point to a particular *attitude* that lies underneath this wandering, a specific mode of relating to the ground on which one moves. For the nomad, the ground is a surface for movement, not a territory as it is for the sedentary (2004, 421; Patton 2010, 37). By opposing nomadism to the sedentary, Deleuze and Guattari draw out two different types of behavior, two diverging ways of doing and approaching things. To the nomad, ground is not a territory; when conceived of as a surface, ground has no borders. At the most, a nomad temporarily occupies a place, takes a place, yet this is a temporary hold—a staying in order to leave. To the sedentary, ground provides the foundation for building a house; ground is something to settle on (Deleuze and Guattari 2004, 419–22). Along with the sedentary, borders emerge, as well as property, and ownership, and in their slipstream so do inclusions and exclusions, inside/outside divisions, in sum: territories.

When observing the world in terms of territory, we cannot but notice that by far the largest portion of the (life)world is organized into territories, whether divided into national borders, territorial waters, parcels and premises, parks, pavements, or pigeon holes. A nomadic relationship with ground is the exception rather than the rule. More accurately: the nomadic *is* the exception to the rule, the counter-force to order, regulation, legislation, to conceptions of normality, standardization, or convention. The nomadic, therefore, is deeply political, hence the many references to resistance, disruption, dis-settlement, and deregulation, terms by which Deleuze and Guattari posit the nomad against the State. The State is the territorial force, and this of course does not only pertain to geographically defined areas but also to economics and finance, political institutions, science, sexuality, educational systems, or any other field in which certain ways of thinking and doing strongly dominate over others. The nomad destabilizes the seemingly self-evident nature of the State, through deterritorialization. Deterritorialization is not the nomad's intention, it is an attitude inherent to the nomadic: it is the nomad's relation to territory. The nomad and the State are co-existent and interdependent. The State seeks to expand on territory and to maintain its power, yet there is always a nomadic counter-force, which sooner or later gets incorporated by the State in turn. However, this does not defy the nomad, because the nomad will appear elsewhere. As the nomad and the State incessantly define and redefine each other, their relation is not oppositional but rather constitutes a continuous becoming; together they create a multiplicity, an infinite series of ruptures, breaks, and assemblages (Deleuze and Guattari 2004, 397–8; Marzec 2001).

To repeat, the nomadic in my view entails a certain mode or attitude, much more than it is a (variation on a) desert-nomad. As mentioned above, one of Deleuze's first essays on nomadism, "Nomadic Thought" (1973/2004b), relates to a philosopher, namely Friedrich Nietzsche. For Deleuze, Nietzsche radically thwarts the hierarchical history of philosophy; the energy and force in Nietzsche's work completely steps off the beaten track of rethinking and reevaluating the already existent, and demonstrates that philosophy is creativity of thought. Reading Nietzsche produces affects, according to Deleuze, a sensation, an intensity, a gaining of awareness of something that eludes description, or analysis, or interpretation; something that escapes the code. In this essay the nomad continuously appears as something that comes from the outside, something that is suddenly there, in the midst of things, and disturbs the existing order of things. Nomadism emerges as something that "gets through" but escapes the code, the code that promises recognition.[11] It is something that flows through and underneath the codes of law, contract, institution, the three main principles that legislate, regulate, and politicize society (Deleuze 2004b, 253–4).

Such nomadic movements rearrange existing conceptions of what can be known, imagined, thought, or done. Nomadic acts, then, have the potential to alter our perception and understanding. Put differently, they are capable of producing a *politics of perception*, as they cause a rearrangement of what Jacques Rancière names the "distribution of the sensible," in *The Politics of Aesthetics* (2000/2004). Rancière uses the term to indicate that our perception and therefore our conception of the world is first and foremost a product of a certain distribution of what can be seen, sensed, or heard and therefore, of what is thought, done, and imagined. Attending to distributions of the sensible implicates a critical investigation of what is to be perceived in the world and what is made imperceptible; to seek the exclusions within the inclusions, and to focus on what previously escaped the light of attention.

Summarizing, Deleuze's nomadology does not, or not only, refer to movement and mobility, but instigates a type of movement and mobility that escapes rule, convention, order—in Deleuze's terms: law, contract, institution—and posits something else in return: experimentation, creativity, and potentiality, related to a politics of perception. Expressed through spatial concepts, such an approach to movement and mobility is, I think, a very inviting and constructive approach through which also contemporary theatre and performance can be taken into view.

Nomadic Theatre: A Concept, a Toolbox

Earlier on in this introduction, I indicated that I regard "nomadic theatre" as a concept, and not as the name of a genre. The concept of nomadic theatre is a tool for analyzing mobile theatre performances, for thinking through practice and for mobilizing theory. In this section, I look a bit more closely at what a concept is, and how one puts a concept "to work." To start with, this study proposes that a mobile phenomenon—movement and mobility in the theatre—should be investigated by means of a mobile theory, a mobile theory that relies on the flexibility of working with concepts. This stance closely affiliates with Mieke Bal's standpoint, in *Travelling Concepts in the Humanities* (2002), namely that interdisciplinarity in the humanities "must seek its heuristic and methodological basis in concepts rather than methods" (5). Bal's account is recognized as very relevant for theatre and performance studies (Bleeker et al. 2009) and this book, which brings in a variety of disciplines, furthers that line of investigation.

In *What is Philosophy?*, Deleuze and Guattari argue that concepts are the creative products of philosophy; at least, that is what philosophy in their view ought to do. Philosophy creates concepts, in response to (philosophical) problems, whereas art produces affects, and science works through percepts (1994, 5). My reasoning is that questions arising from the field of theatre and performance may also invite the invention of concepts (cf. Cvejic 2015). They do not create philosophical concepts though, but quasi-philosophical concepts, concepts at a cross-point of philosophy and art. Accepting then in advance, that a quasi-philosophical concept encounters a different milieu than a philosophical concept and therefore operates differently, I combine Deleuze and Guattari's approach with Mieke Bal's use of concepts as a tool for cultural analysis. So, what is a concept?

For Deleuze and Guattari, concepts are not extant ideas, but newly created products of invention, responding to problems. Concepts have a (zigzagging) history though, and a zone of neighborhood through which they overlap with other concepts. A concept consists of heterogeneous, yet inseparable components; components that:

> remain distinct, but something passes from one to the other, something that is undecidable between them. There is an area *ab* that belongs to both *a* and *b*, where *a* and *b* "become" indiscernible. These zones, thresholds, or becomings, this inseparability, define the internal consistency of the concept. But the concept also has an exoconsistency with other concepts, when their respective creation implies the construction of a bridge on the same plane. Zones and bridges are the joints of the concept … each concept will therefore be considered as a point of coincidence, condensation, or accumulation of its own components … In this sense, each component is an *intensive feature*. (1994, 19–20, italics in the original)

Nomadic theatre is similarly a newly created area *ab*, in which the nomadic fuels concepts and terms relevant to theatre, whereas theatre, as will become clear, intensifies the performative qualities and situatedness of the nomadic.

In *Travelling Concepts*, Mieke Bal explores the potential of existing concepts, by arranging and studying their travels from one discourse or discipline to another, travels which question the very notion of "field" (2002, 4). Although Bal's agenda differs from that of Deleuze and Guattari, she similarly underlines the performativity of concepts: concepts are creative and provisional, they produce something new, they are mobile and bring about change. Bal's cultural analysis demonstrates in detail what concepts are, what they do, how they relate to objects, and how they impact modes and methods of analysis. She observes that concepts appear as words, and "look like words" (24) but actually are "miniature theories" (22). The disciplinary, theoretical, and historical baggage of concepts, when tested and put to work in a new field, produces new meanings, perspectives, and relations. Concepts "do" things because they create focus: they organize phenomena and define the sphere of questions addressed to an object. Through this, consequently, they do something else as well: they (co)produce their objects. A concept works as a searchlight; it focuses interest and installs a certain, articulated perspective, without denying that a different perspective would produce a different object (31–3). In turn, objects "speak back" (45): they determine the specific set of questions that will be addressed to them and, occasionally, they answer by resisting interpretation. Bal therefore sees objects as *theoretical objects* (cf. Bleeker 2008a, 8). This co-constructive relationship implicates the involvement of the critic or observer as well; concepts therefore are intersubjective tools, a triparte event between concept, object, and critic (Bal 2002, 44–5).

In line with Bal, I regard the practices discussed here as theoretical objects. They are expressions of thought, conveying specific ideas about the relationship between theatre, movement, and mobility. However, what compromises this project entirely—deterritorialization in *optima forma*—is that it is impossible to say what comes first: the practice, or the theory. If a concept inflects the object, and the object in turn co-defines the concept, then what is "of" the concept, and what is "of" the object, and how do you prevent these movements from getting into a blurry mess? To make it even worse: if concepts are hailed as the methodological answer to interdisciplinary phenomena, exactly because they are mobile, what happens when the concept in question—nomadic theatre—precisely seeks to investigate that, as its object: movement and mobility? Bal observes that working with concepts can be a risky affair, but also provides a way out of this dilemma: "It is only through a constant reassessment of the power of a concept to organize phenomena in a new and relevant way that its continued productivity can be evaluated" (32). Similarly, this study is an ongoing investigation of what the concept of nomadic theatre does, and how concept and object relate through propagation and contamination, instead of starting with or arriving at a final definition of what the concept is. Bal states that concepts are to be worked through—tested through the analysis of the object (44). Consequently, I attempt to articulate what movements I follow and am involved in; an attempt that starts anew with each chapter, each time with another performance as a theoretical object and aide.

Although I will not—and cannot—explain what the concept of nomadic theatre *is*, as I can only demonstrate the potential of the concept through *use*, I will give an inventory of the accumulative components within the concept. The concept of nomadic theatre first of all deals with *territories* and with processes of *deterritorialization* and *reterritorialization*, with inside-outside connections, and patterns of inclusion and exclusion. In the theatre, such processes may manifest themselves as the disruption of (spatial) conventions or the deregulation of codes. Secondly, nomadic theatre adheres to distinct modes of displacement, that of *traversing* fields and *cutting across* territories.

The concept crosses disciplinary boundaries; performances make use of paths and routes, of navigation, distribution, and way-finding, of temporary spaces, and situations. Thirdly, the concept passes through *tonalities of sensation* and *affective modulations*, attending in particular to sensory modes of spectatorship, where the address to all the senses deterritorializes the dominant role of vision in the theatre. Lastly, the concept affiliates with *experimentation, testing*, and *play*. I regard performers, spectators, and spaces as enfolded into a threefold, flexible constellation: their role and spatial position is not fixed, instead the relationship among them is constantly negotiated and played with.

A concept defines the sphere of questions addressed to an object. Nomadic theatre firstly asks what kind of territories are in play, and which patterns of de- and reterritorialization emerge. These patterns do not advocate the end of territory. Stuart Elden remarks that in relation to de- and reterritorialization, territory is "both its condition of possibility and, in some newly configured form, its necessary outcome" (Elden 2006, 50). These operations turn territory into a process of making and remaking, and point to the continuous reconfiguration of *spatial* relations (Elden 2006). To investigate these spatial relations, I rely on a broad range of theories related to urban theory, cartography, geography, scenography, and architecture. This moving across disciplines is characteristic of what is called a "spatial turn" in performance (Wilkie 2015b; Turner 2015; Turner and Behrndt 2008 195–8; Read 2000). I am also reminded of a remark by Elinor Fuchs and Una Chaudhuri, who in *Land/Scape/Theater* (2002) suggest that the study of spatial relations in performance asks for an interdisciplinary approach, next to a "spatialized consciousness" (4). This study likewise takes space as a primary interpretative window, which also accounts for the many references to (spatial) theories that date back to the late 1960s and early 1970s, especially in the area of continental philosophy. Tom Conley observes a spatial turn in French critical theory in that period, which reveals a strong preference for simultaneity, heterogeneity, dispersion, and openness, seen as the distinct qualities of space (Conley 2003).[12]

A second line of enquiry revolves around the question of how these spatial reconfigurations are *staged*. I investigate how processes of de- and reterritorialization in the theatre are organized and composed, how they position or address the spectator, and what emergent dramaturgies arise from these open-ended processes. The focus on staging creates a tension between nomadic resistance to rule and theatre's imposition of order. Despite theatre's intrinsic nomadism—i.e. the continuous variation inherent in live events—theatre is always concerned with staging and therefore with organizing the relationship between performance and the spectator. By following the argument in its twofold way, I will demonstrate that not only does theatre materialize differently as a consequence of the encounter with the nomadic; the nomadic is also contaminated by the theatre, which manifests itself notably in my emphasis on embodied, situated, and local operations.

Bal notes that concepts encounter a variety of (established) methods along the way. The concept of nomadic theatre amongst others cuts across two prevailing methods in the field of theatre studies: semiotics and phenomenology (Fortier 2002; Pavis 2003). Concepts do not belong to a particular field, and therefore the concept of nomadic theatre cannot be placed within semiotics or phenomenology, or entirely outside of them. Nomadic theatre encounters semiotics through (the deregulation of) codes; it traverses phenomenology by attending to lived space and embodied perception; the concept escapes both methods when reflecting on relations between artworks and theory. It encounters them again, but differently, as a faint echo, when entering fields of geography, cartography, or architecture; and again, but once more differently, when engaging with philosophy.

Theory as Tool: How to Do Things with Deleuze?

Although theatre and performance studies employ a range of Deleuzian concepts, the nomadic is but occasionally mentioned and usually figures somewhere on the backstage or as an aside. A possible explanation for this minor role is that the nomadic can easily be critiqued for being either too romantic, too Euro-centrist and neocolonialist, or too aggressive. I will look into these disqualifications in more detail in Chapter 2, but it should indeed be acknowledged that Deleuze and Guattari present the nomad as a war machine.[13] The nomadic may emerge in art, yet appears as well in real flesh-and-blood guerilla warfare, which is probably as creative as art. When taking the full scope of nomadic tactics into account the concept gets rather uneasy, with the sole redeeming feature being that at least something forces us to think. My stance in the matter is that the nomadic may manifest itself in various ways, either positively or negatively. Nomadism appears as well, for instance, in the ungraspable fiscal and monetary flows of global banking circuits, responsible for the 2008 financial crisis amongst others, and not to everyone's satisfaction, to put it mildly. Notwithstanding such alarming types of movement, this can hardly be a reason for disqualifying the concept of nomadism itself.

The subtitle of this paragraph alludes to J.L. Austin's *How To Do Things With Words?* (1962), his introduction to speech act theory that has issued an extensive discourse on performativity, denoting acts and utterances that constitute or produce that which they present or refer to (Culler 2000; Kattenbelt 2010, 30). Deleuze's words are similarly constitutive and performative. His work "does" things: his style of writing unsettles and disorientates the reader; his texts perform philosophy, and, above all, his language is highly contagious. Contagion, or contamination, is not necessarily a bad thing: it describes a viral type of movement that changes the environment that it partly occupies and is changed by it as well (Bal 2002, 32–3). Yet one can immediately recognize Deleuzian contagion, for instance by an abundant use of Deleuzian–Guattarian concepts, or by a Deleuzian style, and above all, by the insistence on his ontology of events. The latter issue in particular brings forth the question of how to get Deleuze "right." The "Deleuzians" have created brilliant studies that engage far more thoroughly with Deleuzian thought than I do, but in a sense they can also be seen as replications of Deleuze, and repetition-of-sameness is precisely the thing Deleuze rejects (cf. O'Sullivan 2006, 5). So what is "getting Deleuze right"?

For a response to this question I rely on Brian Massumi's foreword to *A Thousand Plateaus*. He emphasizes that Deleuze and Guattari are pragmatists: the book is something to work with, and not intended to fall prey to philology. The book affords to be read randomly and selectively, similarly to choosing your favorite tracks or songs on a record. The same goes for the concepts that buttress the book—they should be evaluated in use: do they work, do they help to solve a problem? In his inspiring introduction, Massumi compares concepts with toolboxes. Concepts should not "add up to a system of belief or an architecture of propositions that you either enter or you don't, but instead pack a potential in the way a crowbar in a willing hand envelops an energy of prying" (in Deleuze and Guattari 2004, xv).

My hand is willing. Doing things with Deleuze here involves the selection of three tools, or songs: performativity, thinking through practice, affirmativity. *Performativity*, firstly, entails a focus on creation and production, in relation to both theory and practice. Nomadic theatre is a performative concept: it requires experimentation and actual use for the concept to work. The second, related, tool is *thinking through practice*. Practices are not mere objects for observation and analysis; they are expressions of thought and, as such, theoretical objects. My encounter with Deleuze is primarily a trajectory of practices, in particular related to play and architecture. By drawing a comparison between chess and Go, for instance, or by describing the logic of qualified labor in the building processes of twelfth-century gothic cathedrals (see Chapter 2), they astutely demonstrate how practice may be conceived of as a form of *material thinking*, a topic I will address in the concluding chapter. Thirdly, I choose an affirmative approach to my research subjects. Instead of the more common critical approach in which the researcher tends to dissect the object of analysis, I am interested in how both concepts and practices *generate* ideas, how they install connections or contaminate each other, and how performances create a sense of potentiality. Simon O'Sullivan presents a rather similar approach, in the context of art criticism, understanding this as the creation of new bricolages or assemblages (2006, 6, 26).[14] Likewise, while demonstrating how the concept of nomadic theatre can be used as a tool for performance analysis, this study creates *affirmative assemblages*. Such assemblages render visible how art criticism or scholarly reflection interfere with the art work, and how a performance invites, and in fact creates, thought. Nomadic theatre fuels this affirmative assemblage by installing connections across a variety of (disciplinary) fields, by the reading of practices through theory and vice versa, and by regarding physical movements in the theatre as stepping stones for theorizing movement and mobility at large.

Spatial Dramaturgy

While testing the concept of nomadic theatre, and in parallel to the recurring focus on spatial reconfigurations, I am interested in unpacking the spatial dramaturgy of the works discussed. *Spatial dramaturgy* describes the multiple ways in which artists create structural coherence and meaningful experiences through the use and arrangement of spaces, sites, situations, and spatial relationships. It is a type of dramaturgy that attends to the coordinates of lived space, to temporary occupations, to ways of navigating through space and creating space through movement; to strategies of merging, juxtaposing, or "serializing" space, of working with routes, pathways, or patterns of distribution, and so on. Such processes emphasize the impermanence of events, which leads to the observation that spatial dramaturgy often equates to *situational dramaturgy*. Situations are the spatial equivalent of events, in my view. When spectators are part of a staged or constructed situation, the situation surrounds them; spectators are placed "in" a situation, they are on the inside of the staged event.[15] Expressed in a formula, we might say that "space + event = situation."

Dramaturgy is notably a slippery and elastic term (Turner 2015, 3; Turner and Behrndt 2008, 18), especially in the context of postdramatic theatre, where the creation of meaningful compositions no longer relies on the structure of a (pre-existing) play. Therefore, I provide a short explanation and reflection on my use of the term. Compatible with my spatial perspective, it is interesting to note that several authors turn to architecture when describing characteristics of (postdramatic) dramaturgy, most notably Cathy Turner in *Dramaturgy and Architecture: Theatre, Utopia and the Built Environment* (2015), but see also Turner and Behrndt (2008) and Lehmann (1997). These authors address, directly or indirectly, the practice and discourse of *performative architecture*, which concentrates on how space is produced through performance, and how designed space invites movement or is created in accordance with use (Filmer and Rufford 2018; Salter 2010; Spurr 2007; Kolarevic and Malkawi 2005). They mention the work of architect Bernard Tschumi, for instance, for whom architecture takes place at the intersection of space, movement, and events (Tschumi 1996). Lehmann also quotes Jacques Derrida, who in response to Tschumi, notes that architecture does not create locations for events, but instead, "the sense of event is woven into the very structure of the architectural composition" (in Lehmann 1997, 57). Lehmann uses these references to distinguish between a dramatic and postdramatic logic of composition, the first dealing with structural coherence, unity, hierarchy, and functionality, the second relying on open composition, fragmentation, deconstruction, or disjunction (1997, 56). Cathy Turner and Synne K. Berndt too call upon Tschumi, in *Dramaturgy and Performance*, when they observe that both dramaturgy and architecture are concerned with "the deliberate deployment of structure in order to provoke live events" (2008, 5). They relate Tschumi's interest for the performance of architecture to dramaturgy's concern with the "architecture of performance" (2008).

How can we analyze a performance's architecture? In a dramaturgical analysis, I distinguish three dramaturgical layers, or "planes of composition."[16] These layers are active in any staged event, whether conventional or experimental, but they are especially useful for analyzing postdramatic performance. I briefly describe these layers, first in general terms, and then translated and applied to spatial dramaturgy.

The first layer focuses on the tactics of composition itself, that is, the staging of actions and elements, the organization of space, and the structuring of time. On this *composition* plane, the researcher basically asks how the performance takes the audience from a begin-point *a* to an end-point *z*; what does a performance do in order to carry the audience through time? What is the structural logic here (classical plot, episodic structure, a set of rules, repetition, juxtaposition, seriality, associative montage, et cetera)? And what are the key tools and stylistic means to achieve this (use of space, time, bodies, actions; of set, costume, light, music, digital media; playing with presence, acting styles, narrative formats, and so on)? Turner and Behrndt refer to it as the "internal fabric" or texture of a text or performance (2008, 5). This layer is always present in almost any performance analysis. Translated to spatial dramaturgy, key questions to ask are: what spaces are used, and how are they used; which spatial relationships are created and how do they facilitate movement? (How) does the performance play with site-specificity, navigational patterns, processes of simultaneity, synchronicity, or co-presence? In connection to one-to-one performances or ambulatory theatre, it helpful to keep Deleuze and Guattari's understanding of the *assemblage* in mind. To them, the assemblage is a multiplicity, an ongoing increase of connections: "A multiplicity cannot increase in number without changing in nature" (2004, 9). Performances unfold in time; the assemblage of the one-after-another and the next-to-each-other qualifies a performance's emergent dramaturgy.

A second plane of composition involves *audience address*. Audiences, whether *en groupe* or singled out, do not just look at or participate in a performance. They are addressed in a specific way, and they are positioned through address, either explicitly or implicitly: they are perhaps confronted, absorbed, or aroused, treated as guests or as outsiders, as sensitive bodies, as citizens, and so on. Spectatorship is not a natural given, but a construction (Bleeker 2008a). Audience address, then, is always a part of any dramaturgical strategy. With an eye to the postdramatic shift from internal communication to external communication, it is not surprising that spectatorship or perception processes themselves often become key themes in performance. Translated to spatial dramaturgy, questions may relate to the connection between audience address and the spectators' position(s) in space. (How) are they seated, or asked to wander around in an installation? Are they addressed as a group or as individuals? Are they at liberty to navigate freely? The works discussed in this book deal with isolation versus connectivity, with proximity versus distance, or with shared spaces, where spectators are deliberately placed "inside" the situation: on stage, positioned within, installed within the work, sharing many similarities with installation art (see Chapter 2). In an analysis, we may examine how these acts of spacing, placing, siting, and positioning create meaning and experience.

Thirdly, a dramaturgical analysis attends to the *context* in which a work is being made and presented, and it can be helpful to distinguish further between a societal and an artistic context. Societal context is an umbrella term for the social, cultural, economic, or political world(s) that somehow reverberate within a work. A performance always resonates with an outer world, even if it behaves like it does not. Referring to Adorno's "Logik ihres Produziertseins" (2006, 104), Lehmann observes that artworks are always exponents of the cultural moment in which they are created and presented. In a similar vein, Alan Read, in *Theatre, Intimacy and Engagement*, suggests that the relationship between an artwork and the "outer world" can be conceived as intensities that cross and re-cross each other's surface (2008, 37). We may also think of Deleuze and Guattari's analysis of the assemblage, when they observe that "an assemblage, in its multiplicity, necessarily acts on semiotic flows, material flows, and social flows simultaneously" (2004, 25).

Next to the societal context, a work is created within a specific artistic biotope, which equally could be part of Read's intensities or of Deleuzian flows. This biotope is the artistic environment in which a work is made, an "atelier" in the widest sense of the word, consisting of source materials and the artist's archive; affinities with other artists, thinkers, or political ideas; preferences for certain styles or working methods; restrictions; recurring themes or motifs, and more. Connecting this contextual layer to spatial dramaturgy, I observe that the works discussed in this book stand in line with an increased spatiality of cultural practices, in which (global) mobility leads to the reassessment of place and space. This manifests itself in a renewed interest in the complex interactions between spatial, social, and political practices, or between place, memory, and identity (Gallagher and Freeman 2016; Wilkie 2015a; Tompkins 2014; Levin 2014; Fischer-Lichte and Whistutz 2013; Birch and Tompkins 2012; Hill and Paris 2006; McAuley 2006). This attention to place and to localized action is shared with contemporary developments in urban theories, cartographic practices, and performative architecture; theoretical climates that encounter each other as the concept of nomadic theatre passes through them. A focus on space not only forces open the dramaturgy of a work, as Turner and Behrndt observe (2008, 197), but also instigates new alliances, and exposes cultural domains, spatial theories, and design practices as being connected and webbed in many ways.

Since *staging* also pertains to a deliberate deployment of structure and certainly to the architecture of performance, the question arises of the extent to which staging differs from dramaturgy. They are not mutually exclusive terms. I often refer to "staging" when I focus on composition strategies or spectatorial positions, and tend to prefer the term "dramaturgy" when reflecting on how the combination of composition, audience address, and the wider context produces meaning and experience. These terms, therefore, are instruments with which to switch focus, rather than entirely different concepts.

Points Are Relays on a Trajectory: Chapter Overview

To summarize the aim and approach of this book: in this study I investigate movement and mobility in theatre and performance through the concept of nomadic theatre. I will examine patterns of de- and reterritorialization, and inquire into how movement and mobility are staged. These patterns point to a continuous reconfiguration of spatial relations, and my approach to both theories and case studies can best be understood as being informed by a spatial perspective. I conceive of the chapters to follow as relays, as temporary points of condensation. Every chapter is a new trajectory, a new assessment of the potential of nomadic theatre. These chapters can be read separately and randomly. Yet despite the pleasure that hopefully derives from such an arrangement of the text (Barthes), and in line with my focus on staging, dramaturgy, and composition, I think it is time to revive the author somewhat (Barthes again[17]). Not in order to position the author center-stage again, but as a way of acknowledging that the author cannot entirely escape the linearity of the page and composes the order of sequences. The next chapters are kaleidoscopically arranged: in each chapter, the performer–spectator–space constellation is "shuffled" differently, each time putting a new angle on the dynamics of this constellation and its myriad configurations. Such an arrangement intends to demonstrate that, in each case, elements that are often similar are at work, although they are not always equally highlighted. Every chapter discusses a different territory or spatial register and another staging strategy, which also activates other components within the concept of nomadic theatre and creates a different milieu of references.

In Chapter 2, **Encounter**, I discuss Dries Verhoeven's *No Man's Land* (2008–14), a performance that liaises with cultural or social mobility by taking migration as its subject matter. It is an ambulatory performance that carefully confronts spectators with the uneasy ways in which wealthy nations deal with migrants and refugees. In *No Man's Land*, migrants take single spectators on a walk through the city, and I use this walk also to examine the theoretical consequences of ambulatory works with regard to the most characteristic territory within the theatre: the *stage*. The stage, in its simultaneous fixity and mobility, becomes a very useful device for contemplating nomadic conditions. I explore how Verhoeven uses the *encounter* as a staging strategy, and how this encounter between mobile performers and spectators deterritorializes the stage. As a consequence, the positions of performers, spectators, and spaces reterritorialize on each other, which results in observing performers, staged spectators, and smooth spaces. I also pursue the encounter with the (Deleuzian) nomadic, including critical inquiries into the concept. Inherent to these inquiries is the question of whether the concept of "the nomadic" is a metaphor, which also puts referentiality and representation on the agenda. Representation is certainly not a main subject in this study, but the topic knocks persistently at the door, and since nomadic theatre has no doors, it is already in.

Chapter 3 introduces **Displacement** as a staging strategy, and looks into the mobility of information, goods, and services in view of global economy, in relation to Rimini Protokoll's *Call Cutta* (2005) and its follow-up, *Call Cutta in a Box* (2006–12). As call-center employees in India guide spectators through Berlin, the stage is distributed over several locations across the globe. The stage cuts across both physical and virtual spaces, and traverses conceptual territories such as the global market, outsourced labor, urbanism, and fluid citizenship. Although globalization is a key frame for this audio play, the concept of nomadic theatre helps to expose how *Call Cutta* counters globalism by producing "locality," due to its persistent attention on the site-specific context. I describe how nomadism in the theatre surfaces as a series of local operations, which produce the theatre space while one moves through it. As a theoretical object, then, *Call Cutta* paves the way for conceiving of theatre spaces as profoundly relational and performative; they are not fixed in space but instead emerge through seriality. Since these spaces are produced in use, I look into Henri Lefebvre's notion of *lived space*, a concept that refers to spaces that (become) matter as they are used, practiced, and experienced in everyday life. This chapter points at the relevance of Lefebvre's urban theories and concepts, also because Lefebvre values lived space for its imaginative and representational potential. Through Lefebvre, I take some distance from Deleuze's anti-representational image of thought, not only to account for the fact that theatre always deals with representation but also to inquire how our mobile condition shapes our way of thinking and imagining a world on the move.

The fourth chapter, **Cartographies,** discusses a second performance by Dries Verhoeven, which is *Trail Tracking* (2005). This ambulatory performance plots a route through an abandoned railway station and deals with (imaginary) traveling, which invites a brief comparison between the nomadic and travel as cultural tropes. In this chapter I look into *navigational spaces*, while approaching spectatorship as both an embodied and embedded practice. This early work of Verhoeven is used to enquire into (performative) cartography as a staging principle. I conceive of this performance as organized through a set of cartographic layers, calling attention to the co-creative relationship between maps and users. Cartographic theory in turn is used to analyze how cartographic qualities such as the interconnectedness of space, place, movement, and subjectivity fuel the spatial dramaturgy of *Trail Tracking*. As a follow-up to the attention given to locality and lived space in Chapter 3, I here briefly discuss the (feminist) concept of *politics of location*. These joint observations mount to the argument that the nomadic is a situated practice rather than a rootless wandering, thriving on the ongoing assessment of one's relationship to place.

The first three chapters all question the theatre as a domain of opsis and make room for other modalities of spectatorship, that is, the materiality of embodied, sensory, and lived relations. This materiality is explicitly addressed in the fifth chapter, **Diagrams**. Ontroerend Goed's *The Smile Off Your Face* is the primary theoretical object here, in which the stage primarily materializes through sensorial experience. If *Trail Tracking* was already concerned with close geographies, in this chapter the scale of encounter is even smaller, as it investigates *spaces of proximity*. By highlighting the multiple senses through which spectators engage with performance, *The Smile* deterritorializes the theatre as a seeing-place and turns the stage into a sensorium. Of all the cases in this study, in *The Smile* the spectator seems the least mobile, yet this speeds up the movement of thought. The explicit address to (all) the senses proves to be a magnificent agent for mobilizing theory. In this chapter I introduce the (Deleuzian) *diagram* as a staging strategy that on the one hand invites spectators into a fundamentally open process, while at the same time provides the conditions for spectators' mode of engagement. Such operations also characterize play and games, but here I focus on Deleuze's approach to architectural diagrams, to explore the tonalities of sensation within spectatorship, while also exposing the territorial forces at work in these experimental processes.

Chapter 6, **Architextures**, continues with passing through places, positions, and perspectives, this time in connection to processes that deal with building performance and that are inspired by play. The starting point is Signa's *The Ruby Town Oracle* (2008), a nine-day non-stop event that portrays a community of outsiders living in a semi-permanent village in a "temporary autonomous zone," sited in-between an abstract "North" and "South"—inviting associations with refugee camps or the Calais Jungle. This performance installation plays with (trespassing) borders in all sorts of ways, both thematically and performatively. *Ruby Town* challenges the (fluid) boundaries between actors and spectators, obfuscates clear-cut distinctions between play and reality, and, quite similar to games, deals with rules and with breaking the rules. The stage here is literally a playing arena. Joining theatre studies and game discourse, I conceptualize the stage as a *rhizomatic game board*, which allows spectators to enter and exit at will. In this chapter I introduce the term "architextures" as a staging strategy, denoting a web of intersecting spaces and shifting perspectives. Whereas the other chapters are "experimentations in contact with the real"—Deleuze's qualification of cartography—this chapter experiments with fictionality. Signa's imaginary world is used to test the concept of nomadic theatre in the less obvious context of a fictitious, narrative environment—again making room for theatre's alliance with representation, contrary to Deleuze's point of view. I show that fictionality is excellently suited to think through the role of limits and borders in view of the nomadic. The chapter ends by arguing that rules and boundaries—characteristic of both play and architecture—as well as the excess of those limits, form the backbone of this performance, and of the concept of nomadic theatre.

I conclude with **Distributed Performance**, in which I highlight some of the resonances between the chapters, while pointing out how performance distributes itself across other disciplinary domains. I reflect on how the concept of nomadic theatre facilitates a back-and-forth movement between theory and practice, and how this assists in understanding theatre and performance as forms of material thinking.

Playgrounding

In this introductory chapter, nomadism has been aligned with movement, mobility, flexibility, and changeability. There is one association that I saved for last, which is the observation that these are also the terms frequently employed in neoliberal discourse. Dance scholar André Lepecki refers to this connection as well, in *Exhausting Dance: Performance and the Politics of Movement*, observing that movement tends to participate in a "general economy of mobility that informs, supports and reproduces the ideological formations of late capitalist modernity" (2006, 16)—which explains his interest in dance that disrupts or "exhausts" movement. Although I focus on movement and mobility, I certainly do not intend to celebrate global acceleration, post-Fordist flexibility, or the mobility required of the flexi-worker in an age of advanced capitalism. To support this stance, I call upon the notion of *playgrounding*, a term that once was mentioned by David Micklem, artistic director of Battersea Arts Centre (BAC) in London. He used the term to explain BAC's way of renovating the huge former town hall where BAC resides. Playgrounding involves the maintenance and improvement of the building by engaging theatre practitioners and performance projects in the work. It is actually a very specialized brand of site-specific performance, one might say, as the building is gradually adjusted, repaired, and enriched as part of theatre production processes. Micklem explained his concept of playgrounding to me while we were sitting in the beautifully painted and decorated foyer, which, for instance, turned out to be part of the scenery of a former Punchdrunk show.[18] Playgrounding is attuned to sustainability and long-term investment: it produces relational spaces and attentive architecture, and charges space with memories.

Already present in this introduction, elaborated in the chapters to follow, is the affinity with play. Play involves mobility, in the sense that it offers a place for movement. Hans-Thies Lehmann remarks that the German word *Spiel* actually has three meanings. It encompasses both "play" and "game" but also refers to the tiny, unnamed, or empty space, the void "that the wheels of any machinery (including social machinery) need in order to function properly" (2007, 53; cf. Raessens 2010, 15). In this study, performers, spectators, and spaces are "in play": their roles and spatial positions are constantly negotiated and subjected to experimentation. The emphasis is on the performance as a process, instead of a finished work, a process that each time unfolds in a unique, precise, and specific way: instead of the theatre as a social gathering space, it is the enactment of social machinery.

The concept of play, and the notion of "grounding" will both emerge throughout the chapters to follow, as a response to neoliberal abstractness, trying to answer the question: how are we able to attach ourselves to fluidity? This question is inspired by the introduction of *Metaphoricity and the Politics of Mobility* (2006), in which the editors Maria Margaroni and Effie Yiannopoulou argue, following cultural geographer Tim Cresswell, that mobility theories in the twenty-first century should not celebrate mobility for mobility's sake, but need to "do justice to our diverse, historical and geographically concrete experience of movement" (9). The authors ask how we are able to create affective bonds between everyday experience and a world that is on the move, between global mobility and situated, local histories and practices; how, to put it in other words, we might be able to attach ourselves to fluidity. They call for a mobile theory that preserves the destabilizing power of mobility, but also incorporates concrete, lived experience and situated practices, and initiates an ongoing negotiation between material and discursive movements. This stance tunes in with the emerging attention to embodied space produced by mobile media (Farman 2012), or the localized, embedded positions in mobile critical paradigms (Gallagher and Freeman 2016; Levin 2014). All these authors advocate a politics of mobility that aptly meets my approach to movement and mobility in the theatre. Nomadic theatre invites a focus on situated practices, on processes of articulating particularity, and on the investigation of embodied relationships with the places and spaces through which we move and that through movement we create.

2

Encounter

Meeting Multiplicity in *Dries Verhoeven's* No Man's Land

Of Horses and Wasps

It's impossible to understand how they made it all the way to the capital, which is nonetheless quite far from the frontier. But there they are, and every morning seems to increase their number ... Impossible to converse with them. They don't know our language ... Even their horses are meat-eaters! (Kafka in Deleuze 2004b, 256)

As abruptly as I open this chapter, with very little context, this quote suddenly appears in Deleuze's "Nomadic Thought" (2004b). This quotation style is demonstrative of the disruptive force of the nomadic, which is precisely the content of this short excerpt of a story by Kafka: suddenly they are there, in the middle of a town—nobody knows where they came from, or who "they" are. What deterritorializes the center even more: even their horses eat meat.[1] Encounters in a Deleuzian universe do not follow principles of quiet transformation. Meeting someone or something else always implies a change of situation: through the encounter, one's lifeworld expands. Encounters therefore facilitate the creation of new assemblages. For Deleuze, encounters occur when territories are "traversed by a movement that comes from the outside" (2004b, 256); when something incomprehensible slips through and escapes the code of recognition.

In this chapter I investigate the *encounter*, as a staging strategy, in relation to *No Man's Land* (2008–14). In this ambulatory performance, created by Dutch director and scenographer Dries Verhoeven, a single spectator follows a migrant on a walk through the city.[2] *No Man's Land* stages encounters between performers and spectators, but also between theatre and everyday life. The performance takes place in an urban environment. Such an encounter, in which performance takes to the streets, bears similarities to the Kafka story quoted above. There is something strange to the town, something other, something that adheres to different laws, codes, and conventions than those that regulate the urban environment, even when taking into account that urban space itself is unpredictable and polymorphous. Although on a much more modest scale than Kafka's nomads, a performance in the city deterritorializes the urban environment, and due to this encounter, it forms a *rhizome* with that environment. In *A Thousand Plateaus*, Deleuze and Guattari describe the rhizome as an a-centered, non-hierarchical network, that comes into existence through principles of connectivity, heterogeneity, multiplicity, and deterritorialization. A rhizome is always in a state of *becoming*, as it continuously changes and has no fixed points or positions. The rhizome therefore is the opposite of territory; it is always in the middle, it has neither beginning nor an end (2004, 7–10; Colman in Parr 2010, 232-4). Urban environments, then, are always rhizomatic, as there are many ways of living in or understanding a city; there are numerous pathways and entry and exit points—both practically as well as conceptually. A theatre performance nevertheless manages to bring something other to the urban environment, as will be shown in relation to *No Man's Land*, something which escapes, changes, and yet reverberates with the codes of the city.

The theatre deterritorializes the urban environment, but meanwhile the city changes the *stage* as well. While performers and spectators traverse the city, they render the stage into *a state of continuous variation*, as the urban scenery changes with every step and consequently the stage, as a platform for performance, unfolds alongside their trajectory. The stage is the primary territory of enquiry in this chapter, a stage that materializes within and emanates from a mobile threefold constellation of performers, spectators, and spaces. I will follow the pathways of this constellation, which also catalyzes encounters with theatre conventions, nomadic games and science, spectatorship in fine arts and the theatre, installation art, and Deleuze's anti-representational image of thought. This trajectory of encounters demonstrates how the concept of nomadic theatre stages connections across a variety of (disciplinary) fields.

Encounters may be sudden, as seen in Kafka's "horses" statement above, or they may be smooth, as in Deleuze and Guattari's often-quoted example of the a-parallel evolution of the orchid and the wasp:

> The orchid deterritorializes by forming an image, a tracing of a wasp; but the wasp reterritorializes on that image. The wasp is nevertheless deterritorialized, becoming a piece in the orchid's reproductive apparatus. But it reterritorializes the orchid by transporting its pollen. Wasp and orchid, as heterogeneous elements, form a rhizome. (Deleuze and Guattari 2004, 11)

Deterritorialization, inseparable from reterritorialization, is the equivalent of encounter. The wasp and the orchid deterritorialize each other because something passes between two heterogeneous movements—a force, a flow of intensity—and produces a mutual becoming: the becoming-wasp of the orchid and the becoming-orchid of the wasp. Such a becoming does not work through imitation or resemblance but through a capturing of code. Encounters bring about change; however, the orchid and the wasp do not change into one another. Instead, they evolve in relation to one another; their encounter is an instance of an "aparallel evolution" (Deleuze and Guattari 2004). In *A Thousand Plateaus*, Deleuze and Guattari describe a range of such a-parallel evolutions and they qualify those encounters between two heterogeneous elements as a process of *entering into composition* with the other (2004, 289).

No Man's Land brings such encounters into play. The stage captures the codes of the city and, in turn, the intensities of the urban environment traverse the stage. Performers, spectators, and spaces enter into composition with one another, in the collaborative maintenance of a smooth stage. Performers and spectators are neither orchids nor wasps, but they too are engaged in a heterogeneous, a-parallel evolution: they enter into composition with each other while they explore contrasting ways of living and experiencing a Western city.

The Rhythms of a Smooth Stage

Standing beneath the vast, blue departure board at Utrecht Central Station, I watch the crowd in front of me—a hurrying, eating, and strolling crowd—in anticipation of things to come. It is the start of *No Man's Land*. Approximately twenty other spectators are lined up with me, each of us wearing headphones and holding a piece of cardboard with a particular name on it. We are waiting for the migrants who will be our guides in this performance. I am waiting for Abderraghman, apparently. Through the headphones I hear sounds of a station concourse—occasionally drowned by the noise in the actual concourse—spliced with faint music fragments, like a radio tuner searching for a clear channel. Our condition resembles that of performers on a stage: while we are standing in a row, with name cards on our torsos and headphones adorned on our heads, we attract quite a lot of attention. Instead of being seated in a darkened auditorium, we are being gazed at and observed by passengers. Unwillingly, we have created a gulf in front of us, a gap of about two meters that is perhaps unconsciously avoided by travelers and other people present in the hall.

Amidst the continuous movements, I suddenly notice that a few people are standing still, their eyes closed. They are on the other side of the gap, as it were, approximately three to five meters away from us. The longer I look, the more people I see, highlighted by this still and silent position, opposite to us, their eyes closed. These "still lives" juxtapose the hasty and fast-paced movement that surrounds them, and create a fissure that changes my perspective on the incessantly moving crowd: it turns the movements in the hall into a choreography of conscious and unconsciously passing travelers. Expectations rise: these are most likely the people we are going to meet. The music through the headphones slowly drowns the sounds from the station concourse and it seems the soundtrack has finally located the right tune. While we listen to a Purcell aria, these people suddenly open their eyes, look straight into ours and begin to sing along with the aria—or so it seems, as we are unable to clarify this because of our headsets.[3] Whether it is Purcell's score to this urban choreography, or the apprehension of the encounter about to take place I am not sure, but this is an enthralling moment, which deeply moves me, even in my stationary position. One-by-one, the performers cross the gap and approach each of the spectators; they nod in a friendly way and with a little wink invite a spectator to follow them. Each migrant–spectator couple disperses through the hall, in varying directions. Abderraghman is late; I have time to watch at least twelve couples dissolve into the crowd. I wonder what he will look like. The next moment I am approached by a man with dark friendly eyes, about 40 years old, dark hair, a short beard, dressed in black jeans and a black leather jacket. He nods silently and invites me to follow. We quietly walk toward and across platform number four and leave the station. Although I am guided, I feel slightly lost: I am unsure what to expect of this, I have no idea where we are going, and I must put my fate, and faith, in the hands of a stranger.

No Man's Land stages an encounter between migrants and theatre spectators—an encounter that is taken quite literally in the opening scene. The performance takes the spectator out on a walk through Lombok, an Utrecht district with a dense population of immigrants with varied cultural backgrounds. The performer leads the way, through busy and quiet streets, past shops, squares, and park benches, as if showing the spectator around in his or her habitat. Meanwhile, the spectator hears an audio track through the headphones, which conveys a range of different stories and experiences, providing an impression of what it means to be a migrant in the Netherlands. In this performance the political-ethical subject matter of migration and integration is (en)countered by the mundane rhythms of everyday life, the hybrid of which I regard as exemplary of Henri Lefebvre's understanding of *lived space*. In the posthumously published *Rhythmanalysis: Space, Time and Everyday Life* (2004), Lefebvre proposes to study urban, lived spaces by analyzing the rhythms of cities, which may help to understand how contemporary cities arise from and are produced by the polymorphous flows of everyday life. These rhythms, just as in *No Man's Land*, involve both the repetitious movements of daily routine as well as the contrasting and conflicting flows of social space.

Already present in the opening scene, but more distinctively in the trajectories to follow, the stage of *No Man's Land* has no fixed boundaries, and instead becomes a *smooth space*. Opposed to *striated* or closed space, Deleuze and Guattari qualify smooth space as an open space without divisions or clearly defined borders; it is a directional space rather than a dimensional, metric space; a space which orients rather than contains movement. Smooth space is the realm of the nomadic, whereas striated space is the product of the sedentary (2004, 528–9). Similar to the difference between a nomadic and a sedentary attitude as discussed in the Introduction, the distinction points to two diverging ways of relating to space. The nomadic mode is that of being "distributed into smooth space," a type of distribution which does not divide in parts, whereas striated space is based on compartmentalization, structured and organized by law, and marked by inclusions and exclusions (Patton 2010, 37). Nomadic practices both contaminate and escape sedentarist striation; their pattern of distribution is that of occupying a borderless domain, without possessing it entirely (De Kesel 2006, 2). Like many of the conceptual couples of Deleuze and Guattari, the smooth and the striated are two absolutes. They refer to two different attitudes, yet in reality they cannot be strictly separated (Deleuze and Guattari 2004, 523).[4]

The concept of nomadic theatre ignites attention to smooth and striated spaces in the theatre. Next to investigating processes of de- and reterritorialization, nomadic theatre asks whether spaces are treated as smooth or striated, and whether the theatre space itself is a smooth or striated space. *No Man's Land* distinctively opts for smoothness. The performance distributes the stage over the city and occupies the borderless domain of urban space, without possessing it entirely. Also the auditorium, which usually assembles and seats the public in one place, is deterritorialized and now reterritorializes as twenty synchronous trajectories that run in parallel through town, each with slightly different rhythms and coordinates.[5] On the smooth stage of *No Man's Land*, at least one pattern of striation known from the conventional theatre has disappeared, or more precisely is being addressed, which is the separation of performers and spectators. This (abandonment of) separation is intrinsically linked to the spectator's relation to the stage, and as the stage is the primary space of inquiry in this chapter, I suggest investigating the opening scene more closely (Figure 2.1).

Figure 2.1 Opening scene of Dries Verhoeven's *No Man's Land* in Athens, 2014. Courtesy Studio Dries Verhoeven, photo Stavros Petropoulos.

Mind the Gap

In *Visuality in the Theatre: The Locus of Looking* (2008a), Maaike Bleeker uses Roland Barthes' concept of the (photographic) *punctum* to point at certain details in performance that "puncture" the viewer's experience and hence draw attention to the relationship between the seer and how the seer is addressed by the stage (16, 93–7). Such extraordinary details can serve as a portal for analysis. The opening scene of *No Man's Land*, and in particular the caesura taking place when the performers announce themselves by standing still, is precisely such a punctum. Therefore, while the performance proceeds into town, let us linger here, at this semi-spontaneous gap between performers and spectators. In the opening scene, performers and spectators are simultaneously joined, separated, and defined by this gap, a relatively empty yet energetic space, unnoticed by the majority of the crowd in the station hall, hardly visible, but definitely felt by those who do pay attention. As this breach is so explicitly addressed by first installing and later by crossing the gap, it helps to explore how *No Man's Land* tackles spectatorship and, consequently, exposes how this performance becomes active as a theoretical object.

This gap between performers and spectators is a historical and theoretical variable, as it has been the motor for numerous innovations and evolutions in performance. It has been closed by the fourth wall convention, paradoxically to draw the spectators into the world on stage; the gap has been maximized by Wagner, placing the audience in the dark to immerse them into the world on stage (Groys 2008). There have been various efforts put in place to crush the distinction, as in the Futurists' attempts to shift the live event from the stage to the auditorium and onto the streets outside (Fischer-Lichte 1997). The gap has been politically and dramaturgically addressed by Piscator and Brecht, for instance, requesting the spectator's intellectual and critical involvement. We can think of efforts to minimize the gap, as in environmental theatre, or attempts to vaporize the distinction, as in Artaud's theatre of cruelty which sought to unite performers and audience into one energetic, orgasmic body; which in turn brings the work of Living Theatre or La Fura dels Baus to mind, and so on, and so on.

As if it were a counterpart to Peter Handke's *Publikumsbeschimpfung* (Offending the Audience, 1966), in which four actors on stage face and confront the audience, playing with stage conventions and expectations, *No Man's Land*'s performers cross the gap and warmly invite the spectators to come along. Responding to that invitation, the spectator steps onto the stage. Although the spectator enters an extremely smooth stage—as it is not clear at all where the stage starts and stops—the spectator enters a situation which is obviously staged, and which shields both the performer and the spectator from the daily reality in the station concourse. They both occupy this daily reality, they are part of this everyday-ness, yet simultaneously they are separated from it, by means of the "contract" that is the theatre performance. As a result of this shared agreement, they are separated from the daily events by way of an invisible, extremely porous membrane.[6]

By stepping on the stage, the spectator occupies and becomes physically part of the work, reminiscent of *installation art*. In fact, all the performances discussed here could be called installations. Although installations in fine art and performance are not always similar, a brief elaboration will support the inquiry into *No Man's Land*'s dealing with spectatorship.

Performance Installations

No Man's Land and other instances of immersive theatre bear resemblance to installation art, in the sense that many art installations require visitors to enter a space, to move around, to do something in order to make an installation "work," or to provide input in order to complete the work. Such works literally install the spectator within an environment or situation. The installation is notoriously difficult to define; in fact, the most stable characteristic seems to be that of indefinability (Bishop 2005). Installation art often occupies an in-between position, situated in-between (art) disciplines, genres, or mediums. For the purpose of the present discussion, I understand installations as artworks that rely on the active contribution of visitors and/or the physical presence of spectators within the work, which underlines their process-character; installation art is by default a time-based art. Vito Acconci's installations, for example, do not "work" without the visitor-spectator. Acconci designs spaces that invite action and response, and which change in response to those actions. His work needs to be performed by the visitor-spectator (Spurr 2007, 120–34). The same could be said of Tino Seghal's *This Situation* (2007) and other conversation pieces, or Rimini Protokoll's *Situation Rooms* (2013), Julian Hetzel's *Schuldfabrik* (2016), or Ontroerend Goed's *A Game Of You* (2010), performance installations in which the spectator passes through several interrelated rooms. Performance installations are staged *situations*, combining characteristics of installation art, theatre, and performance, in which the spectator-artwork relationship often fuels the (situational) dramaturgy of the work.

Performance installations disrupt the convention of frontality, which prevents spectators from observing the work from a distance. Throughout history, the notion of (aesthetic) distance has often been associated with objectivity, rationality, truthfulness, and with "the possibility of seeing it 'as it is'" (Bleeker 2008a, 5). Instead, the installation offers partial, fragmented perspectives: it collapses subject–object distinctions and foregrounds the relationship between the viewer and the artwork (Bouchard in Oddey and White 2009, 168; States 1992, 371). Art always necessitates the presence of spectators, but installation art seems to make this explicit. This leads Claire Bishop to remark that installation art should perhaps be defined along the lines of spectatorial address, rather than by the attempt to point out characteristics of the work itself. For Bishop, the various modes in which installations address and understand the relationship between viewing and subjectivity could be a way to envisage the *medium* of installation art (2005, 8–10). This seems certainly relevant for the work of Dries Verhoeven. In his work the performer regularly disappears out of sight, to facilitate a focus on the spectator's experience and engagement. Verhoeven likes to model the theatre spectator on the visitor in a museum or art gallery, seeking to provide spectators with time to explore their own response to the work. An overt focus on performers often produces a sense of awe: spectators tend to admire performers, instead of examining their own perceptual process. To illustrate this, Verhoeven once aptly remarked that paintings do not need applause (Groot Nibbelink 2007).

Installation art emphasizes the relationship between the artwork and the viewer-visitor. In performance installations, however, the encounter with the artwork often involves another living entity: the performer. Along with the performer comes the notion of the *stage*, which brings a set of quite specific conventions into play.

Staging the Spectator

What is a stage, exactly, and what is staging? These are much-used words but they are not often precisely defined. Usually the stage is presented as the counterpart of the auditorium (McAuley 1999, 25). The stage is where the performers present themselves to the public; the stage is where the spectators are not. The stage is often easy to distinguish, when marked by a proscenium arch, or looked down upon in black-box theatres or arena settings (Balme 2008, 49–50). The stage becomes smoother in environmental theatre or street theatre, but even then, there is still a stage. As soon as a street theatre artist starts doing something that deviates from everyday behavior, people stop, form a crowd, gathering around, and there it is: the stage. When attending the 2013 edition of *No Man's Land*, again in Utrecht, many travelers stopped to watch the line-up of spectators, pointing at us, taking pictures with their cell phones. These simple acts reveal that spectators are as much responsible for a stage coming into existence as performers are. A stage emerges from the activation of a *theatrical frame*, a set of conditions that marks or frames the presented things or events as being staged; they are presented in order to be seen, and to be seen *as* performance (Carlson 2004, 35–7). As such, the stage can extend toward all kinds of domains in life: to political arenas or social media, to commercials, or corporate industries. I regard the stage as a platform for performance, which can materialize in many different ways; the stage does not always concern an elevated height, but it produces a heightened attention.[7]

This heightened attention closely relates to what media scholar Chiel Kattenbelt names the "aesthetic orientation" of the spectator (Kattenbelt 2010, 31). Aesthetic orientation refers to the awareness of spectators being witness to a staged or framed reality, instead of actuality itself, which invites the spectator to perceptually transcend the constraints of daily life (31). This orientation, precisely through the confrontation with the art object, installs a type of reflexivity which is both oriented toward one's actual experience and toward the exploration of the imaginative, the possible, and the potential. The aesthetic orientation is the precondition for every performance event to come into existence (31–3). It is precisely the condition through which we may recognize a theatre performance as such. This orientation installs the notion of the stage and, simultaneously, a stage invites this aesthetic orientation to become active. This dialectical process is an indicator of the potential smoothness of the stage and may serve to understand the conventional stage–auditorium divide as the striated version of both stage and auditorium instead of as a prerequisite of their definition.

These reflections bring Peter Brook's often-quoted opening lines of *The Empty Space* (1968) to mind: "I can take any empty space and call it a bare stage. A man walks across this empty space whilst someone else is watching him, and this is all that is needed for an act of theatre to be engaged." From a scenographic perspective, a space is never empty, and seeing or watching is not always a precondition for theatre, as I will suggest in Chapters 3 and 5. More relevant to the present discussion, however, is the observation that in *No Man's Land*, the spectator walks Brook's bare stage as well, a space that now is significantly crowded with traffic, with sounds, smells, and scents of the city, and with other users of public space. Here we touch upon an interesting paradox. When I conceive of the spectator in *No Man's Land* as being positioned onstage, the spectator is both on the stage and the "other" of the stage, the "other" who is needed for the stage to come into existence. We can abandon the notion of stage altogether to dispose of the problem, but then we would dispose of theatre, in my opinion. I propose to use the paradox, instead, to argue that the presence of the spectator onstage brings forth an utter strangeness, reminiscent of the nomads in Kafka's story with which I started this chapter, who are suddenly perceived to be in the center of the town. Due to the spectator's aesthetic orientation, a spectator will always remain a stranger to the stage, even when s/he is *on* the stage. Even when there is hardly any physical distance between performers and spectators, the aesthetic orientation of the spectator still will provide a certain (aesthetic) distance. A spectator on the stage does not automatically transform the spectator into a performer, or a character. The spectator, in my view, remains a spectator; a spectator who somehow is not supposed to be on the stage, yet nevertheless is there.

This paradox perhaps explains the sense of uncanniness that often occurs at the start of performances like *No Man's Land*. The spectator does not know what to expect or what is expected: what am I to do? Am I doing "it" right? Am I doing it "right"? Contrary to (most of) the performers, who tend to arrive well-prepared on the stage—even in improvisational performance— the spectator often wonders what to do, how to behave, what to say, or not to say. Contrary to the performer, the spectator did not rehearse. Staging the spectator produces a strangeness that cannot be captured, precisely because the spectator brings a certain exteriority along: a spectator cannot be placed on the stage like an object, or in a similar way be directed or in control like a performer, nor can the spectator be designed like lightning or sound. The spectator can be guided, and severely manipulated, but always carries along a certain unpredictability. Next to the performer, now there is another living presence on the stage, a force or energy which deterritorializes the stage from within. The spectator destabilizes the stage by bringing the auditorium "along," which turns the stage into a space where multiple perspectives are active at the same time. This by definition creates an unstable situation, a kind of theatrical cubism, in which the spectator is both participant and reflexive observer at the same time. Here we see the collapse of object–subject distinctions that is so characteristic of installation art. As a consequence of these deterritorializing acts, spectatorship itself becomes the object of heightened attention.

Walking with Abderraghman

Let's follow Abderraghman, with me in tow, as we leave the station concourse and walk across the platform toward one of the many exits of Utrecht Central Station. Abderraghman walks before me, equipped with a small audio set and a tiny earplug, while I wear large white headphones (Figure 2.2). Again we attract attention, as I follow the footsteps of my guide. We are on our way to Lombok, but I do not know that yet. I feel amused and uncomfortable at the same time, curious about what will happen and uncertain because I do not know what to expect. I wonder whether I even *like* performances such as this one … But why do I want to know what will happen? When attending a conventional theatre performance, I do not know what to expect either. That type of suspense,

Figure 2.2 Leaving the station, in *No Man's Land* by Dries Verhoeven, Utrecht 2013. Courtesy Studio Dries Verhoeven, photo Maarten van Haaff.

however, is part of a convention. It is institutionalized suspense, a remnant of age-old traditions: the curtains rise, on stage a magical world will unfold, a world that will draw you in. In *No Man's Land*, however, the unknown is not framed within a context in which not-knowing has its own, orderly place. A reassuring frame is absent. This is not the time to sit quietly in the dark; the safe plush seating has disappeared and so have my fellow audience members.

Halfway down the stairs Abderraghman stops and turns around. We look straight into each other's eyes. Through the headphones I hear the following text:

This is me.
These are my hands.
These are my legs.
This is my face.
This is not a theatre costume.
This is not a Dutch appearance.
I am a foreigner—or migrant, that sounds better.
A refugee.
Political or economical—you don't know that yet.
And maybe even a Muslim.

Or I'm just here on holiday, that's also a possibility.
That is the most cheerful version.

This is not my voice. This is not my language.
This is the voice of an actor.
See, I may still look like a stranger,
Like some kind of character from a comic strip from a distant country, who stands in front of you, a little uncomfortably.

Someone who wouldn't normally speak English this fluently.
But because of the English voice you will regard me differently, listen differently.

Clearly, I could let you hear my own voice.
I could talk with a slight accent, Goodevenink.
How nice that he speaks English.
That you would be touched when I pronounce the English word "lemon curd" … without making a mistake.
You probably wouldn't really listen to the words.[8]

The text raises many questions concerning the identity of the man standing in front of me, and the voice through which he is represented—some of which I will address below. In the meantime, the eye contact at close distance settles the atmosphere for things to come; there is sympathy involved in the exchange of looks, the eye contact is actually quite intimate, and pleasant. Next we move on, walking rhythmically on the merry *raï* music now played through the headphones, toward one of the station's exits and onto the street, setting course for Lombok district. During the next half an hour or so, we alternate between walking through Lombok and moments when Abderraghman stops, turns around, and looks at me, while I hear a voice on tape. The voice tells of "his" land of origin, of how "he" has dreamt of living in the West, of tedious asylum procedures, of first experiences in the Netherlands, and of living in the Netherlands for 22 years and still being called a migrant. While I gradually get used to this mobile duo-performance, in which Abderraghman and I together establish a similar pace, the nature of the story changes. This time Abderraghman does not look at me, when the voice reports a gruesome memory of being held by militia while his daughter is raped and burned. Slowly we start walking again. While I need some time to digest this story, we pass through other streets, occasionally observed by residents who seem to vary between curiosity and suspicion. There are cheerful moments as well. At a certain moment Abderraghman dances lightly on the beat of the music, when out of the blue two more dancing performers appear around different corners, each of them followed by a slightly dazzled spectator. The sudden duplication of the situation, including my own spectatorship, brings Henri Bergson's essay on laughter to mind, where he observes that any human behavior that resembles mechanic repetition invites us to laugh.

As the performance's title reminds us, a migrant's life often is a no man's land, a life in-between homes, marked by displacement, lacking one-ness or wholeness. While walking through the streets of Lombok, it appears that the stage as well has transformed into a kind of no man's land. The stage is distributed onto urban space and unfolds as the trajectory progresses. Meanwhile life in the city follows its routes, ruptures, and routines. The theatre space and the urban space are separated by an invisible, yet extremely porous and permeable membrane. A boy loitering on his bike asks me what we are doing. The membrane dissolves. Well, I am in a performance, listening to stories that you may know by heart … This is one of those few, odd potentials of performance in public space, where the rules of play become the object of observation itself. In the second half of the walk, the story's tone changes again and deliberately bypasses cultural-political tensions, to make room for social connectivity on a more personal or intimate level. The voice muses on how we might relate to each other, how we could discuss books or films, or share a meal. If it gets late, I could stay the night, the voice says, and although he has to leave early in the morning, I can take my time and let myself out. He provides me with trust, and the key to his house, with the kind request to put the key through the letterbox when I leave. He promises to serve breakfast to me. Abderraghman then places a small orange tangerine on the pavement. I pick it up and return again to the here and now of the walk.

Throughout the trajectory, the stage and the urban space continue to destabilize each other. They merge into urban scenery and proliferate through their mutual interference. They frame each other, as the urban space becomes the set and the stage reterritorializes on the streets. They unfold again, but differently, when the porous membrane that separates the two domains suddenly dissolves, due to curious inquiries of passers-by, or, simply, at a traffic light. These patterns of de- and reterritorialization render the stage of *No Man's Land* into a smooth space, and put Abderraghman and me into a state of continuous variation.

Triads and Constellations

During our joint walk, Abderraghman and I are constantly engaged in a process where we (re)position ourselves relative to the other and to the spaces through which we move. While this becomes truly significant on a dramaturgical level, as I will discuss below, the continuous reconfiguration of spatial relations also instigates a theoretical movement. This act of continuous repositioning invites us to exchange the dualistic stage–auditorium divide for a much more flexible way of looking at the relations between performers, spectators, and space. In their Nomadology chapter in *A Thousand Plateaus*, Deleuze and Guattari draw a comparison between Go and chess, pointing at two different logics at work in these games, one connected to the nomadic, the other to the sedentary. Their comparison inspires my preference for looking at the performer–spectator–space triad as a flexible, threefold constellation. I will briefly explain how. For Deleuze and Guattari, Go is attuned to a nomadic war machine, in contrast to the State apparatus of chess, when comparing respectively the functions of the game pieces, the internal relationships between pieces, and their spatial orientation.[9] On the level of *functions*, chess pieces are coded and have pre-established identities and functions, while Go pieces are simple, anonymous units, without intrinsic properties; they have only situational functions. Therefore, the *relations* between pieces are different. Chess pieces have "bi-univocal relations with one another, and with the adversary's pieces: their functioning is structural" (2004, 389). Go pieces on the other hand work through the formation of constellations. They derive their function from their position within this constellation; they perform functions such as "insertion ... bordering, encircling, shattering" (2004). Also their *spatial orientation* is different: chess defends space and is oriented toward closing the space, whereas Go is concerned with

> arraying oneself in an open space, of holding space, of maintaining the possibility of springing up at any point: the movement is not from one point to another, but becomes perpetual, without aim or destination, without departure or arrival. The "smooth" space of Go, as against the "striated" space of Chess ... The difference is that chess codes and decodes space, whereas Go proceeds altogether differently, territorializing or deterritorializing it (make the outside a territory in space; consolidate that territory by the construction of a second, adjacent territory; deterritorialize the enemy by shattering his territory from within; deterritorialize oneself by renouncing, by going elsewhere ...). Another justice, another movement, another space-time. (Deleuze and Guattari 2004, 389–90)

Go and chess do not differ from each other in terms of their open-endedness or the absence of rule sets. One cannot predict the outcome of a chess game, and also a Go game has rules and a grid. Rule sets and grids do not fix positions in space. Instead, they provide the conditions for play. The differences between the games, however, enable us to distill two varying modes of play, connected to two diverging logics of practice.

The Go game provides a model for understanding the performer–spectator–space triad as a mobile threefold constellation that in each specific performance evolves through particular, changing configurations and situations. I am not implying, however, that I regard performers and spectators as anonymous Go pieces. The Go game points to situational relationships and to a specific spatial orientation, namely one of being distributed into smooth space, of playing with shifting territories, of renouncement and going elsewhere. Analogue to the strategies in Go, a performance like *No Man's Land* places performers and spectators within an open space, and their respective territories—the stage and the auditorium—are active as interfering spheres, subject to deterritorialization. Although performers and spectators are not the exact equivalents of game pieces, the comparison suggests a certain affinity between the stage and the game board, which I will elaborate in relation to Signa's *Ruby Town*, in Chapter 6. This game board occasionally is on the move itself, as is the case in *No Man's Land*. The smooth stage of *No Man's Land* occupies the urban space without possessing it entirely. The stage distributes Abderraghman and me into an open space, creating situations that are temporary relays, always maintaining the possibility of going elsewhere.

A Problem of Referentiality

It seems utterly romantic and quite naïve to speak of Abderraghman and me as being distributed into an open, smooth space, in times of involuntary migration, political exile, and cultural displacement—topics that are at the heart of *No Man's Land*. Posited against this sociopolitical reality, one can even wonder whether nomadology as a tool for analysis is inappropriate, if not politically incorrect. Robert Marzec introduces this moral dilemma in his essay on Deleuze's nomadology, referring to critical remarks by Caren Kaplan and Gayatri Spivak, amongst others, who criticize Deleuze for being a-historical and nostalgic (Marzec 2001). Although Deleuze and Guattari explicitly distinguish between the nomad and the migrant, this dilemma is tenacious and needs a few words of explication.[10] Caren Kaplan, for instance, argues that the idea of a perpetual transcending of boundaries actually repeats a Western Enlightenment dream, closely connected to a (European) history of colonial expansion and exploitation (2002, 35).

Looking into more recent discourse, both Tim Cresswell and Mark De Kesel criticize the use of nomadist vocabulary in relation to postmodern, global citizenship, where it is often applied to appreciate ourselves as dynamic globe-trotters. De Kesel (2006) points to the aggressive nature of Deleuze and Guattari's nomadic war machine instead, which indeed leads one to imagine a radical terrorist rather than a fashionable cosmopolitan. Cresswell critiques the "nomadist metaphysics" of mobile theories, including those of Deleuze and Guattari, which not only take a-world-on-the-move as subject matter, but seek to incorporate mobility in the very structure of thought itself. For Cresswell, those theories tend to celebrate mobility for mobility's sake, while they ignore the fact that access to mobility is unevenly distributed, due to reasons of class, race, or gender. Such theories tend to flatten out differences and fail to do justice to social inequality, ignoring the "racialized root of the metaphor" (2002, 18).

These are serious accusations, asking to inquire into the ethics of nomadology. To this end, we need to dive a little deeper into the arguments. Cresswell sees the nomad as a metaphor, an issue that is critically dissected by Paul Patton, in "Mobile Concepts, Metaphor, and the Problem of Referentiality" (2010). Patton discusses the critique of Caren Kaplan and Christopher Miller, amongst others, who accuse Deleuze of perpetuating (neo)colonial dreams of expansion, coupled with a fascination for the primitive Other (cf. Bogue 2004). To Kaplan, these myths perpetuate the "rhetorical structures of a modernist European imaginary" (Patton 2010, 39). Patton offers an insightful answer to these and other accusations, arguing that these problems do not pertain to the nomadic per se but actually expose a problem of referentiality: "the real issue here is that of the relationship of their concepts to their apparently empirical claims" (36). Deleuzian concepts only contingently relate to empirical facts; their real source lies in philosophy (37). Vital in Patton's argument is the question of whether Deleuze and Guattari use the nomad as a metaphor, which, according to Patton, they do not: "To persist in treating nomadism [and] the war machine ... as metaphors is simply to fail to recognize their nonrepresentational practice of thought" (36). For Deleuze and Guattari, the nomad is not a metaphor, but a conceptual persona, a concept with which to mobilize thought. To them, a metaphor expresses one thing through another, which not only suggests the independent existence of things, but also distinguishes between an original and its derivative (24–6). Deleuze strongly rejects such a representational, hierarchical image of thought.[11]

My approach to the matter closely aligns with Patton's remarks. Already implicit in the various examples discussed here, the nomadic manifests itself in many different ways, no one more true or close to the "original" than the other. The nomad in science is not closer to the nomad than the nomadic tribes in the desert. Deleuze and Guattari observe that "the nomads do not hold the secret: an 'ideological,' scientific, or artistic movement can be a potential war machine, to the precise extent to which it draws ... a creative line of flight, a smooth space of displacement. It is not the nomad who defines this constellations of characteristics; it is this constellation that defines the nomad" (2004, 466). Nomadism surfaces in war tactics, but also in art and philosophy. Some of these practices raise ethical questions, but however contested these practices may be, they do not disqualify the concept of the nomadic itself.

This Is Not My Voice: A Problem of Referentiality, Part 2

Next to this problem of referentiality, *No Man's Land* offers a second problem, which pertains to the obscure relationship between the physically present migrant-performer and the manner with which he is represented by the prerecorded voice of an absent performer. Although I started the performance with a sense of insecurity, not knowing what my role as a spectator would be, the activities required (walking, listening, observing) are, all in all, quite familiar. Instead, the instability of spectatorship surfaces elsewhere, namely in the failing attempts to connect the text provided through the headphones to the performer in front of me. This is not his voice. This is not his story. The story is inconsistent. It is not the tale of one person, but of many. Actually, the story is a collage of all the stories told by the various migrants who participated in the project.[12] Each spectator hears the same story. Although I know or suspect all this, a part of me projects the stories onto the man in front of me, trying to bring the various elements together into a coherent whole. But it doesn't work. The two types of address, one by the voice on tape, one by the physical presence of Abderraghman, stay in conflict. And the conflict multiplies: who is this man that I walk with, who is the "real" Abderraghman? Is he a performer or a migrant, or both? On the one hand I feel disappointed about this "missed" encounter; on the other hand we *do* still have an encounter. Paradoxically, the audio equipment both separates and unites us. We do not speak to each other; yet we are both silent witnesses, listening to the prerecorded voice on tape.

The text is composed according to the principles of a dialogue, and contains phrases such as "I could have," "you may wonder why," and "you probably think that." Personal pronouns such as "I" and "you" are deictic markers; they organize social relationships. Precisely because they are empty forms, deictic markers allow the partners involved in the discourse to *appropriate* these terms for themselves (Bleeker 2008a, 19). It is a smart strategy for rendering the spectator present within the work, and it probably explains my sincere urge to speak during the performance, or rather, my acute awareness that I am silent. Both the stories and the "direct" address by the prerecorded voice cause a wish to express my willingness to comprehend "his" situation, to explain my sense of guilt—for being in a privileged position, for being unharmed. I know that I am manipulated into these feelings, yet this leaves me with an actual sense of incapacity: I will never be able to put myself into Abderraghman's shoes, or to capture his situation entirely; full comprehension is impossible.

The intervention of the mediating voice raises an ethical dilemma. To deprive a person of a voice can hardly be called a suitable means for arranging a successful encounter, especially when thought of in relation to Spivak's well-known essay "Can the subaltern speak?" (1988). It is easy to argue that the prerecorded voice of a professionally trained actor installs the migrant as Other. In addition, the actor-mediator appears to be an all-knowing figure, who repeatedly predicts my response, always one step ahead in articulating possible observations, feelings and thoughts. He even addresses this specific dilemma, and once more the mediator's thoughts are faster than mine, as he also provides an explanation. The voice, by way of the paradoxical utterance "I could have used my own voice," explains how that latter choice probably would invite compliments on how well the migrant-performer has mastered the Dutch language.[13] Even after living in the Netherlands for over 22 years, he keeps receiving that compliment: "How excellent is your Dutch!" It is difficult to describe the intonation of that comment. It is a combination of the positive appraisal by a native speaker who willfully ignores the stuttering language of the other, and of the tone one uses to compliment a child—but that actually does the trick. It makes me realize that this is what "we" do—I have to include myself, I'm afraid. The comment is not a neutral one, it is the expression of difference. This interpretation of the scene is strongly affected by the cultural-political climate in the Netherlands at the time of this performance, in 2008. Ahead of the widespread nationalist and anti-refugee sentiments that currently define political agendas throughout Europe, a growing animosity towards foreigners had invaded the Netherlands and Dutch politics at that time, which led to polarized debates about the failure of the multicultural society and to increasingly rigorous asylum and integration procedures. Within light of those events, the nearly mastered Dutch language had become a sign for failed integration, and "How excellent is your Dutch" precisely the confirmation of not being "Dutch." Suddenly I wonder whether my participation in this performance is not an equivalent of this sentence, a "How good of you to tell your story to me." It makes me realize that the subject-matter—Dutch native meets migrant—is thoroughly perverted, as there is no best choice when it comes to which voice to use. In either way the migrant is deprived of his voice, whether by the actor-mediator or by an ongoing political debate-as-mediator, a debate that I cannot escape, and which, although I may conceive of myself as open-minded, has perverted my way of listening as well. This encounter with Abderraghman confirms our distinct positions, as if we are both struck in a perpetual repetition and reconfirmation of (social) difference.

No Man's Land seems to promise an encounter between a migrant and a spectator. The personal tour through the Lombok district suggests that we will get to know each other. But instead of the expected encounter, the performance installs a feedback loop, through which spectators are invited to experience and reflect on their own, often unconscious ways of perceiving and thinking about migrants. As a consequence of the isolation brought about by the headphones, and the commentary voice, the performance manages to bypass the ethical questions raised above and instead redirects the attention to how spectatorship is the product of personal projections and prejudices, and influenced by cultural baggage. There is a second, related strategy that causes this self-reflexivity to emerge. By obscuring the relationship between migrant and performer and by the hybridization of stories, *No Man's Land* escapes dominant imagery and puts the very idea of "the migrant" itself into a state of continuous variation. Instead of presenting a coherent story or a clearly identifiable character, the performance shows that actually there is no such a thing. The problem of referentiality itself thus becomes the subject matter of this performance. This strategy is in a way similar to Deleuze's account of the work of Carmelo Bene.[14] In "One Less Manifesto," in which Bene's work is discussed, Deleuze asks:

> Might not continuous variation be just such an amplitude that always overflows, by excess or lack, the representative threshold of majority measure? ... Might not theater, thus, discover a sufficiently modest, but nevertheless, effective function? This antirepresentational function would be to trace, to construct in some way, a figure of the minority consciousness as each one's potential. (1997, 253–4)

For Deleuze, perpetual variation entails a process of continuous differentiation. This is not a repetition-of-sameness or re-presentation, but instead a threshold of potentiality; it points to things in a state of change, to the option of the always-otherwise. The problem of referentiality in *No Man's Land* similarly creates openings to other horizons and other modes of encounters, as I will elucidate below. Perpetual variation does not imply, though, that we arrive at a reality that is "more true." Instead, spectators are invited to explore the conflictual relationship between a body-without-voice and a voice-without-body, and their own responses to this conflict. Such a mode of audience address characterizes postdramatic dramaturgy, which often relies on a multiplication of frames or perspectives, compared to the "operation of the single frame" of dramatic theatre (Bleeker 2008a, 8). Maaike Bleeker observes that Lehmann connects the subsequent ambiguity to the political potential of (postdramatic) theatre. Politics in this case does not pertain to what is represented on stage, but resides in the perceptional processes involved, as this mode of address "draws attention to the problem of representation itself, to representational forms and how they are perceived, or not" (2008a, 8; cf. Lehmann 2007, 53).

Deleuze values (Bene's) theatre for its anti-representational potential. In *Visuality in the Theatre*, however, Maaike Bleeker points out that theatre always deals with representation. Although there have been many attempts to conceive of a pure, unmediated presence in the theatre, for instance by Antonin Artaud and in 1960s and 1970s performance art, Bleeker argues that presence in the theatre always operates within principles of representation, because "presence relies on other signifiers and thus remains within the realm of the already constructed. Derrida's 'always already' left deep marks" (2008a, 21). Theatre cannot escape representation. Theatre does not necessarily depend on the "as if" but always relies on the "as theatre." Therefore, in a departure from Deleuze, and other authors in his slipstream, such as Simon O'Sullivan (2006) or Nigel Thrift (2008), I do not think that an emphasis on process, experimentation, or continuous differentiation leads us *beyond* representation. This is demonstrated by *No Man's Land*, which, in line with Bleeker's observations, renders representation itself into the subject of investigation.

Fractured Reciprocity

Representation in the theatre is closely connected to conventions of spectatorial address. *No Man's Land*'s staging of the spectator plays with and thus exposes these conventions. The encounter between performers and spectators is not only frustrated by conflicting stories or by the ambiguous body-voice assemblage, but also by the simple fact of the close eye contact between performers and spectators, through which the performer returns the gaze of the spectator. This eye contact is an inversion, and deterritorialization, of Brook's notion that "someone else watches and that is all that is needed for an act of theatre to be engaged." A performer who looks back at the spectator destabilizes spectatorship, and renders the contract between performer and spectator visible (Ridout 2006, 80–7; Klaver 1995). This exposure of the contract between beholder and beheld relates to Barbara Freedman's use of the term *theatricality*, in her study *Staging the Gaze* (1991), discussed by Maaike Bleeker, in *Visuality in the Theatre*. For Freedman, the theatre is always marked by and works through the tension between seeing and being seen. For her, theatricality refers to "[t]hat fractured reciprocity whereby beholder and beheld reverse positions in a way that renders a steady position of spectatorship impossible. Theatricality evokes an uncanny sense that the given to be seen has the power to both position and displace us" (in Bleeker 2008a, 9). Bleeker elaborates on Freedman's use of the term "theatricality," by pointing out that theatricality renders visible how theatre addresses and positions the spectators. Address entails spectators being invited to adopt a particular point of view from which to look at what is being presented on stage. This does not imply that the spectator always accepts or identifies with the presented perspective. As Freedman points out, such a suggested point of view can also cause a sense of displacement. Next to theatricality, Bleeker posits the term *absorption*, which indicates another, opposite mode of address, namely one in which the spectator is drawn into the world on stage, precisely because the traces of mediation are erased (2008a, 21).

Although Bleeker elaborates her thoughts in relation to performances that work with the conventional stage–auditorium divide, her observations provide further insight into the fractured reciprocity in *No Man's Land* and expose that theatre is always involved with representation, and with a process of staging the spectator. For Bleeker, staging involves the construction of a viewing position for the audience, which she terms the *subject of vision*. Paralleled to the function of perspective in painting, this subject of vision entails a specific, suggested point of view, which mediates between the seer as subject and what there is to be seen (80). Seeing, therefore, is always a relational act and actively involves the body of the seer-spectator as the locus of looking. In addition, Bleeker uses the (narratological) concepts of internal and external focalization to describe how the relationship between stage and audience is organized. Internal focalizers invite the audience to take up a performer's or character's points of view (28). External focalization relates to the anonymous agent through whose eyes we look at the events presented on stage (31). *No Man's Land* uses various, conflicting focalizers, playing the physically present performer against the mediating voice of the absent actor: one is looking, the other is talking. Through the contrast between a body-without-voice and a voice-without-body, and by returning the gaze, the spectator is prevented from absorbing into the "world on stage." However, despite the many strategies that point to theatricality as the dominant mode of address, *No Man's Land* also makes use of absorption, as a culturally conditioned mode of viewing.

In order to elaborate on this argument, it is helpful to look a bit further into Bleeker's analysis of perspective. She draws a parallel between perspective painting and dramatic theatre. Analogous to the strategies of absorption in dramatic theatre, perspective painting draws the viewer into the represented world, precisely by suggesting the beholder to be absent (21). Perspective obscures the framing devices through which the physical presence of the spectator is replaced by an "ideal" looking position, the subject of vision. This way, perspective suggests direct access to the things presented, showing the world "as it is," which conceals the representation *as* representation (48). Although we have come to see perspective as a particular representational technique, Bleeker observes that the promise of perspective is quite persistent, namely that there is such a thing as "an objective world existing independently of our subjective point of view" (36).

No Man's Land stages a situation in which the spectator, other than in perspective paintings or conventional stage set-ups, is literally invited to step inside, to share the stage with the performer. Despite the many external focalizers, this invitation incites a culturally coded and conditioned response, one in which "stepping inside" has become associated with direct access, immediacy, truth, and reliability. Bleeker observes how absorption invites the spectator to take up the position of a character or performer, or to empathize with performers presenting "themselves": "We are invited momentarily, to forget the relationship between ourselves and the other we are seeing. It is as if we experience directly what the other feels, seeing the world through his or her eyes" (33). This may explain why I expected this encounter to be a genuine encounter, in which I would have direct access to a "real" migrant, and why I felt such a strong urge to feel empathy. Previously I described how my response to this performance was tainted by a specific political climate and societal debate. The tension between absorption and theatricality exposes again how spectatorship is a culturally conditioned process. *No Man's Land* produces an encounter in which two people are quite close, but ultimately, this creates a fractured reciprocity, where "beholder and beheld reverse positions in a way that renders a steady position of spectatorship impossible" (Freedman), and where the spectator, and his or her response to spectatorial address, becomes the object of observation.

Building Performance

At the end of the performance, we arrive at yet another variation of a no man's land. This takes the form of an empty field near Utrecht Central Station, covered with a silver-colored sand beach, on which twenty beach houses stand (Figure 2.3). Each migrant–spectator couple enters one of the houses, where the headphones are taken off and the migrant sings to the spectator. Abderraghman's voice is raw, low, and a bit squeaky. It is strange but

Figure 2.3 Closing scene of *No Man's Land* by Dries Verhoeven, Utrecht 2013. Courtesy Studio Dries Verhoeven, photo Maarten van Haaff.

nevertheless comforting to know that this sound is "really real." After having been isolated by the headphones for the preceding three quarters of an hour, the live voice is strikingly intimate. At the end of the song, Abderraghman leaves the beach house, only to return in front of the house a few minutes later. Through a small hole in the door the old projection technique of a camera obscura is revived. I see Abderraghman projected upside down on the wall in front of me. First I see a blurred image but when it sharpens I notice that he holds a small cardboard sign, with my name on it: Liesbeth. It is both a literal, visual inversion, as well as an inversion of the performance's beginning, and indicative of the performance's self-reflexivity. Seeing my name on the cardboard is somehow a sign of recognition, not in an Aristotelian sense but in the sense of a mutual acknowledgement, indicating that we don't know each other, that in this encounter we did not get to know each other better, but that we nevertheless have shared time and space together. We have looked into each other's eyes; perhaps we shared some thoughts and feelings. Together we were involved in quite an intimate situation, despite the mediating technology. In *No Man's Land*, the headphones intermediate and obstruct the encounter but also invite re-appraisal and awareness of lived and shared time.

Nicolas Bourriaud remarks that relational art produces situations in which "it is no longer possible to regard the contemporary work as a space to be walked through ... It is henceforth presented as a period of time to be lived through" (1998/2002, 15). This focus on lived experience pertains to this performance as well. The trajectory leading from the station, to the streets, and to the beach house installs a perceptual awareness, which in the end surpasses *No Man's Land* political agenda. More precisely, the spatial dramaturgy is oriented towards approaching the topic from a different angle. Instead of installing a critical, distanced reflexivity regarding social and political inequality and other ethical questions, the performance asks what can be shared, despite the obvious differences. This interest in lived experience and in theatre's potential to install a sense of connectivity, marks much of Dries Verhoeven's work. The performance achieves this by, amongst other ways, leading the performer–spectator–space constellation through a range of spatial configurations; varying from installing and crossing the performer–spectator division in the station concourse, to the joint walk, to the interiority of the (temporary) house. Throughout these configurations, the performer and spectator together are involved in a process of *building* performance, drawing on lived experience.

In their Nomadology chapter, in *A Thousand Plateaus,* Deleuze and Guattari mention a twelfth-century practice of building Gothic cathedrals, in which the building process is not based on (the reproduction of) static and pre-designed templates, which are the instruments of the State, but on the embodied knowledge and experience of the craftsmen engaged in the work. They present this practice as an instance of nomad science, grounded in (collaborative) experimentation. Deleuze and Guattari describe how craftsmen create architectural volume and structural coherence through squaring, approximation, and qualitative calculation, generated by the material and the work-in-progress: "One does not represent, one engenders and traverses" (2004, 402). The qualified labor in nomad science relies on experience that is built up in time and is stored as corporeal knowledge. State science instead works through reproduction, regulation, and the generalization of labor, which produces an unequal power relationship between those who commission the work and those who execute it (2004, 401–2).

Engendering and traversing the work: this is a remarkably apt description of *No Man's Land*'s architecture and its emergent dramaturgy. Performers and spectators are not engaged in an act of constructing a building, of course, yet they are mutually involved in a process of building performance. While navigating the streets of Utrecht's Lombok district, they traverse the paradoxes inherent the dis-settled life of a migrant in the Netherlands. Both performers and spectators engender the work by bringing their corporeal knowledge and sensibilities to the work. *No Man's Land* generated a range of responses, varying from spectators reporting they had a joyous walk, or an alienating experience, or were moved to tears.[15] Each trajectory joins two particular lives and produces heterogeneous encounters. Building on experience also brings the *Experten des Alltags* to mind, the experts of daily life, a term coined by Rimini Protokoll but also relevant in relation to *No Man's Land*. As an alternative to working with professionally trained actors, Rimini Protokoll collaborates with non-actors who present a particular (professional) expertise: truck drivers, local politicians, the elderly, or factory-workers who have lost their job (Dreysse and Malzacher 2008). It is a wonderful concept, I think, as of course everyone is an expert of his or her own everyday life. *No Man's Land* likewise presents non-professional actors, builds on the expertise of migrants, and works with the experience of the spectator.

When the song has ended, Abderraghman leaves the beach house. After a while I leave the beach house as well, only to find the field empty, with the exception of fellow wandering and wondering spectators; spectators who do not want to leave yet. They seem to be in search of their guides, to enter into dialogue with them, the guides who have already disappeared into town. All in all, *No Man's Land* is not a politically correct performance in which migrant and native are brought to an increased, mutual understanding.

The performance doesn't provide an encounter. At least not in the ways one might have expected. Instead it queries what an encounter is, or might be. How do you get to know a person? What is "knowing" exactly? Meanwhile, *No Man's Land* experiments with a different kind of encounter, in which two people with quite different backgrounds share a similar rhythm and spend some time together, bringing their own experience to the work. Is this, then, the "real" encounter? Well, no. The encounter itself is subject to a dramaturgy of perpetual variation. After my walk with Abderraghman, Abderraghman will invite someone else, and then again someone else. This *assemblage* of the one-after-another and the next-to-each-other qualifies *No Man's Land*'s emergent dramaturgy.[16] A performance that uses the format of a one-to-one encounter extends itself in time, compared to conventional performance. As each spectator will respond differently and each trajectory is a different trajectory, the performance multiplies in number, and changes in nature.

Expanding Spectatorship

In this chapter, I examined various ways in which *No Man's Land* deterritorializes the stage. Evolving from the station hall, to the streets of Lombok, to twenty beach houses in a row, the stage loses the usual structural integrity and reterritorializes as synchronous trajectories. *No Man's Land* puts the stage into a state of continuous variation, by distributing performers and spectators onto the smooth space of the urban environment, while they traverse the rhythms of a migrant's life in a contemporary European city. The scale of the encounter swings from horses to wasps and back again, as the performance variedly shifts from large-scale sociopolitical contexts connected to immigration and multiculturalism, toward the tiny details of the everyday, the quality of shared time, and the intimacy of the house. I have characterized this trajectory as a process of building performance, a process of co-creation, in which both performers and spectators traverse and engender the work. Traversing and engendering the work also characterizes my involvement as a researcher. In this chapter, I built an argument through a series of approximations, suggesting that analyzing performance is equally a process of squaring and scaling, partly relying on corporeal and subjective experience, partly relying on how the material generates response.

No Man's Land promises an encounter with a stranger, only to backfire toward the spectators in the end, as they primarily encounter themselves and are invited to self-reflexively explore their response to ambiguous spectatorial address. Staging the spectator in *No Man's Land* produces a situation in which spectatorship itself is brought to the light of attention and renders visible how spectatorship is (always) staged. In *No Man's Land*, the relation between performers and spectators is full of inversions and reversions. This fractured reciprocity also involves an exchange of activities and, ultimately, an expansion of spectatorship. The usual activity of the performer—presenting oneself in front of an audience—and that of the spectator—watching, listening, witnessing—are shared with one another. Abderraghman performs, but is as well engaged in looking and listening. Similarly, I am observed by Abderraghman, by passers-by, and feel an urge to express myself. We do not exchange roles. Abderraghman is still the performer, albeit a confusing one, and I am still the spectator, albeit a confused one. However, we do take over some qualities or characteristics of that other role and integrate this with our existing role or function.

This mutual encounter resembles Deleuze and Guattari's account of the orchid and the wasp, mentioned above. The orchid–wasp assemblage consists of a mutual becoming. In *No Man's Land*, performers and spectators enter into composition with one another, which produces situational functions: a *becoming-spectator of the performer*, and a *becoming-performer of the spectator*. The spectator does not become a performer, does not transform into a performer, but rather, enters into composition with those aspects and functions that we usually relate to performing in the theatre: to present oneself to another person, to step on a stage in order to do so. The spectator enters a zone of proximity with the performer, by living in symbiosis with these aspects. Likewise, the becoming-spectator of the performer signals a performer who looks and listens and thus cuts across the usual area of expertise of the spectator, on his own terms. The goal is not to arrive at new positions, but this negotiation itself. Both the performer and the spectator are engaged in *becoming-space* as well, as they enter into composition with space by means of way-finding, navigating, and by maintaining the coordinates of the theatre space, a process which will be further investigated in subsequent chapters.

Setting up situations that focus on the (apparently) trivial produces a "poetics of encounter," to use a phrase by Nigel Thrift, "which both conveys a sense of life in which meaning shows itself only in the living, and which, belatedly, recognizes that the unsayable has genuine value and can be felt 'on our pulses'" (2008, 147). A last return to *No Man's Land*, place of memory: the station concourse. Recall for a moment the situation in which spectators and performers are waiting, each on either side of the gap. They are looking into each other's eyes, waiting for the encounter that is already taking place. A no man's land is a smooth space. The gap between spectators and performers too is a no man's land: it belongs to nobody in particular. It is a space without borders, open for any traveler in the station. But the gap is not empty, as it is already taken by those who pay attention to it. The gap defines performers as performers and spectators as spectators, and as well performers as becoming-spectators and spectators as becoming-performers. These elements together form the image of a gap that is both present and absent, a gap that both divides spectators and performers, and connects them. This is the after-image of *No Man's Land*, which will be active in the following chapters. A gap, on the verge of being traversed and dissolved, embodied and multiplied.

3

Displacement

The Situated Pathways of Rimini Protokoll

Urban Moves

In this chapter I revisit *Call Cutta* (2005), produced by Rimini Protokoll, a German collective of performance artists consisting of Helgard Haug, Daniel Wetzel and Stefan Kaegi.[1] I will use this performance to trace the whereabouts of the stage in relation to the *theatre space, urban space*, and the domain of global economy. As mentioned in the introduction, *Call Cutta* connects a walking spectator in Berlin with a performer aka call-center employee in Kolkata (Calcutta), India, with the help of a mobile phone. In a short interview, Rimini Protokoll's Daniel Wetzel remarks that "[s]ince we increasingly spend more time on our mobile phones, it is only natural that it becomes a place for theater" (Hansen-Tangen 2006). In *Call Cutta*, the mobile phone not only becomes this place for theatre, but functions as a primary deterritorializing force, as the phone engages the performer–spectator–space constellation into a dynamic process of ongoing shifts and multifaceted movements. *Call Cutta* employs various modes of *displacement*, as a staging strategy: spectators are involved with physical displacement, whereas the performers are displaced from their usual location at center-stage. Also the stage is subject to displacement: instead of bringing performers and spectators within a distance of a few meters, the gap between them now stretches over 10,000 kilometers. The performance focuses on call-center work, both as subject matter and as dramaturgical format, and charges real call-center employees with carrying out the task. *Call Cutta* thus operates through outsourcing labor, another form of displacement, which in this case can also be seen as a form of "outsourcing performance."

Although *Call Cutta* deals with globalization, the performance cuts across the local conditions of both performers and spectators and renders perceptible how places are practiced and lived. Therefore, in this chapter I turn to Henri Lefebvre's notion of *lived space*, by which Lefebvre counters prevalent conceptions of space, where space is primarily theorized in terms of the perceived and the conceived. Through its focus on lived and situated practices, *Call Cutta*, as a theoretical object, serves to demonstrate how nomadism in the theatre surfaces as a series of local operations, which produce the theatre space as one moves through it. Deleuze and Guattari affiliate the nomadic with localized actions and spaces, rather than the globalized. They point to the nomad's absolute and "nonlimited locality," adding that for the nomad, "the coupling of the place and the absolute is achieved not in a centered, oriented globalization or universalization, but in an infinite succession of local operations" (2004, 422). Lefebvre's spatial analysis helps to render visible how these local operations involve processes of articulating particularity, as a countermovement to all too general or dualist conceptions of the global versus the local, or of space versus place.

As mentioned earlier, Lefebvre's work is involved with the study of the polyphonic rhythms of everyday life, in the context of expanding urbanization, globalization, and commercialization, and impacted by developments in media and information technology, housing and infrastructures, and much more (Lefebvre 2004). At the basis of his rhythmanalysis, however, is his understanding of social reality as an inherently spatial practice. In *The Production of Space* (1974/1991), Lefebvre counters the abstractness of fast-growing urban, global, and capitalist agglomerations by making room for the mundane realities of everyday life. Drawing on both Marx and Heidegger, he employs a triadic spatial analysis of how the perceived, the conceived, and the lived are collaboratively involved in a process of production, that is, the production of social space (Elden 2004). *Perceived space* involves the concrete reality of material and physical spaces; it concerns spaces that can be seen, touched, mapped, or measured. *Conceived space* relates to how we think, imagine, and conceptualize space. This abstract and mental space is the instrument of, amongst others, urban planners, designers, social engineers, but also the domain of philosophy, law, and politics. *Lived space* points in particular to how spaces are actually used and experienced by different (groups of) people, how they modify over time and are molded by political and social developments, and get infused with symbolic meanings, embodied memories, and situated histories. Of vital importance in Lefebvre's work is that these three spatial domains can be distinguished, but never separated. They are always produced through one another, and their interrelations create trialectic pathways that transcend dualism (Lefebvre 1991; Soja 1996).

Although Lefebvre wrote *The Production of Space* in the early 1970s and builds upon even earlier work, his spatial analysis is still relevant for contemporary performance.[2] All the practices I discuss rely heavily on this specific understanding of lived space, in which spatial experience is linked to the production of social space. Such a social space is put on the agenda in Rimini Protokoll's *Call Cutta*, which glimpses backstage at call-center work and counters notions of floating, fluid globalism by firmly locating call-center employees at the place where they work and live. Lived space also surfaces in the time spent together in Dries Verhoeven's *No Man's Land* (Chapter 2), or in the corporeal memories through which we are tied to habitual places of passage, as in for instance Verhoeven's *Trail Tracking* (Chapter 4). Lived space equally materializes in Deleuze and Guattari's account of twelfth-century cathedrals, mentioned in Chapter 2, where collaborative experimentation and embodied knowledge are the backbones of the building process.

A more contemporary urban example is parkour, in which physical displacement is used to counter the affordances of the built environment by personal expression of use. Parkour, also referred to as *l'art du déplacement* or the art of displacement, involves the act of traversing the city in a fluid and continuous manner, as quickly and effectively as possible, through improvisation and the creative use of the obstacles and restraints one finds on the way (Kidder 2012; Ortuzar 2009; Fuggle 2008). John Urry uses the term "affordance" to explain how objects and environments invite, discourage, and constrain human behavior (2007, 50–1).[3] Against the perceived and conceived realm of the affordance, the practitioners of parkour, or *traceurs*, are "jamming" their way through the city through improvisation, by climbing over fences, scaling walls, swinging on railings, or walking on roofs. Parkour is an explicit example of how users and inhabitants perform the city: instead of an abstract or functional space, the city emerges as a lived space, constructed in use. Both parkour and (ambulatory) performance in urban, public spaces point to the possibility of using spaces otherwise, and reveal the urban environment as always open to a different use than what is intended or programmed by design. "It's about a change in perception," says a *traceur* in a newspaper article, "We move our bodies, and learn to move our minds" (Feldman 2008). This displacement of perspective is precisely the basis for Lefebvre's argument that lived space functions as a space of (alternative) representation. In line with this reasoning, this chapter suggests that physical displacement is linked to perceptual displacement and provides, next to parkour, a number of *parallax* practices to sustain this argument. Parallax involves "the apparent displacement of an object caused by the actual movement of its observer" (Foster 1996, xii). I will rely in particular on Alan Read's use of the term, which focuses on the appearance of the minimal difference within an object of perception, rather than an oppositional point of view, when taking a slightly different perspective (Read 2008, 17).

As in my discussion of the installation in Chapter 2, the comparison here with parkour does not suggest that in the theatre exactly the same processes are at work. Instead, both the installation and parkour are parallax practices, which invite a slightly different perspective on the object of enquiry, and help to point at specific characteristics or qualities. Whereas the installation pivots around the relationship between the viewer and the artwork, parkour explores alternative modes of engaging with the (urban) environment. Parkour's urban pathways also point to the situationality of the (performance) event. Parkour foregrounds improvisation, whereas *Call Cutta* stages processes of improvisation. Yet they both deal with displacement as a strategy for reimagining the city as a space where qualitative difference is produced and lived, through performance.

Performance scholar Jimena Ortuzar critically describes parkour as a "kinetic utopia" which repeats the (modern) myths of free mobility and the transcendence of (physical) restraints, but in that quest is also utterly unfree. To support that argument, she points to parkour's need for continuous movement, which seems to express a state of constant emergency—leading her to inquire what is actually the rush? (2009, 60). Indeed, let us slow down. Let's walk.

The City as Stage

In *Call Cutta*, a single spectator embarks upon a journey by foot through Berlin's Kreuzberg district, guided by a call-center employee who is based in Kolkata, India. After purchasing a ticket at the HAU Theatre (Hebbel Am Ufer) in Berlin, the spectator is handed a mobile phone and instead of being invited into the theatre, is asked to wait outside. Within a few moments, the phone rings and after a short mutual introduction, the spectator sets off on a tour that lasts for about one hour. With the aid of the cell phone, the employee navigates the spectator through nearly abandoned parking lots, shopping malls, play areas, and courtyards adjacent to dreary housing blocks. *Call Cutta* had an "offshoot of afterlives" (Bastajian 2008) in the many reviews and scholarly essays it engendered; a common theme is the ambivalent, yet thoroughly intriguing awareness that even though the call-center employee is situated thousands of kilometers away, simultaneously one expects to see the employee behind the next corner. While the dialogue emphasizes the distance between them, the intimacy of the voice produces an effect of presence, and creates a sense of proximity.

Initially, the call-center employees behave like average call-center workers, as they introduce themselves by a Western name and in a flawless Western accent. But it doesn't take long before the employees reveal their true names and start disclosing information about working and weather conditions in

Displacement

Figure 3.1 The call-center in Calcutta, in Rimini Protokoll's *Call Cutta*. Courtesy Rimini Protokoll.

India (Figure 3.1). Through *Call Cutta* Rimini Protokoll investigates the phenomenon of outsourcing. In the global economy that characterizes advanced capitalism, tele-services are often transferred to low-wage countries. When calling a helpdesk service or taking out an insurance policy, one often does not realize that this service may be carried out on another continent. The distance is concealed through the use of Western names and accents—and telephones of course. Call-center employees in India, for instance, often work at night, to meet Western timetables. This phenomenon is referred to as translocality, by Arjun Appadurai (in Whybrow 2010, 253).

Contrary to the style of reporting in the previous chapter, this time I will use an over-the-shoulder-perspective, to demonstrate that the address to the individual spectator does not necessarily require a first-person perspective to reflect on it. I will rely in particular on essays by Heiner Goebbels (2007) and Susan Leigh Foster (2008), occasionally supplemented by my personal account of the box-version of this performance, attended in Brussels in 2008.[4] *Call Cutta* is composed as a loosely scripted telephone conversation, which starts off with the revealing of true names. And so it happens that Heiner Goebbels walks with Priyanka, who initially introduced herself as Prudence, and Susan Foster finds herself in the company of Aisha. Goebbels reports a multifaceted dialogue, that apart from the very precise instructions through which Priyanka maneuvers him through the streets, meanders from political-historical relationships between India and Germany, to an exchange of opinions regarding the interference of the public and the private, to a description of the actual working conditions in the call-center. When Susan Foster enters a vacant area, Aisha asks her to look for some pictures attached to a tree. These pictures show Aisha's great uncle, so she is told, who came to Berlin during the Second World War to seek assistance for setting up an Indian liberation army. The history of colonial India's struggle for independence is tagged onto various objects, hidden in dustbins or under park benches.

Aisha leads Susan across abandoned train tracks and a loading dock, explaining how these sites were used to transport armaments to the various war fronts, during the Second World War. The archeological remains, the intimacy of the remote voice and Aisha's "uncanny connection to Hitler" create a "new cybernetic world, one that requires new kinds of skills to navigate" (2008, 171). The "new cybernetic world" Foster refers to, is the product of various patterns of de- and reterritorialization, in which a remote-controlled layer is placed over the urban environment and where the city turns into a stage. Similar to *No Man's Land*, and parkour, the performance appropriates the

Figure 3.2 On the road in Berlin, in *Call Cutta* by Rimini Protokoll. Courtesy Rimini Protokoll.

territory of urban space, without occupying it completely. Urban space too reterritorializes on the theatre as the streets, lots, and vacancies define the scenography and the *mise-en-scène* (Figure 3.2). And yet, the theatre and the urban space are separated by an invisible membrane, which produces a minimal difference between staged and daily reality. Performance scholar Alan Read describes this perceptual displacement caused by the theatrical frame as the "minimal parallax condition": the process of staging itself installs a "stage rhetoric" that distinguishes the stage from daily life (2008, 16). Such rhetoric is also at work in *Call Cutta*. Except, this performance is almost invisible, hardly distinguishable from daily reality. Most of the passers-by probably will not even have noticed that it took place. This situation actually comes even closer to Read's use of the term parallax. In *Theatre, Intimacy and Engagement*, he refers to the appearance of the *minimal* difference within an object of perception, rather than a diametrically opposed one, when looking at an object from a slightly different point of view (2008, 17). I will return to Read below; I have evoked his observations here to further enquire into this minimal stage rhetoric.

Since mobile phone theatre is primarily noted by the ones engaged in it, these performances can be characterized as a form of "secret theatre" (Balme in Chapple and Kattenbelt 2006, 118). This notion of a secret theatre helps to expose the slight change of perspective caused by a type of theatre that nests within a city, rendering the urban environment into *urban scenery*. Christopher Balme, drawing on Shuhei Hosakawa's "The Walkman Effect" (1984), argues that ambulatory spectators in audio theatre come quite close to Hosakawa's Walkman users. Mobile audio devices produce a secret theatre, as spectators are shielded from the (urban) environment, traversing the city with an altered perception. The isolated listener is corporally affected by an acoustic, invisible source, which causes small changes in pace and behavior. The soundscape makes the walk "more poetic and more dramatic" in Hosakawa's words, and turns all the passers-by into figures on a theatre stage (2006, 119). Heiner Goebbels gives a similar account of *Call Cutta*, as he reports an increased corporeal awareness, induced by the mobile phone: his walking, listening, seeing, occasionally singing body produces an experience of being at the center of an acoustic envelope (2007, 122).[5]

This secret theatre is a portal to both a vertical and a horizontal genealogy of urban displacement. Ambulatory performances like *Call Cutta* can be regarded as follow-ups of Baudelaire's *flâneur* and as contemporaries of pervasive games. In *The Arcades Project* (1982/1999), Walter Benjamin describes the flâneur as someone who wanders around in the city with no goal other than to observe, without being noticed himself. Drawn by the sounds and the scents of nineteenth-century Paris, the department stores in the arcades, attractive women, and particularly the unknown behind the next corner, the flâneur loses himself in the crowd, while at the same time observing and thus distancing himself from the crowd. The crowd functions as a veil from behind which the city appears; a city that by then sparkles with commercial, technological, and artistic innovations that beckon the flâneur to keep dwelling, and which provide the stage upon which he entertains his daydreams (Benjamin 1982/1999, 416–24).[6] Due to the experience of immersion and intoxication, Baudelaire's flâneur seems to be engrossed into a *phantasmagoria*. The phantasmagoria is often regarded as a pre-cinematic invention, as it suggests an encapsulating environment that offers distraction through optical illusion (Buck-Morss 1992). Benjamin, however, uses the term for environments that establish a sense of interiority, or an experience of being indoors.[7] As such, flânerie also can be seen as a forerunner of the invisible, secret theatre that is at work in *Call Cutta*, where passers-by do not know that they figure on a theatre stage. Not only ambulatory performances create secret theatres; I had a similar experience in the box version, which took place in an abandoned office building. When closing the door of the office after my one-hour talk with Souptic Chakraborty, I realized that nobody would come to know what I had been doing in that particular hour. This is a peculiar thought, in a way, since I spend lots of hours at home or in my office, without someone knowing what I actually did during that time and without me wondering what others think I am doing.

A contemporary example of a parallax condition can be found in pervasive games. Pervasive games, and related forms such as mixed reality or augmented reality games, place an extra, virtual layer on the urban fabric of a city, using mobile media that facilitate navigation, geotagging, biomapping, and so on (Farman 2014, 2012; Verhoeff 2012; Benford and Giannachi 2011; De Souza e Silva and Sutko 2009). This layer pervades or augments—deterritorializes—daily reality. Game theorist Markus Montola defines a pervasive game as one that "has one or more salient features that expand the contractual magic circle of play socially, spatially or temporally" (2012, 121). This contractual magic circle has many similarities with the (dramatic) stage, further demonstrated in relation to Signa's *The Ruby Town Oracle* (Chapter 6). Pervasive games, similar to *Call Cutta*'s theatre space, often do not have clear physical or geographic boundaries; the gaming area is truly a smooth game board that is on the move. Both pervasive games and ambulatory performances deterritorialize the urban space, as they unfold within the city, but follow a different rule-set than regular urban traffic. Both reterritorialize on the urban space, as—keeping the flâneur in mind—life in the city becomes perceptible as (always) staged, and as engaged with the performance of place.

Theatre Goes Global

Similar to some pervasive games, *Call Cutta* is organized through remote control: spectators are navigated through Berlin by a performer who resides on the other side of the world. In comparison to a performance like *No Man's Land*, the most remarkable difference is, of course, that in *Call Cutta*, the stage and the theatre space have gone global. The stage is shattered to pieces; the theatre space is deterritorialized by means of mobile technology and redistributed over the globe. The stage resurfaces in several joint locations: Berlin, Kolkata, and a Hertzian space in-between. *Call Cutta* thus captures the code of the particular time-space reconfigurations that mark a globalized world, where "synchronization substitutes the unity of place, where interconnections supersede the unity of time" (Weber in van Eikels 2011, 9).

In early theories on globalization, space and time were seen as liquid or even void categories. Globalization was perceived as a process by which the world seemed to be simultaneously shrinking and expanding, in increasing degrees over the twentieth century, due to the accumulation and intensified use of various mobility systems. Shrinking, since these mobility systems brought places closer together, and expanding, as the area in which one is able to move was rapidly enlarged (Cresswell 2002).[8] John Urry notes, in *Mobilities* (2007), that contemporary mobility systems do not so much engage with physical or vehicular mobility, but counter distance with tactics of simultaneity, co-presence, or networked connectivity (cf. Verhoeff 2012), often by using mobile communication technologies, in particular mobile phones (De Vries 2012).[9]

Co-presence and connectivity are precisely the registers explored and exploited in *Call Cutta*. One of the defining characteristics of theatre as a live event is the simultaneous presence of performers and spectators in the same room. *Call Cutta* radically rethinks this convention, or, rather, appropriates the networked co-presence of wireless communication technology by establishing connections across the globe. Such an act of reterritorialization puts forward the question of what "the same room" exactly entails, in a globalized context. Instead of regarding the stage as shattered to pieces, we could also argue that global society always puts us in a shared space— which gives a rather new flavor to Shakespeare's famous dictum that "all the world is a stage". *Call Cutta* thus seems an emblem of cosmopolitanism, as it incorporates various mobility systems, organizes displacement through digital technology, and makes the stage go global. Throughout the tour, however, emphasis is put on the local specificities on both ends of the line. Distance is the omnipresent given and there is an ongoing exchange of information about the two locations. Both performers and spectators invest in making themselves known to the other and making themselves present through the ongoing negotiation of distance and difference. *Call Cutta*'s local perspectives slice through a globalized world, rendering abstract globalism and related assumptions of universality back to the scale of lived space.

The Production of Space

Call Cutta counters abstract globalism by exposing the location of call-center employees' work and private lives, juxtaposing this lived space with that of the spectators. At the start of this chapter, I briefly introduced Henri Lefebvre's notion of lived space. I value his concept because Lefebvre not only links lived space to spatial experience but also connects this experience to the social conditions of a changing lifeworld. In this respect, Lefebvre shares an agenda with *Call Cutta*. In *The Production of Space*, Lefebvre describes how social space is produced through everyday practice and lived experience, yet also is shaped and molded by political processes and global economies, and socially constructed and transformed by use. Social practice does not only take place *within* a space, but produces space itself.

In *Understanding Henri Lefebvre: Theory and the Possible* (2004), Stuart Elden meticulously discusses the influence of both Marx and Heidegger in Lefebvre's work. He describes how Lefebvre uses Marx's analysis of economics to enquire into the politics of spatial relations, shifting the attention from the production of things *in* space toward the production *of* (social) space itself. Production does not only refer to the creation of things, but as well to the production of society, knowledge, institutions, and so forth. Through Heidegger, Lefebvre contends that technological and scientific developments have created a reductive world view in which space is primarily understood in a geometrical, calculated, and mathematical sense. Consequently, the world is regarded as "a substance which can be ordered, planned and worked upon—instead of worked with" (Elden 2004, 189). Heidegger uses the concept of *dwelling* to suggest a way of inhabiting the world as a matter of concern, in a lived, experienced manner. Both his terms *dwelling* and *habiter*—approached as verbs, indicating an activity or temporal situation rather than a fixed or permanent state (Elden 2004, 190)—resonate in Lefebvre's approach to lived space, yet Elden suggests that Lefebvre's "pluralist Marxism" much more explicitly addresses the connections between politics and space, in relation to modern capitalism (189).

These influences join forces in Lefebvre's severe critique of abstract space—demonstrative of the ultimate dominance of conceived or mental space—which according to Lefebvre is the result of technological acceleration, economic expansion, and increasing rationalization and bureaucracy. Abstract space "transports the body outside of itself in a paradoxical kind of alienation," and instead foregrounds "the primacy of the written word, of 'plans', of the visual realm ... analytic intellect ... 'pure' knowledge; and the discourse of power" (Lefebvre 1991, 308). Everyday life thus is consumed and exhausted by capitalism, and lived time has vanished from social space (1991, 95-6). *Call Cutta* and also *No Man's Land* render back this lived time, by providing performers and spectators with an opportunity to explore social space. *Call Cutta* turns globalization into a rather concrete phenomenon, and, taking Goebbels' and Foster's occasional impressions of disorientation into account, provides the opportunity to physically experience the space-time reconfigurations of a globalized world.

In *Thirdspace: Journeys to Los Angeles and Other Real-and-Imagined Places* (1996), cultural geographer Edward Soja reframes and rephrases Lefebvre's spatial analysis in relation to contemporary human geography, feminist theory, and Foucault's heterotopology. He coins the terms firstspace, secondspace, and thirdspace—respectively connoting perceived, conceived, and lived space—to introduce spatial thinking as a methodology for critical analysis, or, in Soja's terms, a "critical thirding-as-Othering" (1996, 10). I prefer Lefebvre's terms and rhizomatic approach; however, Soja provides a clear insight into Lefebvre's triple dialectics, or trialectics. Spatial thinking does not divide in parts, but instead transcends dualism by favoring a "both/and also" way of reasoning over an "either/or" mode of thinking (7-13; cf. Elden 2004, 32-3). Lived space both encompasses and also exceeds perceived reality and the mental realm of the conceived, and involves real-and-imagined space. The radical openness of lived space disturbs and defies dominant readings of space, and allows for alternative epistemologies (Elden 2004, 190; Soja 1996, 81). Such a "both/and also" logic is also present in parkour, which does not reject the material or conceptualized urban environment, but surpasses these realms to explore other ways of using a city. A fence is still a fence, *both* a physical object and a token of propriety, but can *also* be used as a jumping board. I call upon parkour to serve as a parallax practice for a second time, now to expose how *Call Cutta* and other ambulatory performances are engaged in the production of theatre space.

Lefebvre was interested in the *production* of space, the kind of production that is grounded in use. Parkour is a good example here, since it relies on the (alternative) use of space, which produces alternate urban space. Implicit in Lefebvre, yet much more common in contemporary (spatial) theory, is the coupling between production and performance. To understand production as a creative and performative practice now is widely accepted, recognizable in the performative turn in many (spatial) disciplines, for instance in architecture. Performative architecture does not only pertain to the performance of buildings, but also stresses that space is produced through performance. In a Lefebvrian mindset, architect Bernard Tschumi argues that "there is no architecture without everyday life, movement and action" (Tschumi 1996, 23). Parkour's moves precisely touch upon this intersection; they are compositions in and of lived space. Similar to Ian Borden's approach to skateboarding, parkour may be regarded as a form of performative architecture (cf. Kidder 2012, 237; Spurr 2007, 58). Likewise, ambulatory performance produces ephemeral theatre spaces, spaces that are created in and through movement.

Parallax to parkour, and similar to *No Man's Land*, *Call Cutta* challenges the convention that a theatre space has clearly demarcated boundaries and takes place at a fixed spot or location. The theatre space instead follows relays—points that are reached in order to be left behind. This space is produced along the way. The theatre space takes a place, and it takes place: it no longer *is*, but takes place. The theatre space becomes a *navigational space*, a succession of local operations. Performer and spectators together maintain the coordinates of this procedural theatre space. When taking the Heiner–Priyanka and Susan–Aisha vortexes into account, two fluid axes that form but a fraction of the multiple grids of *Call Cutta*'s theatre space, we can see a continuously morphing movement-space, a performative architecture that is built on the gestures, displacements, and changing viewpoints of those who are involved in the act of maintenance. An assemblage of mobile and talking bodies and navigational spaces, which cuts across commercial contracts, political pathways, Hertzian space, embodied coordinates, and situated histories.

Performing Locality

Through its emphasis on distance and local differences, *Call Cutta* ties in with a larger development of practices and theories that are "getting back to place" (Cresswell 2002, 18) with the acknowledgement that global space is always active in those local places. The focus on place and location in both practice and theory pays tribute to an increased awareness of the complexity of place and the myriad interactions between spatial, social, and political practices, or between place, location, memory, history, and identity, within a world in motion (Wilkie 2015a; Tomkins 2014; Fischer-Lichte and Wihstutz 2013; Cresswell and Merriman 2011; Hill and Paris 2006; Margaroni and Yiannapoulou 2006; Massey 2005). This awareness asks for reevaluation of, and a non-dualistic approach to, place. This is also the central argument in "Theorizing Place" (2002), in which geographer Tim Cresswell traces a history of thought in spatial theory, in which place has been tied to fixity while space was clothed in fluidity. Place has come to be associated with a specific location, with a distinctive identity and history, whereas space was alternatively celebrated and rejected as unlimited, abstract, and anonymous (cf. Massey 2005; Augé 1992/1995). Such a distinction also informs Michel de Certeau's approach to place and space, in his often-quoted essay "Spatial Stories" in *The Practice of Everyday Life* (1984). In this essay, de Certeau compares places and spaces to the distinction between *langue* and *parole* in linguistics. Space is like the word spoken (parole) and involves the actual use of a system (langue). Places are defined by and fixed on particular locations; they exist next to each other and cannot overlap. Space on the other hand, as the practice of place, can take infinite forms. Place is location, whereas space is operation (1984, 117).

In line with more contemporary approaches, and with Lefebvre's lived space in mind, we may see that both place and space are (always) practiced and performed. Anthropologist Arjun Appadurai advocates a similar understanding in relation to the concept of location. He uses the term *locality* to counter prevalent (anthropologic) conceptions in the 1990s, where the local was often seen as a simple given and portrayed as an "inert canvas upon which the global and other forces produce changes" (in Whybrow 2010, 249–50)—rather similar to de Certeau's approach to place. Instead, locality envisions the local as a product of creation and imagination. For Appadurai, locality is not so much a spatial structure but a work of the imagination, a *technology* for producing a "structure of feeling" through which people are able to relate to the contradictory and circulatory flows that mark our contemporary cities (in Whybrow 2010, 252–3). He stresses that imagination is a social practice:

> the imagination [is] something more than a kind of individual faculty, and something other than a mechanism for escaping the real. It's actually a collective tool for the transformation of the real, for the creation of multiple horizons of possibility. The production of locality is as much a work of the imagination as a work of material social construction. (250)

Much in line with Lefebvre, in my view, Appadurai argues that people need everydayness; they live through attachments, intimacies, and daily routines. People "simply cannot work with entirely abstract, or virtual, or mediated ... communities" (251). People do not necessarily need face-to-face experiences but they need to be able to relate to local and global situations in a "material, embodied, sensory manner"; rather than roots, they need (spatial) engagement, which necessitates "some spatialized local" (251). Parkour is a modest example of Appadurai's locality-as-technology, where the city never ceases to be a horizon of possibility and gets charged with embodied relations. Appadurai sees the local and global as intertwined, circulatory flows (252–3). This comes close to the "global sense of place" as described by feminist geographer Doreen Massey, who sees place as a meeting ground or a node in a network of social, economic, political, and cultural relations (1994; 2005, 192). Place is always much more than what we can directly perceive or conceive, leading Massey to observe that "a larger [pro]portion of those relations, experiences and understandings are constructed on a far larger scale than what we happen to define for that moment as the place itself" (1994, 154). Place therefore is not the other, or the outside of global space. Instead place is precisely defined "through the particularity of linkage *to* that 'outside' which is therefore itself part of what constitutes the place" (155).

This global sense of place is actively at work in *Call Cutta*, as Kolkata becomes a force of energy in Berlin, and vice versa. *Call Cutta* brings place to the call-center employees, while the spectator in Berlin is invited to perceive the city as a network of both Western and non-Western spatial operations— or to give up the notion of "the West" altogether. Both performers and spectators are engaged in a process of performing locality, in creating Appadurai's "structures of feeling" that reverberate in the many rhythms of *Call Cutta*. When Heiner Goebbels crosses the Möckernstrasse in Berlin, Priyanka imitates the multiple sounds, noises, and voices she would hear when crossing a street in Kolkata (Goebbels 2007, 122). Goebbels, who is both a scholar and an internationally renowned director of music theatre, discovers that they share knowledge of the same Indian song, a song that he used for one of his operas. Despite the time lapse they sing together, while passers-by in Berlin are puzzled with this man who suddenly starts to sing (119, 129). Goebbels thoroughly enjoys this way of being "on the road," and experiences a "*Lust des Findens*" while navigating through unknown parts of the town (121).

Susan Foster reports a slightly different experience. After an hour-long walk, being led through busy streets, across empty parking lots, past unkempt bushes, tattered housing projects, multi-story flats, across a bridge, into a shopping mall, and onto the street again, she feels entirely disorientated and displaced. The reassuring presence of another participant whose trajectory more or less matched hers, is also gone. Probably the most uncomfortable moment occurs when Foster enters the grungy backyard of a tenement and stumbles upon a picnic of, based on the looks of their dress, Turkish inhabitants. She feels like an intruder who probably will be perceived as privileged and as a voyeur, without her being in control of her actions (2008, 172). Toward the end of the tour, when Goebbels stands in front of a street mirror, Priyanka describes his looks in detail, to his discomfort. Not because the description is not accurate enough but because he doesn't know the location of this viewpoint. The script then proceeds to actual visual encounter. Susan Foster enters a shopping mall and discovers the face of Aisha waving to her, from a screen that is displayed in the window of a multimedia store. She is invited to take a picture of herself, to complete the visual exchange. She is taken back to the theatre by bus, while others report on entering the HAU at the rear end, which is also quite telling, dramaturgically, as *Call Cutta* radically rethinks the conditions of theatre. These reports show how locality each time involves and emerges through a different performance, dependent on the societal and material flows that distinguish this co-creative event from the next encounter, to the next, and to the next.

Navigating Representation

Performing locality seems close to how Michel de Certeau conceived of spatial practices as a way of writing the city, in which walkers' trajectories become spatial stories, expressive of individual use and singular style, in an unlimited diversity. In his often-quoted essay "Walking in the City," in *The Practice of Everyday Life* (1984), de Certeau pits the infinite trajectories of the walker on the streets below against the city as representation, seen from above— in de Certeau's case, the city seen from the 110th floor of the World Trade Center.[10] For de Certeau, the bird's eye view produces the city as an image or as a map to be read, which implicates a viewing position that privileges a single, stable point of view (1984, 92–3). *Call Cutta* complicates and adds nuance to de Certeau's analysis in an interesting way. By replacing the bird's eye perspective with a geographically remote and culturally different point of view, Rimini Protokoll produces multiple, fractured, and parallax views of the city, exemplified in the experiences of ambiguity and disorientation in both Foster's and Goebbels' accounts. For de Certeau, spatial practice rebels against the regime of the visible, the panoptic, the reproduction, and the representational. He argues that the spatial stories of everyday life remain "below the threshold of visibility," adhere to an "opaque and blind mobility," and make use of spaces that cannot be seen or known (1984, 93). I argue, instead, that these spatial practices can be regarded as spatial representations and I revisit Lefebvre to flesh out this argument.

Lefebvre's main project was to investigate, in particular, representation itself, acknowledging that representations are internal to lived, social space

(Soja 1996, 34). Lefebvre's triad of perceived, conceived, and lived space is actually a stepping stone to another, more profound and politically informed triad concerned with rethinking our understanding of social space, in which he distinguishes between spatial practice, representations of spaces, and spaces of representation (Lefebvre 1991, 38–9). *Spatial practice* relates to perceived space and involves material, socially produced space, where space is both a product of and a mediator for behavior. It concerns empirical space as it takes physical form, the spaces that we use and inhabit, providing certain cohesiveness to daily life. *Representations of space* are the products of conceived space, relating to space as it is represented in, for instance, urban design, certain paintings and literature, philosophy, city planning, or law. Conceptualized space tends toward the verbal and the intellectual, it is the space of "savoir (knowledge) and logic" (Elden 2004, 187). It has been, and to a large extent still is, the dominant space in society (Elden 2004; Lefebvre 1991, 39). Edward Soja describes these representations of space as "epistemological storehouses," strongly involved with control, regulation, power, ideology, and surveillance (1996, 67). *Spaces of representation* encompass both perceived and conceived space but also transcend these spaces by foregrounding lived space.[11] It is "the space of connaissance," which, other than the space of savoir, involves "less formal or more local forms of knowledge" (Elden 2004, 187). Lefebvre does not explicitly define this latter realm, apart from and because of the unknowability of its potential. Spaces of representation involve the territories of imagination that disturb or interrupt dominant modes of representation. Lefebvre calls upon the arts, and "certainly theatre" (Soja 1996, 48), in order to restore homogenized space to ambiguity, to make room for diverting corporealities, to render the nonverbal and the rhythms of everyday life a counter-force against the overestimation of texts, writing, the readable, and the visible (Lefebvre 1991, 391).[12]

Soja remarks that these three realms each correspond to a particular type of epistemology. Lingering on Soja's terms for a moment: firstspace epistemology tends to a positivist, deterministic fixation on the material forms of things in space, often accompanied by claims of objectivity, pretending to describe "how things are." Secondspace epistemology, on the other hand, places the "true" knowledge of space in the mind, assuming that spatial knowledge is primarily produced through discourse, interpretation, or conceptualization (Soja 1996, 79). In both these modes of knowledge production, the experience of space is removed and replaced with scientific calculation or abstract thought. Thirdspace epistemology is not based on a set of distinguishable operations. The knowledge inherent to lived space can only be neared, not fully grasped, "through an endless series of theoretical and practical approximations, a critical and inquisitive nomadism" (82), which "builds cumulatively on earlier approximations, producing a certain practical continuity of knowledge production that is an antidote to the hyperrelativism and 'anything goes' philosophy often associated with such radical epistemological openness" (61).

Such approximations describe as well my way of working with the concept of nomadic theatre, and, next, bring Deleuze and Guattari's twelfth-century cathedrals back in mind, as discussed in Chapter 2. Although the radical openness of Lefebvre's lived space to a certain extent ties in with Deleuze's nomadology, their theoretical trajectories show remarkable differences as well. Both Deleuze and Lefebvre approach space in terms of open, rhizomatic networks, and Deleuze's "vibrations, rotations, whirlings, gravitations, dances or leaps" through which he characterizes Nietzsche's theatre of philosophy, match well Lefebvre's understanding of rhythms. They both have their roots in the May 1968 protests and their work is representative of a de-hierarchized, spatialized consciousness in the aftermath of those events (Conley 2003). Nevertheless, in the books that I consulted, cross-references are sparse.[13] Perhaps they would not have been the best of friends. Both Deleuze's and Lefebvre's work is grounded in the idea of production, but for Deleuze, this concerns the creation of thought, whereas Lefebvre rejects abstractness and consequently connects production to social practice. The most obvious dissonance lies in their approach to representation. Deleuze's work is thoroughly anti-representational, whereas Lefebvre describes his own work as meta-philosophy, which "differs from philosophy most notably in its acceptance of the world of representations. It analyzes representations as such, as internal to their world, and from this analysis comes the critique of representations" (Lefebvre in Soja 1996, 34). It must be acknowledged that Lefebvre is not very explicit on how exactly he defines the (lived) space of representation. Through his emphasis on lived space, as *another* category next to the perceived and the conceived, Lefebvre primarily seems to question the conditions of representation itself, asking what is actually represented, or representable, and what remains unseen. His approach affiliates with Jacques Rancière's "distribution of the sensible," mentioned in the Introduction. Lived space then can be regarded as a space that allows for the appropriation of representation—a strategy that is also at work in *Call Cutta*, as I will elucidate below. Therefore I take some distance from Deleuze's anti-representational image of thought, to account for the fact that theatre always deals with representation.

To illustrate the representational potential of lived space, I shortly discuss a pervasive game by the British company Blast Theory, who are well known for their interactive mixed reality games such as *Operation Black Antler* (2016) or *I'd Hide You* (2012). In *Rider Spoke* (2007), participants are sent out on the street, alone at night, on a bike with a handheld computer mounted on the handlebars, which is connected to a headset with a microphone.[14] The biker is asked to look for a hiding place, a place where one feels at ease; the computer functions as a positioning system, signaling to the rider any hiding place nearby. When at a hiding place, a personal question appears on screen. The participant records an answer onto the device, after which this data is tagged to that particular location. Now the biker can continue the journey and start looking for geotags that signal the hiding places of other participants. In these specific locations, the recordings and stories of other participants are revealed. The (nightly) isolation of the biker, separated from the daily routine, induces an increased self-awareness, which gradually expands toward the other participants, with whom one shares secrets and stories. This produces a sense of connectivity, even though one does not share the same space or timeframe. Gradually, the city becomes a depository of voices, an archive of identities coinciding with space. *Rider Spoke* produces an "other" city, a newly imagined and embodied city, which offers a re-acquaintance with a (usually) well-known environment. *Rider Spoke* thus transforms and performs the city through lived experience, and uses both the realm of the perceived and the conceived to explore alternative forms of representation.

In an interview, Blast Theory's Matt Adams explains how the company seeks to explore the "ethos of social interconnectedness in the face of often quite commercial technologies that have no real interest in the ethos that they create" (in De Souza e Silva and Sutko 2009, 77). *Rider Spoke* thus equally probes the qualities of (Lefebvre's) lived space:

> Given the rise of more and more participatory spaces, particularly online ... some of the questions we've been asking ourselves is, "who is able to speak in those spaces?" and more importantly, "what is able to be said in those spaces?" ... "what kind of modes of address do they allow?"
> (De Souza e Silva and Sutko 2009, 72)

Such questions point to a Rancièrian mindset, in which the redistribution of the sensible does not only pertain to the game itself, but also to social reality. In *Rider Spoke*, the assemblage of bikers, bikes, technology, and spaces creates a hybrid social space, a product of intertwined locations and relations, through which both the game and the city materialize in a process of co-creation and become perceptible as an Appaduraian work of the imagination. *Rider Spoke* produces "structures of feeling" through which participants can relate to the city in an embodied and sensory manner.

Through this discussion, two different but intertwined interpretations of the term "representation" emerge: that of being represented, and that of envisioning (new) ways to perceive, conceive, and experience the world, in order to make sense of it. In the next section, I will discuss how *Call Cutta* uses similar strategies but, even more so than in *Rider Spoke*, employs a both/and also strategy in order to investigate representation itself.

Outsourced Performance

Call Cutta is directed from within a call-center and is performed by call-center employees. This particular locality is a vital part of this performance, not only as subject matter but also in relation to *Call Cutta*'s dramaturgical strategies. The spectators are addressed as clients and the performer–spectator relationship is firmly tied on the grid of capital. Rimini Protokoll investigates the contemporary service industry, and the related practice of outsourcing labor to low-wage countries, by appropriating the system under investigation itself. Rimini Protokoll too offers a service and draws on the DIY-principles of personal customization, but alternative to a commercial customer service, the service is now a theatre performance. Instead of professionally trained actors, the collective hired call-center employees for the project—who are equally professionally trained performers of course. By employing these *Experten des Alltags*, Rimini Protokoll literally outsources performance. The spectators encounter these experts of the daily life in their actual workspace. In the box version that I attended, my dialogue partner Souptic used a web camera to show me around, pointing to the various clusters of small cubicles, in which teams working for respectively the Australian and American markets were executing regular sales work, next to Rimini Protokoll's call-workers.

Throughout the tour, it is quite obvious that the conversation is scripted, and also the tone of address follows the format of call-center sales work.[15] The employees maintain a friendly and cheerful conversation, chatting easily and making flirtatious remarks. It is a playful conversation, which provides a perverse pleasure, as it facilitates awareness of how the spectator is subjected to manipulation. Souptic told me for instance that I have a very pleasant and agreeable voice, assuming that I would be a very friendly person. His remarks made me smile, despite knowing that he was just playing the game, and it definitely increased my willingness to sing a song, in the middle of an abandoned office building. This feel-good strategy also seems to encourage participants in the ambulatory version to jump onto a deserted platform in a grey courtyard and shout out loud, or to reveal personal information (Dutt 2005). However, in this respect conversation fell short between Susan and Aisha. When Aisha asks whether Susan could imagine falling in love with someone over the phone—a scripted question—she learns that Foster is involved in a steady lesbian relationship. Aisha then tries to "switch sexual orientation" and claims a flirtatious interest in Susan herself, which Susan experiences as disingenuous (Foster 2008, 172).

These various responses show that *Call Cutta*'s mode of spectatorial address is a peculiar version of *personal customization*. Personal customization is a term closely connected to digital technology, and demonstrates that *Call Cutta* is not only fastened on the grid of capital, but also scripted by digital culture. Media theorist Lev Manovich uses the term to identify a distinct logic of postindustrial society and digital media: the variability and the modularity of the bits and bytes that distinguish digital media from older media allow users to arrange and program media content according to their own preferences— although often limited by formats (2001, 29–37). Manovich notes that users' choices are "both free and constrained" which implicates that "customization involves individuals not so much choosing freely but applying standard ready-made suggestions for consumption" (37). Giving witness to a process of cultural transcoding, another of Manovich's terms, one-to-one performances such as *Call Cutta* are customized on the single spectator, as performances reach their definition in relation to spectators' choices, responses and behavior, while at the same time this process is structured by certain formats and procedures. Such performances, in other words, transcode a procedure that originally refers to computer-generated processes, onto a cultural practice. Personal customization is only partially a neutral term, also demonstrated in *Call Cutta*, as there is a distinct flavor of commodification in the dialogue between performers and spectators.

Heiner Goebbels additionally describes feelings of uncanniness, in his case caused by the awareness of being led around Berlin by someone on the other side of the globe who has never been to this city. This "mis-guide" calls the Situationists' *dérives* to mind, urban wanderings based on the counter-strategy of the *détournement*: walking the streets of Paris not with a conventional city map but one that charts desire and affects, for instance. Here we are at the other end of the "commodity spectrum" since the Situationists radically critiqued the consumer culture of capitalism. I refer to the Situationists not only because their urban displacements are part of the family of "walkers in the city" traversing this chapter, but above all to show how *Call Cutta* chooses a distinctively different approach to processes of commodification. The detours of the French neo-avant-garde movement Situationist International (SI) were directed against the late 1960s mass media and consumer society. In *Society of the Spectacle* (1967), SI's front man Guy Debord describes the human condition as thoroughly perverted by capitalism. Capitalism exchanges the use-value of objects for their exchange-value and severs objects from their material existence: objects become images. The world of commodities thus becomes a spectacle, where appearance prevails above material experience. The spectacle does not refer to reality but solely to itself and its goal is only to establish itself. For Debord, the spectacular not only relates to concrete products of mass consumption; it has become the dominant *model* for the relationship between subjects and world (Debord 1967/2005, 8). SI envisioned a unitary urbanism in which collaborative projects, ephemeral or "constructed situations" and playful experimentation or *détournements* were vital tactics to re-appropriate urban life (Doherty 2009; McDonough 2002, 255–7).[16] The *dérives* and the use of playful maps were based on the principles of psychogeography, a way of moving about in the (urban) environment that deliberately bypasses functionality or efficiency and instead is motivated by desire, curiosity, or chance (Bishop 2012, 85; Wigley 1998, 18–19). Psychogeography involves intuitive displacement, attempts to get lost, or navigation on the basis of scents, ambience, or atmosphere (Pinder 1996).

Whereas SI firmly rejects totalitarian capitalism, Rimini Protokoll appropriates the system—not in order to change it exactly, but to offer a parallax view. Through this, *Call Cutta* makes representation itself part of the process under investigation. The dramaturgical strategies in *Call Cutta* come close to what Claire Bishop calls *delegated performance*, in the context of contemporary arts. Bishop defines delegated performance as "the act of hiring non-professionals or specialists in other fields to undertake the job of being present and performing at a particular time and a particular place on behalf of the artist, and following his/her instructions" (Bishop 2012, 219). Conversely to hiring actors in a theatre or cinema context, artists "tend to hire people to perform their own socio-economic category, be this on the basis of gender, class, ethnicity, age, disability, or (more rarely) a profession" (219).[17] Bishop aptly points out that this mode of outsourcing is also an act of outsourcing authenticity, rather different than the rhetoric of direct, unmediated presence that surrounded performance art from the 1960s till the 1980s. In these earlier forms, performance artists often presented themselves as true, authentic "selves," frequently by applying an aesthetic of risk. In delegated performances, the hirelings "just" carry out instructions, as "themselves," but, at the same time, these activities are authored and directed by the performance artist. Meanwhile, the artist hands over part of the control over the event, as these experts of daily life are the ones in charge of the actual execution of the process, which also creates a sense of unpredictability. It is precisely through this paradoxical situation, argues Bishop, that authenticity is "invoked, but then questioned and reformulated" (2012, 231).

Call Cutta received some critical evaluations and part of this critique involved the supposed lack of authenticity. Susan Foster, for instance, although positively intrigued by the performance, criticizes the conversation for being too scripted, adding that perhaps she and Aisha should practice improvisation more together. The performance is not really an equal two-way dialogue or a shared experience due to the fact that Aisha remains hidden behind the "persona of the call worker" (Foster 2008, 177). In another review, Tina Bastajian speaks of a flattening of subjectivities, a commodification of personal subjectivity that is placed on top of the profession of the call-center worker (2008). These responses precisely give witness to the perverse play that is at work here. Bishop uses the (psychoanalytic) term "perversion" for similar strategies in contemporary art, where unease and discomfort on the side of the viewer give witness to the artists' choice to investigate systems of exploitation precisely by using the rules of this system for organizing the art event. Artists use existing formats or systems in order to criticize, discuss, and thematize these formats or systems themselves. They expose the contemporary labor conditions underlying contemporary art, in order "to defy not only agreed ways of thinking about pleasure, labour and ethics, but also the intellectual frameworks we have inherited to understand these ideas today" (Bishop 2012, 239).[18]

In line with Bishop, and as a response to the critical remarks above, *Call Cutta* in my view focuses not on call-center employees as individual subjects, but rather on their socio-economic position. Although the conversation involves personal stories, and Souptic showed some family pictures, the main focus is not, I would argue, on the personal biographies of the call-center employees. *Call Cutta*'s spatial dramaturgy aims at questioning the socio-economic conditions of the service industry by offering a theatre service and organizing this service on precisely the same grounds. This both/and also strategy creates ambiguous situations, raises attention for the multiplicity of lived space, and examines existing perceptions and conceptions of outsourced labor. Somewhat similar to the staging strategies of *No Man's Land*, the performance questions notions of authenticity and stable identity. *Call Cutta* enquires into the representation of call-center workers precisely by obscuring the relationship between "real" call-workers and their professional personas, thus thematizing representation itself. In doing so, Rimini Protokoll does not oppose customer service industries but instead provides a parallax view.

Parallax

As mentioned above, Alan Read regards the stage as the minimal parallax condition, which invites us to look at things from a slightly different perspective. *Call Cutta* offers a range of these slightly different perspectives, as this performance de- and reterritorializes not only the stage, but also urban, global, and economic space. Alan Read remarks that, in its simplest form, parallax is "the common experience of an apparent displacement that occurs to an object when we change the position from which we view it" (2008, 16). Parallax is, however, not restricted to aesthetics or visuality. In *Theatre, Intimacy and Engagement* (2008), Read uses the term as an alternative to obsolete dualistic relations between performance and politics, in which theatre is thought to have either retreated from politics or still is presented as a society-changing political theatre (2008, 25–7). Parallax strategies provoke an increased sensitivity for qualitative difference, argues Read, a sensitivity that can amplify the relational capacity of human beings and contribute to social cohesiveness. Parallax practices—both inside and outside the theatre—work with strategies that expose minimal differences, typographically indicated by Read as the difference between this and *this*.[19] *Call Cutta* similarly maps the differences between this locality and *this* locality, in the trajectories of Heiner Goebbels, Susan Foster, and all the other spectators.

Although his strategy and scope is quite different from mine, Read's use of the term parallax, which he in turn derives from Slavoj Žižek, is helpful to point out how parallax strategies open up new spaces of representation, spaces that work through the production of qualitative difference and foreground singularity instead of generalization. *Call Cutta* provides us as well with a parallax view on representation. This ambulatory performance on first sight alludes to Deleuze's resistance to representation—regarded as the repetition of sameness—as each encounter between single spectators and performers produces a different spatial practice, which never gets back to "the same." On the other hand, the strategy of personal customization and outsourcing performance also reveals the grid of capital on which this performance is built, a grid that in turn is deeply embedded with reproduction and repetition, and thus with representation. But thirdly—both/and also—*Call Cutta* opens up a space of representation in which this situation of "being caught in the system" can be experienced and explored, in a material, embodied, and sensory manner, and in addition, demonstrates that such a system can be turned inside out, appropriated, and played with. This is the radical openness of Henri Lefebvre's and Edward Soja's lived space, the appearance of a small difference that escapes and extends beyond conceptualized representations of space and that points to the potentiality of the always otherwise.

These various perspectives, which are not put against each other but work through one another, present us with a (dynamic) parallax view. Reviewer Peter Michalzik remarks that Rimini Protokoll's experimental set-ups show a profound interest in the "perception and the knowability of the world, in particular the knowability of human beings. The aim is to break open the complex that constitutes our reality, showing it in all its facets as a way of enabling us to interrogate it" (2006). Alan Read too observes that theatre is able to, and perhaps should, function as a human laboratory, by testing the faithfulness of representations, while keeping an eye to what is included and excluded in representation (2008, 197). *Call Cutta* may be understood as precisely such a laboratory, showing that representation is not the exclusive domain of the dramatic theatre. This is illustrated by Rimini Protokoll's view on theatricality:

> Theatricality, as we understand it, doesn't have to do with obvious role-playing. This is a widespread misunderstanding. Theatricality is a process between me and the other while I watch him or her or it—in a state of interruption, fascination, openness—I call theatricality the process of an aesthetic experience. It's a process of creative perception. That is why theatre is political. (Lindt 2008)[20]

Wetzel's remarks relate to Bleeker's understanding of theatricality, when she observes that theatricality exposes the conditions of staging itself. The display of these conditions also informs Claire Bishop's analysis of delegated performance. One may wonder whether such strategies, in which artists adopt the system they seek to criticize, bring us back to a postmodern superficiality, in which the world is nothing but an endless repetition of simulacra. *Call Cutta* takes a slightly different route, in my view, and should be regarded as an Appaduraian work of the imagination, involved in the creation of structures of feeling through which spectators are able to relate to *Call Cutta*'s subject matter and strategies, on the scale of lived space.

Call Cutta emphasizes the difference between particular locations; differences that are felt and noticed through embodied displacements. Susan Foster feels that the differences were not acknowledged enough because Aisha, for instance, could not foresee that she would stumble upon the picnic with Turkish tenement occupants. In my view, that experience exactly demarcates local differences. Heiner Goebbels' trip turned out to be a joyful one and was concerned with giving trust. Foster's trajectory seemed to be concerned with control and loss of control. These differences are of course relevant with regard to personal experience, but in the end the one experience is not more true, or closer to "the" performance than the other; they are both parallax versions of *Call Cutta*. Read suggests, drawing on Žižek, that parallax is more than just a subjective point of view, as it shows that "subject and object are indubitably tied and mediated. A changing point of view for Žižek will always reflect 'an ontological shift in the object itself'" (2008, 16). This observation comes close to Maaike Bleeker's discussion of the concept of movement vision (see Chapter 4), but also characterizes the parallax practices discussed in this chapter.

"There is little point in putting theatre in a wider context when it already shows the complexity of that context within its own acts," remarks Alan Read (2008, 43). This observation is also an apt evaluation of *Call Cutta*'s staging strategies, in which theatre space, urban space, and global, social, and economic flows continuously displace and redefine each other. In this chapter, the encounter between the nomadic and the theatre proceeded through traversing a range of displacements, leading to a reevaluation of place, the investigation of practices of appropriation, and, ultimately, the production of parallax views. This trajectory provides us as well with a parallax view on both the terms that encounter each other within the concept of nomadic theatre. Nomadic variability exposes the theatre as an open-ended laboratory, in which local attachments, global connectivity, and spaces of representation can be explored and experimented with. In turn, the theatre redefines the nomad's nonlimited locality by placing emphasis on lived spaces and situated practices, and, through that, draws nomadism into the realm of both Lefebvre's and theatre's "meta-philosophy."

Call Cutta engages performers and spectators into a process of *becoming-space*, as they enter into composition with (globalized) urban environments and appropriate the city through the performance of locality. Spectators enter into composition with space, through embodied displacements and acts of way-finding, by navigating and performing space, by establishing a relational space together with the call-center employees. Simultaneously, the call-center employees take care of the connection between the locations. They perform their own location by providing site-specific stories, they are tour guides, they create nearness. In *Call Cutta*, becoming-space keeps being tied on the grid of capital but also produces structures of feeling through which spectators and performers may attach themselves to fluidity, in a material, embodied, and sensory way. This type of engagement is also explored by (feminist) enquiries on the "politics of location." I will discuss this concept in the next chapter, but will cite one related observation by Kathleen Kirby here, as it astutely captures the lived spaces addressed in this chapter. Whether we think of parkour's urban moves, *Call Cutta*'s commodity-flavored theatre space, or the hybrid social space of *Rider Spoke*:

> [space] forms a medium for reconnecting us with the material, but it also maintains a certain fluidity, a mobility: if we are speaking of space in the abstract it is susceptible to folding, division, and reshaping. A space persists only as long as the coordinates holding it open are deliberately

maintained, and the shapes and boundaries modeling space are, at least ideally, open to continual negotiation. (Kirby 1993, 175)

In the next chapter, I will further chart these negotiations in relation to cartography. I will then show that the focus on place, space, and local operations calls attention to embodied and embedded spectatorship. Already shimmering below the surface of this chapter but more explicitly addressed in the next, I will discuss how the performer–spectator–space constellation is drawn and configured through corporeal archives, situated knowledge, and the affective tonalities of becoming-space, and how these forces collaborate in maintaining the coordinates of a smooth stage.

4

Cartographies

Trail Tracking *and Map-Making as Staging Strategy*

You Are Here

A few years ago, I had taped a small flyer on the front window of my house, which displayed the text "You are here."[1] Passers-by and people about to board buses nearby often stopped walking in order to read the text. They seemed to freeze for a moment, as if they gained sudden awareness of themselves, on that particular spot—of course: I am *here*, and *I* am here. Learning this seemed to prevent movement. It was my favorite living-room sport to observe that process, in which passers-by had their feet nailed to the ground, figuratively speaking. Performing "You are here" is a modest, yet multi-layered event. It implicates a short interruption of an ongoing movement, a temporary pause within everyday routine, in which passers-by are invited to make an active connection between these words and their actual location. "You are here" is a deictic utterance, in which the reader appropriates "you" as "I." The linguistic term *deixis* points to how certain words organize subjective and social relationships in discourse. Personal pronouns such as "I" and "you" are deictic markers: similar to adjectives such as "here" and "there," they articulate a subject's specific spatial and temporal position. Precisely because they are empty forms, deictic markers allow the participants to appropriate these terms for themselves (Bleeker 2008a, 19). Therefore, "You are here" only becomes meaningful in relation to a subject who takes up the position of "I," in connection to a particular time and space (Verhoeff 2012, 55). The flyer-event thus points to the close relationship between place, location, movement, and subjectivity.

The text on the flyer was actually written in Dutch, reading "U bevindt zich hier." The subtle nuance gets lost in translation. The Dutch verb *zich bevinden* is a rather formal way of phrasing and bears associations with finding oneself and with discovery. The text thus can be read as a concise version of a phrase like "You are hereby cordially invited to discover yourself on this particular spot." It raises awareness of oneself in relation to a specific location ("here") and of the particularity of that location ("not elsewhere"). The same relationships are investigated, in much more detail, in *Trail Tracking* (2005) by Dries Verhoeven.[2] Similarly to the flyer-event, the performance aims for awareness of place and plays with various meanings of discovering oneself, while being on the move. In this performance, the spectator walks alone through an empty railway station aka museum, equipped with a mobile phone and a suitcase. Like in *Call Cutta*, the mobile phone is used for navigating the spectators through space. However, whereas *Call Cutta* foregrounded connectivity, co-presence, and dialogue, *Trail Tracking* redirects the attention back towards the spectator and, as a theoretical object, focuses on situated, embodied spectatorship.

Trail Tracking brings a set of particular territories into play. Whereas the previous chapters dealt with urban space, *Trail Tracking* instead takes place in a former railway station, a highly symbolic place, strongly associated with travel, mobility, and physical and vehicular displacement. Being a museum, though, it also brings movement to a standstill. The site-specificity of the place, which links past, present, and futurity, fuels the dramaturgy of this performance. Similarly to the previous cases, however, this performance deals with a smooth stage and a mobile theatre space, and the staged displacements place an added layer of reality on top of the site of the railway museum. In this chapter I approach the theatre space as a *navigational space*, a space produced through movement, in which the stage emerges as a set of temporary, changing coordinates, maintained by both performers and spectators. In *Mobile Screens: The Visual Regime of Navigation* (2012), media scholar Nanna Verhoeff remarks that mobile navigation devices, such as mobile phones, remarkably conflate navigation and creation: navigating through space at the same time produces these navigated spaces themselves (14). Although her study focuses on (urban) mobile screens and digital interfaces, her approach to navigation reverberates in interesting ways with *Trail Tracking*'s navigational and much more analogue moves. Verhoeff takes a *material* approach to navigation: she favors a relational instead of an object-oriented understanding of mobile screen practices, investigating how users are dialectically, creatively, and corporeally engaged with the sites and screens in which they are situated, and that therefore are also produced by them (18). These practices produce "screenspaces," engaging the user in a manner that "is not visual, fixated and distanced, but haptic, fluid and procedural" (150, 163).[3]

Trail Tracking in turn is involved with the production of a fluid and procedural theatre space, rather similar to Verhoeff's screenspaces, and focuses in particular on the affective tonalities of navigational space. The spectator is the only moving subject in a large industrial space that has "mobility" as a theme deeply entrenched within it but that now seems to be put on hold, a configuration that solicits sensory and spatial awareness. With the help of the mobile phone, the spectator is guided by a performer who is nowhere to be seen, but suspected to be near. This invisible and presently unlocatable performer plots a trajectory through the actual space of the railway museum. Soon after the start of the performance, though, this trajectory is intersected by another path, namely that of a route the spectator has often travelled in the past and which is now mapped and remembered, and queried by the performer. By way of charting and exchanging locative data, simultaneously oriented toward the past, the present, and the future, performers and spectators use and produce (site-)specific maps, based on the situated knowledge they bring to the map. Due to the various ways in which they are involved with mapping and map-making, I regard *Trail Tracking* as a performance that uses *cartography* as a staging strategy. Cartography concerns the use, design, creation, and conceptualization of maps. *Trail Tracking*'s maps are products of co-creation, as they evolve out of the collaboration between user and site, and between performers and spectators. The performer–spectator–space constellation, therefore, is particularly involved with the *performance* of cartography, and exposes cartography *as* performance. As a theoretical object, *Trail Tracking* tunes in with the performative turn in cartographic theory, where maps are studied as (interactive) performances and as products of co-creative relationships between maps and users, an approach which contends the idea of maps as objective representations of the world (Dodge et al. 2009; Crampton 2010; Verhoeff 2012, 137–42). Performative cartography instead sees maps as inherently open to use. Cartography, as a staging strategy, organizes time and space by setting up a playing field for the actions of performers and spectators, without predicting the outcome, keeping the field open to the potential inherent in the map.

Cartography: Fifth Principle of the Rhizome

The performative turn in cartographic theory has been highly influenced by Deleuze and Guattari's view on cartography, and their understanding of maps as assemblages of heterogeneous connections. In *A Thousand Plateaus*, they present cartography as the fifth principle of the rhizome, next to principles of connection, heterogeneity, multiplicity, and deterritorialization. Instead of defining what a map *is*, Deleuze and Guattari characteristically describe the map's potential, by pointing out what a map *does*:

> A rhizome is ... a map and not a tracing ... What distinguishes the map from the tracing is that it is entirely orientated toward an experimentation in contact with the real ... It fosters connections between fields ... The map is open and connectable in all of its dimensions; it is detachable, reversible, susceptible to constant modification. It can be torn, reversed, adapted to any kind of mounting, reworked by an individual, group, or social formation ... A map has multiple entryways, as opposed to the tracing, which always comes back "to the same." The map has to do with performance, whereas the tracing always involves an alleged "competence." (Deleuze and Guattari 2004, 13–14)

In retrospect and prospect, the reader may recognize the various chapters in this study as open-ended maps, as acts of staging connections both inside and outside the chapters, rendering observations and statements open to processes of revision and reshaping. All the performances discussed in this volume—and my approach to these performances—can be regarded as "experimentations in contact with the real," as experimental set-ups for the exploration and production of lived space. The flyer-event mentioned above helps to demonstrate how cartography (always) involves both experimentation and performance. A single reader executes "you are here" and situates oneself in that act; each encounter with these words will result in a different map, and involves a singular way of making sense of oneself in relation to one's situation. The act of locating oneself may have interrupted the return back to one's house, or delayed a visit to a hospital; it may have evoked a sense of pleasant surprise, or irritation. These potentialities are inherent in and brought forward by the map: they belong to what I will call the *virtuality* of the map, which may or may not be actualized in the encounter.

James Corner, in "The Agency of Mapping: Speculation, Critique and Invention" (1999), equally connects a performative, Deleuzian cartography to lived space. Although Corner uses cartography as a model for urban design and city planning, his observations are quite relevant for the present discussion. Corner argues that (urban) mapping is not an instrument for mirroring reality, but a tool for the construction of lived space; it is a means to engender the process of shaping the worlds in which people live. The underlying argument here is that maps do not represent a field or terrain, implicating the territory to be already existent. Instead, mapping is co-constitutive in producing these territories (225). In a Lefebvrian mode of thought, Corner argues that urban design should not only take the physical attributes of terrain into account; this is just the surface expression of a complex and dynamic set of interrelationships of natural processes, histories, local stories, and economic or political forces. Instead of devices for empirical description, urban maps should be regarded as creative practices and conduits of possibilities, "uncovering realities previously unseen or unimagined, even across seemingly exhausted grounds. Thus mapping *unfolds* potential; it re-makes territory over and over again, each time with new and diverse consequences" (213, italics in the original). Corner connects this potential to the fact that maps are both analogue and abstract. They are analogous to actual environments or events; simultaneously maps are abstract because they are products of scaling and projection, selection, and translation. This leads Corner to observe that "[a]s both analogue and abstraction, then, the surface of the map functions like an operating table, a staging ground or *a theatre of operations* upon which the mapper collects, combines, connects, marks, masks, relates and generally explores" (1999, 215, my emphasis).[4]

Corner's remarks depict the type of encounter between the nomadic and the theatre, and between performance and cartography, that I will pursue in this chapter. In this encounter, the theatre functions as a staging ground for local operations. In the theatre of operations, the map is not a mirror of reality, but co-constitutive of reality. This *theatre* of operations puts forward the question of what kind of cartographic realities are being staged, and how we are invited to perceive and understand these realities. This encounter, then, inevitably puts the topic of representation back on the operating table, in line with theatre's indubitable connection to representation, despite Deleuze's anti-representational understanding of the map.

Throughout history, maps have been used to chart and depict "the world," yet maps are never neutral representations of the world. Instead they are epistemological tools, strongly involved with the creation of a particular understanding and knowledge of the world that is being mapped. In their introduction to *Rethinking Maps: New Frontiers in Cartographic Theory* (2009), the editors Martin Dodge, Chris Perkins and Rob Kitchin remark that cartography is both "epistemological but also deeply ontological—it is both a way of thinking about the world, offering a framework for knowledge, and a set of assertions about the world itself" (1). This observation exposes again the close connection between theatre and cartography, since theatre can equally be regarded as offering a model for understanding the world and, in the act of modelling, produces certain assumptions about that world. Giving consequence to both theatre's and cartography's epistemological force, this chapter not only presents cartography as a staging strategy but also utilizes cartography as a method for describing and analyzing what is actually being staged in the act of mapping. Therefore, before continuing my discussion of *Trail Tracking*, I will first take a closer look into cartography's worldmaking capacities, by way of a short exploration of the history of cartography, seen from the perspective of theatre.

The Theatre of Cartography

There is a certain subtlety attached to the observation that the first atlases were called *theatres* (de Certeau 1984, 121). Atlases were a means to show the world in pictures, but implicit in this act of showing is that atlases *stage* a particular view and in doing so *produce* a certain understanding of the world. Maps are intriguing phenomena, because although they are products of manipulation, selection, and abstraction, simultaneously they are to a large extent kind of obvious. Maps work incredibly well because they do what they say they are doing. A road map, for instance, doesn't pretend to be anything other than a road map; it is what it is: a roadmap. The this-is-just-a-roadmap logic tends to obscure what is left out of the picture, and—truly living its paradoxical life to the max—the map could not do otherwise: without selection it cannot function as a map (Crampton 2010, 6). In *The Power of Maps* (1992), Denis Wood convincingly disarms this self-evident nature of maps, by exposing how the apparent view from nowhere presents a particular point of view and interest, while it obscures the fact that maps have authors and are regulated by specific, cultural codes and conventions. Remarkably similar to Maaike Bleeker's analysis of the absorptive strategies of perspective drawings and dramatic theatre, maps tend to absorb the user into the representation, since they presume to have an autonomous life, existing entirely independently from either author or user. Equally analogous to Bleeker's analysis, maps are products of perspective: precisely through the claim of objective representation, maps often remain invisible as a particular way of presenting the world (Wood 1992, 31; Crampton 2010, 12–21).

An often-quoted but nevertheless well-serving example of the theatre of cartography is the sixteenth-century Mercator projection. The Mercator map places Europe at its heart and takes the Greenwich meridian as the central point of reference. In the Mercator projection, the meridians that in "reality" converge around the poles—meridians are products of European, Euclidian geometry—are projected as rectangles on a flat surface. This creates enormous distortions of landmasses and, as a result, the areas occupied by Western civilizations are depicted as being much larger—read: more important—than non-Western areas (Wood 1992, 57).[5] Despite being widely regarded as a symbol of Eurocentrism now, the Mercator projection still regularly appears in atlases, classrooms, and, significantly, lives on as a digital, easily downloadable image-of-the-world, used in newspapers, prints, and on the internet (Monmonier 1995, 18–23). The Mercator example reveals map-related processes such as geometry, scaling, and projection as being far from neutral. But even when maps are more "accurate," they remain products of perspective. Denis Wood argues that maps are always products of history, culture, and politics, regulated by conventions that are barely questioned: "So surely is this the north toward which cartographers point that they take its presence for granted, as though the neutrality of the general reference map were a fact of nature, a common truth" (1992, 22).

Such claims of self-evident transparency and objectivity date back to the fifteenth century, an era marked by scientific progress and technological innovations, in which European nations used maps and charts to discover and colonize the globe (de Certeau 1984, 115–30). Both de Certeau and Deleuze and Guattari refer to the fifteenth century as the point of emergence not only of science but of a scientific worldview, in which rationally produced, centralized knowledge gradually becomes the norm (Deleuze and Guattari 2004, 529). In *Mapping: A Critical Introduction to Cartography and GIS* (2010), Jeremy Crampton observes that this scientific approach dominated geometry and cartography until well into the late 1970s. Crampton portrays a cartographic history in which technological progress, generalization, and standardization have been repeatedly put to use for claims of greater accuracy and hence objectivity (49–61). This emphasis on rationally produced, centralized knowledge and related claims of objectivity, universality, and truth reveals a Cartesian, dualistic logic, suggesting the world to exist independently and separately from the observer (Dodge et al. 2009, 5; Verhoeff 2012, 137–40). From the 1980s onward, influenced by the work of Barthes, Derrida, and Foucault, maps were increasingly seen as products of discourse, power relations, and ideology. Critical cartography challenged maps as transparent windows to the world, and instead showed them to be vehicles of territorialization, communicating values instead of facts (Crampton 2010, 44–7, 84–5; Dodge et al. 2009, 1–5; Wood 1992). Recent developments in cartographic technology have caused a shift from seeing maps as representations of power and ideology toward maps as *practices*, which focuses on the actual *use* of maps and the (local) contexts in which they are used. Mapping technologies have become widely available to the masses: open source and collaborative mapping tools are easy to download and use; the collaborative use of geomedia, location-aware mapping technologies, GPS, and Geographic Information Systems (GIS) allow amateurs to create, hack, modify, and mash-up maps. Such participatory and digital mapping practices challenge cartography as a specialist, scientific discipline practiced by experts, and produce alternative counter-knowledge (Crampton 2010, 27–40; Verhoeff 2012, 138–9). These practices challenge Cartesian logics and expose how maps conflate production and use. Maps are not autonomously existing objects; instead they are subject to co-creative processes of reshaping, redefinition, mutation, and contestation (Dodge et al. 2009, 16–20). As "theatres of operations" (Corner) maps produce the world for us, while at the same time we bring (situated) knowledge to the map. Such a performative understanding of maps questions the ontological security of maps. Dodge et al. therefore prefer to speak of the ontogenesis of maps, and of maps as "becomings" (2009, 20).[6]

It is worth observing that within the various understandings of what a map is and does, shifting from the map as an objective, transparent window, via maps as representations of power and ideology, to the practice of maps, the theatre of cartography respectively puts the emphasis on perceived, conceived, and lived space. Although these epistemological shifts seem to suggest a chronological development, it is actually a matter of what Crampton refers to as subjugated knowledge, drawing on Foucault: minor knowledge that was placed backstage during certain moments in history, which does not mean that this counter-knowledge was not there (Crampton 2010, 4). Performative cartography, for instance, sheds a new light on medieval mapping practices, as I will discuss below, through its focus on embodied, situated knowledge.

As a function of use, "the map is not fixed at the moment of initial construction, but is in constant modification where each encounter with the map produces new meanings and engagements with the world" (Dodge et al. 2009, 20). This observation aptly characterizes the cartographic encounters in *Trail Tracking*, where both performers and spectators are co-creatively engaged in the use and production of maps, inscribing themselves into the performance, as much as the performance inscribes into them.

Performing Cartography

Imagine yourself wandering around a large railway station, full of tracks and train carriages. Now, erase all the people that may have crowded your trains and platforms in this mental picture. Imagine you are completely alone, the sole living creature amidst an environment of machinery, technology, timetables, waiting rooms, train tracks, and other traces of travel. It feels like you are moving in a vacuum, as if the world has been put on halt, save for you. The only connection to another life is provided by a mobile phone. A friendly voice on the other end of the line first suggests that you loudly shout your name in the empty departure hall and then asks you to cross the hall, to go outside, to step across the track, to turn to the right and to walk toward the end of the platform. While you search for your way through this large space, the friendly voice asks you to remember a path you often walked during childhood. It could be a journey that led from your house to the bakery, or a recollection of the travels across the carpets and halls of your

Figure 4.1 A spectator wandering around in the railway museum in Utrecht, in Dries Verhoeven's *Trail Tracking*, 2005. Courtesy Studio Dries Verhoeven.

grandmother's house. You are kindly requested to remember this route in great detail (Figure 4.1).

Let's suppose for a moment that you had to cross the street adjacent to your house, on your way to school, and then turn to the left, past the huge chestnut tree, past the houses of your neighbors, and past the ominous, dark bushes in the garden of the stern old headmaster. After passing, you look toward the house on the opposite side of the street to see if your friend is leaving for school too. Then you continue to walk, past another six houses until you reach the small stone wall that surrounds the schoolyard. You pass the yard with the three grand old chestnut trees, where you use to play marbles in the spring. Then you arrive at the large front doors of the school; on your left is the bicycle shed, on the right is the place where a classmate once kissed you on the cheek because he was in love with you. And inside you go, past the two classrooms for the first four grades and you enter the third room, because you are in the fifth grade. The fifth grade seats are closest to the door, but next year, in the sixth grade, you will fortunately be sitting next to the windows with a view onto the yard. All the while, the stranger on the phone asks you for details on the houses that you passed, the color of the doorknob on the front door, the smell of the classroom; she seems extremely interested in it all. In the meantime you keep walking through the railway hall: you turn left and right, you type the basic coordinates of the remembered itinerary on a typewriter in an empty phone booth; next you enter an abandoned railway carriage. There you find the drink that you chose some minutes before from four options: tea, hot milk, gin or whiskey— which definitely adds to your impression that this stranger on the other end of the line is actually present in the same hall. Time and time again you are confronted with the actual place of performance when, simultaneously, you are walking in the remembered spaces of childhood.

The imaginary travel described above never actually happened. It is part of what I call the virtual map of *Trail Tracking*. It is the map that could have been performed, had I had the opportunity to "do" *Trail Tracking* myself. To a certain extent, the account above is also a performance of *Trail Tracking*'s map, as the potential inherent in the performance is actualized in my reenactment of this performance. On the basis of interviews with Dries Verhoeven, rehearsal notes, various reviews, and a short film registration, I produced another map, which is nevertheless *a* map: a singular version of *Trail Tracking*, this time based on the encounter between the performance and the critic-observer. This also implies that my account of the performance is not a reconstruction that seeks to depict the performance "as it was" but instead produces an inventory of its potentiality. Next to the first-person perspective (Chapter 2) and the over-the-shoulder-view (Chapter 3), the imaginative reconstitution is a third way of describing a one-to-one performance such as *Trail Tracking*.[7] The emphasis on the virtuality of the map is crucial, not because I did not attend this performance, but because it is inherent in the nature of this work, and other case studies in this book. The map of *Trail Tracking* only comes into being in the encounter between singular performers and spectators, and, in my account, between the performance and the observer.

Trail Tracking was presented at the opening of the Railway Museum in Utrecht, in 2005. The museum is a large space, a former railway station. Some of the tracks are still in use, occasionally. Single spectators, each equipped with a suitcase and a mobile phone, follow a trajectory through the (relatively) empty railway station. From time to time, the spectator catches a glimpse of other travelers in the distance, who also carry suitcases and talk into mobile phones. They are either performers, who are also present in the hall but do not have visual contact with the spectator, or they are other spectators, who started the performance at different intervals and follow a different trajectory. In an interview, director and scenographer Dries Verhoeven explains how his initial encounter with the place inspired his choice for making a performance with one spectator at the time. As the museum was still preparing for the opening, Verhoeven was the only person present in the enormous railway station, a place that was built to transfer hundreds of people and conjures up associations with travel, transport, and mobility, with continuous movement, with being on the road and being somewhere else. The station, as a place of transit, had become a space for dwelling, and each time he stopped walking, it felt like he became part of a world frozen in time (Groot Nibbelink 2007). Together with a team of performers, Verhoeven composed a trajectory that could provide spectators with a similar sensation, a trajectory that created a dynamic interplay between the "here" and the "elsewhere," and works with various senses of scale. Whereas the station, the suitcase, the mobile phone, and the distant performer all signal "elsewhere," the spectator's isolation focuses attention on the here and now of the walk, and the material qualities of the location. Throughout the walk, the scale of the railway station is subverted by the entirely different scale of childhood. Place and space become multi-layered modalities of experience, staged through various layers of cartography.

In "The Agency of Mapping," mentioned above, James Corner identifies four mapping practices in relation to contemporary, creative urban design and city planning. In line with his "theatre of operations," Corner approaches these practices as performances. Corner's operations are quite similar to the staging strategies discussed in this study, which allows for staging a few connections. Corner first describes a type of maps that is modeled on the *drift*, inspired by the Situationists' *dérives* and psychogeographic maps, and the work of walking artist Richard Long. These maps reflect "subjective, street-level desires and perceptions rather than a synoptic totality of the city's fabric" (1999, 231). The practices discussed in the previous chapters can be regarded as guided drifts, whereas a more psychogeographic approach will be encountered in Signa's *The Ruby Town Oracle* (Chapter 6). Second, Corner distinguishes the *game board*, in urban plans that stimulate interaction with the designed environment. These maps orchestrate the conditions for play and function as surfaces for acting out and testing a variety of scenarios (Corner 1999, 240). Such a game board governed Blast Theory's *Rider Spoke* (Chapter 3) and, as a scenario, resurfaces in relation to Ontroerend Goed's *The Smile Off Your Face* (Chapter 5). Third, the Deleuzian *rhizome* installs connections between various (urban) spheres, in line with Deleuze and Guattari's approach to maps quoted above, and transmits intensities across heterogeneous fields. I will join the latter operations when discussing the stage in terms of a rhizomatic game board, in relation to Signa's *Ruby Town* (Chapter 6). Most relevant to the present discussion is the fourth operation, described as a practice of *layering*. Corner refers here to the architectural designs of Bernard Tschumi, Rem Koolhaas, and Peter Eisenman, pointing out how in these designs several, rather independent layers together produce a "heterogeneous and 'thickened' surface ... a complex fabric without centre, hierarchy or single organizing principle" (235). Corner compares these architectural designs with the colored paint delineations on a gymnasium floor, which on the one hand allow for conventional games, based on the internal rule-set of these games, but also offer possibilities for combination, experimentation and montage, creating hybrid games. The four mapping operations show considerable overlap, as they all intend to provide the conditions for open-ended spatio-temporal practices. They invite use, transformation, negotiation; they stage connections and relationships, and seek to accommodate the manifold rhythms of everyday life.

In line with Corner's operation of layering, I distinguish three *cartographic layers* in *Trail Tracking*. These layers have an internal logic, as they can be observed separately, but they also interfere with and redefine each other. I will briefly introduce these layers here and use them as piloting devices for the rest of the chapter. The first layer pertains to the *actual-virtual* map of *Trail Tracking*, already briefly mentioned above. The performance provides the conditions for the encounter, through the design of a particular trajectory, which also implies a specific mode of spectatorial address, and a pre-set list of activities, carried out by either the performer or the spectator. I understand this design as a map, a conduit for action and navigation, which is actualized in the encounter between singular performers and spectators. The actual-virtual map points to the performance's potentiality, as each heterogeneous encounter with the map produces a singular version of the performance. The performance in that sense cannot be traced back to an original, but is always part of a process of ongoing differentiation, of becoming. The second layer involves the *navigational practices* of both performers and spectators. The performer navigates the spectator through the railway station, but there is no visual contact. Therefore, they need to practice a non-digital GPS, so to speak, a verbal exchange of locative data.[8] These spatial operations not only facilitate orientation but also follow the logic of location-aware technology, that is to say: they raise perceptual awareness and address sensory, material modes of spatial engagement; in addition, these operations produce navigational space (cf. Verhoeff 2012). While navigating the railway station, the spectators are asked to remember and describe an often frequented childhood route, as indicated above, as well as to name a place they would like to visit in the future. The performer suggests that the spectator perceive the performance itself as an act of walking between a past and a future. This third layer focuses on *personal geographies*, a term I borrow from Katherine Harmon's *You are Here: Personal Geographies and Other Maps of the Imagination* (2004). Harmon assembled a wide variety of maps, ranging from sixteenth- and seventeenth-century mappings of the mind and the body, to surrealistic dream maps and fantasy drawings. Contrary to the Cartesian map, these cartographies place the people back onto the map; they reveal the "private meridians" of everyday life, intersecting with the larger social realities in which people live and articulating what is of value in that world (10). Personal geographies point to how spectators traverse and engender the performance, how corporeal matter becomes something that matters, and how they bring situated knowledge to the map. These private maps create connections between places, memories, and sensory impressions, between fantasy and geography. As layered maps, the links between past, present, and envisioned futures do not only emerge on the level of personal geographies, but also surface in actual navigation, and in the virtuality of the map.

Charting the Virtual

In *Trail Tracking*, both the dialogue over the mobile phone and the found space of the railway station serve as an interface for the exchange of location-based information. Performers and spectators together form the coordinates of the smooth space in which they are operating, and they can be considered as both co-authors and co-creators of the map(s) of *Trail Tracking*. Dries Verhoeven and his team of performers, on the one hand, author this map, as the trajectory and related actions are pre-designed; these provide the conditions for play. On the other hand, spectators bring situated knowledge to the map: they perform the map, they navigate through their sense of place and they add their personal geographies. The map, therefore, is continuously subjected to experimentation, in contact with the real. In their engagement with the map, both the performer and the spectator do not know beforehand how exactly the encounter will turn out. Therefore, the map of *Trail Tracking* appears in both an actual and a virtual modality. Through the actual encounters with the map, the potential of the map becomes manifest. Potentiality cannot be known before it is actualized; it belongs to the *virtuality* of the map.

To Deleuze, virtuality is the counterpart of actuality—both are part of reality.[9] In *Architecture from the Outside* (2001), Elisabeth Grosz points out that Deleuze's understanding of the term is based on the work of Henri Bergson, who made a distinction between the possible and the virtual. The possible relates to the preformed, predictable version of the real, whereas the virtual is characterized by the unforeseen, the unthought, and the potential to be something other than the actual (Grosz 2001, 12). Bergson developed the concept in relation to time, and in connection with the simultaneous instead of the successive presence of present, past, and futurity. Elisabeth Grosz on the other hand explores the virtual in connection with (architectural) space. The virtual then points to the not-yet-actual, to the latent potential inherent in any design to become other than what is already actualized, to make unpredicted leaps, to function in excess of design or intention (130):

> If virtuality resides in the real … this is because the real is always in fact open to the future, open to potentialities other than those now actualized … Virtuality is not limited to the arena of technological innovation. Perhaps the most conventional of architectural forms and presumptions best illustrates what I understand as the impact, resonance, and richness that the virtual brings to the real: the wall. The capacity of walls, boxes, windows, and corners to function in more than one way, to serve not only present functions but others as well, is already part of the ingenuity and innovation of the virtual. Makeshift, piecemeal transformations, the usage of spaces outside their conventional functions, the possibility of being otherwise—that is, of becoming—must be as readily accorded to the built environment as it is to all futurity. (Grosz 2001, 90)

The practice of parkour (Chapter 2) is of course an excellent illustration to Grosz's remarks. Virtuality does not only relate to objects or concrete environments, but above all calls upon (the sensation of) potentiality. Inherent in *Trail Tracking*'s design is this latency, the potentiality to become something other than it already has become, a potential that presents itself each time the map is actualized in the encounter of singular performers and spectators. *Trail Tracking*'s actual-virtual map materializes in seriality.

Although this actual-virtual map is never finished and never "one," the map is not entirely fluid, because it facilitates navigation and coordinates the performed actions. The map stages encounters and displacements. The performer plots a route through the railway station and simultaneously his or her actions are plotted by that trajectory. During the phone conversation, the performers carry out a range of actions. Apart from directing the spectator, they query and memorize the spectator's memories, pay a visit to the typewriter in the phone booth, prepare a drink for the spectator, compose a story, sing a song, and many more small, site-specific tasks besides. Meanwhile the spectator navigates and performs the actions suggested by the performer and recalls cartographic memories.

Despite these collaborative cartographic efforts of both performers and spectators, their engagement with the map is not symmetrical. Similarly to the a-parallel evolution of the orchid and the wasp in forming a *rhizome*, the map of *Trail Tracking* is one that involves a-parallel heterogeneous movements. This asymmetry manifests itself in particular in the approach to the phone conversation. A mobile phone usually promises dialogue and mutual exchange, as was the case in *Call Cutta*. Verhoeven, however, employs a strategy that prevents the spectator from becoming too interested in the person on the other end of the line. Performers consequently redirect attention back to the spectator: they use a friendly but rather impersonal tone of voice, providing the spectator with a sense of ease and trust, and the invitation to talk freely. Interestingly, Verhoeven's rehearsal notes refer to this strategy as "sales techniques". Different from—or similar to?—*Call Cutta*, the sales technique formula served to prevent the conversation from becoming too private and personal. This strategy enabled the performers to ask personal questions, without getting stranded in casual chitchat, or, worse, in a therapeutic dialogue. The performer thus stays at a distance, which allows the spectator to become the "subject of communication," as Heiner Goebbels put it in response to *Call Cutta* (2007, 123-4). Or rather, the spectator becomes a subject of sensation, as the attention is consequently geared toward embodied relationships to place, and the spectator's situated, local operations.

Navigational Spaces

In *Mobile Screens*, Nanna Verhoeff remarks that "one of the most striking characteristics of screen-based interfaces is the possibility for people in transit to co-create the map of the spatial arrangement in which they are operating. The coincidence of movement and the creation of spatial representations is what I call a performative cartography" (2012, 13). Rather similar processes are facilitated by the much more analogue and auditory interfaces of *Trail Tracking*. Whereas the actual-virtual map is still strongly marked by Dries Verhoeven's signature, the real-time navigations foreground the processes of co-creation Verhoeff refers to. She describes (interactive) navigation as a procedural, experimental and creative act of both reading and making space. Navigation is not only directional, pointing the user where to go, but also an act of construction (138). Although screen-based navigation is different than the act of *staging* navigation, Verhoeff's observations help to demonstrate that *Trail Tracking* uses similar strategies, and also reterritorializes on the logics of (digital) geomedia.

Verhoeff discusses mobile screens and mostly refers to single users. *Trail Tracking* has two types of map-users, the performer and the spectator; hence the encounter with the map sometimes follows a slightly different logic. In line with Verhoeff's observations, the navigational processes in *Trail*

Tracking not only facilitate displacement but equally involve the *production* of navigational space. This navigational theatre space moves along and changes in accordance with the performers' and spectators' evolving itinerary. As performers and spectators are situated in different and changing locations, sometimes distant and sometimes close, and performer–spectator couples start their trajectory at various intervals, the theatre space becomes a strangely morphing entity, its fluctuating coordinates maintained by both performers and spectators.

During the walk, performers and spectators are usually at a distance, but occasionally they are quite close, for instance when the trajectory installs an acoustic proximity. At a certain moment the spectator hears music through the phone, before entering a train carriage. When entering this wagon, the same music can be heard, now live, which suggests that the performer just left the space where the spectator now enters. This example draws on the logic of *geotagging*, as it indicates the performer's (previous) location, in this case by way of an acoustic sign. Geotagging uses digital (GPS) technology to charge locations or objects with digitally stored metadata, which can be retrieved by activating location-specific hyperlinks (Verhoeff 2012, 153). Geotagging facilitates the *plotting* of space, which refers to "marking locations and giving them a layered presence and hence, an added meaning" (Verhoeff 2012). Performers who navigate spectators similarly work with marking and layering locations: stairs, tracks, carriages, and objects in space function as beacons that mark the theatre space; they indicate where the spectator should or can go. Thus, next to their use-value and function as (symbolic) scenery, these tagged objects or places get an added value as temporary coordinates of the stage, used by the performers to plot a route through the station.

Digital, screen-based navigation is able to produce layered and augmented realities.[10] Similar interfaces have been used for theatre performances, for instance in the video walks of the Canadian artist Janet Cardiff and George Bures Miller. *Trail Tracking* too works with such layered, pervasive realities; it places a porous theatre space over the space of the railway station, and, on top of that, adds a remembered-imagined layer of personal geographies. Layering thus modifies space through the combination of material and physical space, interactive communication devices, and navigational processes, which produces hybrid spaces. Verhoeff names this the "mash-up logic" of navigated layered realities, which reveals the "mnemonic, temporal and experiential aspects of mobility" (162). These temporal layers could be regarded as a way of "mnemonic spacing," since navigation draws on data stored in the past and activated in the present (Verhoeff 2012).

Geotags refer to previously stored data but often serve as pointers for future destinations as well. This is why Verhoeff regards geotags as triple indexical markers, which point simultaneously to the past, the present, and the future. This triple logic of geomedia "constructs an urban space in which pervasive presence, embedded pasts, and evolving futures intersect" (152). *Trail Tracking* seems to be governed by a similar (triple) logic, and principles of mnemonic spacing. This is not only achieved by the choice of location—a railway museum about to become an "edutainment" center—but above all by *Trail Tracking*'s specific mode of spectatorial address. The act of navigation, firstly, involves also the places that are left behind and, as the spectator finds out where to go next (in the present), installs an orientation towards the future. Secondly, the isolated spectator lingers in the frozen world of the railway museum. Being alone in an enormous space induces spatial and sensorial awareness in the present, yet the place continuously modulates attention toward the past, while the (stored) trains symbolize futurity, holding a promise of future destinations. Lastly, while the spectator is involved in real-time navigation, at the same time s/he navigates remembered and imaginary spaces, as if simultaneously traversing the past, the present, and a projected future. This assemblage of layered realities allows the spectator to experience the spatiality of time and the temporality of space, and to become aware of the simultaneous presence of past and future in the present.

Trail Tracking not only draws on the (triple) logic of geomedia in order to stage displacement, but also reterritorializes on this logic in view of its spatial dramaturgy. The performance thematically evolves around the intersection of past, present, and future spaces, and, as we have seen, addresses spectators through principles of mnemonic spacing. Verhoeff remarks that navigation produces an experiential, haptic, and material engagement with space. In *Trail Tracking*, this is not only brought about by way of isolating the spectator, acoustic navigation, or dwelling in frozen mobility, but above all, by probing personal geographies.

Personal Velocity

As mentioned previously, next to navigating the actual space of the railway museum, *Trail Tracking* engages the performer and spectator in querying and recounting an often-used path the spectator took during childhood. This usually involves a route that is rather mundane: there is nothing spectacular about the trajectory from school back home or to the swimming pool, for example. Next, this route is traced in great detail, to the extent of seemingly unimportant details such as the color of a door, the tactile memory of a doorknob, the scent of the hall, or the sounds of the attic. Sometimes the actual space of the railway station serves as an interface for the remembered space, when, for instance, the stairs leading towards a platform invite a description of the stairs in the home. The cartographic layer of personal geographies thus foregrounds the sensory and haptic engagement with places and spaces. The haptic refers to touch, derived from the Greek *haptein*, meaning "to touch," but often implicates a broader sensory register that describes experiences of reciprocity, intimacy, and proximity, analogous to touch. Several authors in *The Senses in Performance* observe that haptics is an umbrella term for a range of sense perceptions such as proprioception, kinesthetic awareness, or skin tactility. Haptic perceptions provide a sense of immediate connection with the environment.[11] Deleuze and Guattari allude to a similar immediacy when defining nomad art as being characterized by a constellation in which close-range vision is coupled with haptic space, as opposed to the optical space of long-distance vision. Haptic space does not exclude the eye, but calls upon an understanding of vision and visuality that does not separate the senses, or distinguishes between the looking subject and the object that is looked at (2004, 543–4). Haptic vision instead collapses subject–object distinctions.[12]

During rehearsals and try-outs, Verhoeven and his team discovered that the spectator's imagination was stimulated the most when asked for haptic and otherwise material details of the recounted trajectory: colors, smells, tactile information, proportions, next to memories that coincide with names (Groot Nibbelink 2007). Through the almost exclusive focus on material qualities, the spectator's attention is drawn toward the memories from the perspective of childhood, which prevents these memories from being tainted too much by the evaluation of them from a present, adult perspective. It is important to note that Verhoeven does not aim for nostalgia, i.e., mourning for a childhood that is lost. Instead, he seeks to tap into the intensity of experience that characterizes childhood. Children usually know only a limited amount of spaces, in which they spend a lot of time and that therefore are known to them intimately and intensely. This is the kind of intensity that Deleuze and Guattari connect to smooth space: "Smooth space is filled by events … far more than by formed and perceived things. It is a space of affects, more than one of properties. It is haptic rather than optical perception … occupied by intensities, wind and noise, and sonorous and tactile qualities" (2004, 528). As soon as the world grows larger, one's engagement with the environment tends to become less intensive. By appealing to the vitality of childhood experience, Verhoeven tries to insert a similar intensity into the spectator's current engagement with place and space.

But still, one cannot escape the irony of discussing a performance entitled *Trail Tracking* through a Deleuzian understanding of maps, which fervently opposes trackings, or tracings. To Deleuze and Guattari, tracings are genetic; they are patterns of reproduction and deep structure. Tracings aim for descriptions of "a de facto state, to maintain balance in intersubjective relations, or to explore an unconscious that is already there from the start, lurking in the dark recesses of memory and language" (2004, 13). In *Trail Tracking*, memory is not explored in order to arrive at "the same," or to expose an unconscious that is "already there from the start." *Trail Tracking* performs, experiments with, and (kindly) mutates memory (further elaborated below) and works with minor memories of seemingly unimportant and overlooked dwelling places. It probes neglected pleasures, habitual attachments to the intimacies of the house or the hut, and experiences of being inhabited by space. The performance charts processes of becoming-space, where spectators enter into composition with space; while traversing their personal geographies, they enter a zone of proximity with haptic and affective space. Dries Verhoeven recalls that many spectators greatly enjoyed talking about these memories:

> These are things you never tell to others, because they seem to banal to talk about it. Usually you don't describe the scent of the corridor in your grandmother's house, or the fact that you still know you flushed the toilet by means of pulling an oblong object tied to a chain. But you know all these things! And it gives pleasure to talk about that with someone. (Groot Nibbelink 2007, my translation)

This performance, then, is perhaps a case of, in Deleuzian vocabulary, putting the tracing back onto the map, of plugging the tracing back into the rhizome (2004, 14–16). These remembered movements install heterogeneous connections to forgotten intensities, to thoughts previously un-thought; they release tracings from forces of striation and reconnect them with smooth space.

Similarly to my discussion of navigational practices above, these personal velocities of becoming-space are involved with the production of space. In his writings on the relation between architecture, event, and movement, architect Bernard Tschumi neatly captures *Trail Tracking*'s particular assemblage of personal geographies, navigation, and spaces of affects:

> The pervasive smells of rubber, concrete, flesh; the taste of dust; the discomforting rubbing of an elbow on an abrasive surface; the pleasure of fur-lined walls and the pain of a corner hit upon in the dark; the echo of a hall—space is not simply the three-dimensional projection of a mental representation, but it is something that is heard, and is acted

upon ... Spaces of movement—corridors, staircases, ramps, passages, thresholds; here begins the articulation between the space of the senses and the space of society, the dances and gestures that combine the representation of space and the space of representation. Bodies not only move in, but generate spaces produced by and through their movements. (Tschumi 1996, 111)

Tschumi's words allude to Lefebvre's distinction between representations of space and spaces of representation, and indirectly indicate that *Trail Tracking* experiments with a type of representation that foregrounds movement and embodied relationships to space. This comes close to how Maaike Bleeker uses the term *movement vision*, a term coined by Brian Massumi, in her essay "Massumi, Martin and the Matrix" (2008b). Bleeker critiques the Cartesian understanding of a world that is "there" to be seen, as if existing independently from the viewing subject, a subject who is presumed to look at the world from a more or less stable point of view. In line with Massumi, Bleeker argues that this stable "positionality" marginalizes movement as an activity that merely connects positions or points in time, which fundamentally differs from understanding movement as a qualitative transition and variation in itself. A body always feels and moves, and feels itself moving. Even the most literal displacement evokes a qualitative difference, according to Massumi: "When a body is in motion it does not coincide with itself. It coincides with its own transition; its own variation" (Massumi in Bleeker 2008b, 153). This qualitative transformation necessarily informs our way of understanding and looking at the world. Bleeker argues that this connection between movement and feeling is "essential to how we, as bodies, engage with the world we live in, to how our bodies are involved in constituting our awareness of this world, and also to our awareness of ourselves in relation to this world" (Bleeker 2008b, 152). In opposition to "mirror vision," which conceives of the world as opsis, separating the world as object from the viewing subject, movement vision on the contrary questions the positionality of a stable viewer and the world as opsis altogether. Movement vision suggests that the world can only be known through the "corporeal investments of the ones participating in it" (162). Vision passes through the body into another movement space (163). Movement vision reflects back on my discussion of parkour, in Chapter 2, but is also very relevant in relation to (performative) cartography. The concept particularly draws attention to the corporeal investments in maps and map-making; to ways in which (moving) bodies are intrinsically bound up with theatre's and cartography's epistemological and ontogenetic processes, and open up heterogeneous spaces of representation.

Material Maps

Trail Tracking sets the spectator off on a tour, a tour that is organized through map-making processes. In *The Practice of Everyday Life,* Michel de Certeau presents the map and the tour as two opposite spatial practices, a distinction that is concisely summarized by Nanna Verhoeff: "maps are formalized accounts of spatial relations, whereas tours are spatial movements" (2012, 94). For de Certeau, the map represents the world as if seen from above; it favors a stationary subject and presents geographical knowledge as fixed and static. The map presents places as situated next to each other—the kitchen is next to the hall and left from the bedroom—whereas the tour describes spatio-temporal operations: if you turn left, then you will see the kitchen and if you cross the kitchen you will enter the hall. The map colonizes and territorializes space, whereas the spatial operations of the tour subvert the power relations inscribed in the map. Instead of employing a view from above, the tour approaches the subject as positioned within (de Certeau 1984, 120). De Certeau describes how in line with the emergence of a scientific worldview in the fifteenth century, the map disentangled itself from the itinerary and became the dominant spatial representation at the cost of tours, travel logs, or diaries. De Certeau's account is helpful in connecting *Trail Tracking* to a wider debate in which a (re)appreciation for situated, embodied knowledge counters the hegemony of optical and distanced representations, yet, similar to my earlier discussion of de Certeau (Chapter 3), also invites moving beyond such dualist distinction.

Susan Foster, in her discussion of *Call Cutta,* connects spatial operations such as the tour and the itinerary to both contemporary locative media, and to the medieval portolan chart (Foster 2008, 170; cf. de Certeau 1984, 121). Portolan charts date back to the twelfth to fifteenth centuries; these were collaboratively used and re-used documents that displayed interconnecting rhumb lines and sixteen equidistant intersection points at the circumference of a hidden circle, with which geographical positions could be calculated (Campbell 1987, 376). They can be compared to the function of today's satellites in relation to locative technologies. These charts enabled sailors to determine their location and trajectory *while* they were at sea—which brings the twelfth-century cathedrals back to mind, equally a process of measuring and scaling the work-in-progress while traversing and engendering the work itself. Although portolan charts also play their role in a history of European expansion and draw on Euclidian geometry, they reveal a fundamentally other spatial logic than the static map: "Intended to be rotated, portolan charts have no top or bottom. For most of the early charts ... there is no way of telling which, if any, of the four main directions they were primarily intended to be viewed from" (Campbell 1987, 378). These charts draw on a fundamentally different logic than the "so sure this is the north they point to" principle that Denis Wood critically ascribed to conventional cartography. As these maps were used and re-used by others, portolan charts document the accumulated experience of travel; they draw on embodied, situated knowledge.

Cultural anthropologist Tim Ingold observes how fifteenth-century science obliterated people and their experiences from the map: "Maps as reminders of paths and expressions of experience, as they were conceived in the European Middle Ages, morphed into supposed representations of space through the application of scientific principles" (in Dodge et al. 2009, 20). Both Ingold and de Certeau observe a disconnection between institutional maps and everyday life where people are constantly involved in spatial operations and mapping practices; these paths and experiences, however, escape the conventional map. *Trail Tracking* can be regarded as part of a family of cartographic practices in which maps function as reminders of "paths and expressions of experience" (Ingold), and firmly place people back onto the map. This is a family that links medieval charts to contemporary geomedia, but also includes the maps of the Situationists. According to David Pinder, the Situationists' records of their psychogeographic tours—*The Naked City* is probably the best well-known example—were not stationary maps but documents of spatial practice. These maps were made by cutting up and re-assembling parts of existing maps to create a map that accounts for the experience of atmospheres. Pinder asserts that the Situationists did not reject the map—as de Certeau does—but instead rearticulated what a map can do; they appropriated the map in order to "renovate" cartography, facilitating alternative ways of engaging with the city (Pinder 1996, 414–17). In *Mobile Screens*, Verhoeff observes that with the advent of mobile, digital, location-aware technology, performative and "renovative" cartography has become common practice, which leads to an even greater "convergence of mapping paradigms" in which the tour and the map do not oppose but co-construct each other (Verhoeff 2012, 94).

Both the tour and the map presume a certain subject position. This is also addressed by Susan Foster, who connects the relational cartography of both portolan charts and contemporary geomedia to a particular view on subjectivity. As mentioned above, Cartesian geometry privileges a stationary subject, separated from the object. By contrast, Foster appreciates the portolan chart as a prototype of a relational understanding of subjectivity: "Rather than offering a bird's-eye view of the world as projected from a static viewing subject, the Portolan chart documents identity as a fluid collaboration between reader and landscape" (2008, 170). In a rather similar vein, Maaike Bleeker links movement vision to the relationality of the subject. Instead of a distinctive "I" that looks at the world as if this were an autonomous object, movement vision points to a process of co-construction, in which both subject and world emerge, and also disappear (2008b, 163).

In the twenty-first century, navigation has become a dominant cultural practice (Verhoeff 2012). It is interesting to note the affiliations between contemporary cartography and medieval mapping practices, in that they both reveal a spatial and cultural logic that connects situated and corporeal knowledge to a relational understanding of subjectivity. It is a logic that is also at work in *Trail Tracking* and, closely connected to this, in the concept of politics of location.

Thinking Subjectivity Through Space: Politics of Location

In *Trail Tracking*, the situated knowledge of the spectator is a vital ingredient of the performance, necessary to perform cartography. Situated knowledge is also key to what the poet Adrienne Rich introduced as *politics of location*. Politics of location is a strategy for articulating the particularity of specific locations and (theoretical) positions, often deployed and discussed in feminist theory, as a critical perspective on dominant, homogeneous representations. It is a strategy for accounting for the multiple differences amongst women (Braidotti 2011a, 2004; Kirby 1993). In *Questions of Travel: Postmodern Discourses of Displacement* (1996), Caren Kaplan observes that for "many Euro-American feminist theorists, the concept of location offers a solution to the universalizing gestures of masculinist thought, providing a way of rearticulating marginality or particularity" (144). Politics of location also open up the feminist discourse from within, giving voice to black or non-Western feminists to produce counter-knowledge to Western feminism (Braidotti 2004, 59–60). It is not my intention to use the concept for a feminist reading of *Trail Tracking*; instead I take some of the baggage of this particular field to demonstrate the close yet dynamic links between location and the subject, and to unpack the concept in relation to *Trail Tracking*'s spatial dramaturgy.

The work of Adrienne Rich is discussed by Kathleen Kirby, in "Thinking through the Boundary: The Politics of Location, Subjects, and Space" (1993). Kirby describes how Rich approaches location as a web of different, simultaneously active spatial spheres. When she refers, for instance, to the United States as her country of origin, this implicates a national identity, as well as a nation state, a particular place on the globe, and also works as a frame that inevitably influences the way she observes the world and in turn, the way she is perceived by others. Thus, instead of understanding location as one particular point in space, Rich radically opens up this notion of oneness and shows how location is a product of many interwoven, interfering spatial layers, a "fabric of continually shifting sites and boundaries" (Kirby 1993, 176; cf. Massey 1994). Rich's approach is a way of thinking subjectivity through space: a subject is connected to and produced by all these spatial spheres or "territories of meaning," diverging from micro-political education and schooling to macro-economics and politics (Kirby 1993, 182). As a consequence, subjectivity eludes one-ness too; it has no core or center. Many postmodern theories present subjectivity as a plural collection of subject positions and localities. Kirby finds this approach to the subject somewhat problematic, as it presents subjectivity as only an outer surface on which these positions by coincidence appear, whereas subjectivity also involves a sense of interiority, which provides impulses and records traces of experience. She points at the corporeal, material connections between subject and location: "The subject and its form, subjects and their natures, are tied into political commitments and ethical positions by nature of being tied into particular material spaces, like bodies or countries, ghettos or suburbs, kitchens or boardrooms" (175). In "Transporting the subject" (2002), Caren Kaplan provides a similar argument, when she critically remarks that many mobility theories tend to produce disembodied mobile subjects, through their focus on technological innovation and progress: "The self is believed to have expanded capacities as soon as it is released from the fixed location of the body, built environment, or nation. But the self is always somewhere, always located in some sense in some place, and cannot be totally unhoused" (2002, 34). Both Kirby and Kaplan do not confine the subject to the house, on the contrary; they attest instead to a fluid, yet situated, notion of subjectivity.

In line with this, but taking a strongly vitalist and affirmative stance in the debate, for feminist theorist Rosi Braidotti the politics of location instills a theory of radical difference, and is at the heart of what she terms the "nomadic subject" (2011a). Drawing on Gilles Deleuze and Luce Irigaray amongst others, Braidotti presents a (neo)material approach to the subject as always involved in a process of multifaceted becomings, as it passes through embodied and embedded positions, affects and desires, and emanates through both human and non-human forces of composition (Braidotti 2011a; 2004, 102–20). Nomadic subjectivity suggests a continuous metamorphosis but also draws on "situated cartographies," with which theoretical, historical, and social relations and positions can be mapped, analyzed and questioned, or creatively countered (Dolphijn and Van der Tuin 2012, 14). For Braidotti, the nomadic subject is indubitably connected to a radical ethic of transformation. It is a force of resistance directed against dualist thought, claims of universality, or fixed or stable identities. Her nomadism is not about "fluidity without borders but rather an acute awareness of the nonfixity of boundaries" (2011a, 66). Relevant for the present discussion is that her cartographies are immanently spatio-temporal; she makes way for situated histories and also backward oriented trajectories, for understanding locations as embedded and embodied memories, or as reservoirs of counter-knowledge (2011b, 271).

Trail Tracking brings politics of location into practice, on the much more modest scale of the performance's spatial dramaturgy. The performance reveals location as a densely layered reality, a fabric that weaves together the economic-industrial space of the railway station, the temporary coordinates of the theatre space, the "over there" of the performer, spaces of affects, and places of memory. This morphing "here" is also a way of thinking subjectivity through space, as the maps of *Trail Tracking* draw on the spectator's situated knowledge, invite spatial and sensory awareness, and induce self-reflexivity. Navigation in this performance entails a traversing of various embodied positions, in which the body appears as not only the vehicle for displacement but also as the carrier of memories and the locus of desire, travelling simultaneously in the past, present, and future. *Trail Tracking* exposes navigation as an intersubjective process of collaborative exchange, through which spectators make themselves known to the performer and find their bearings. Subjectivity, then, too is a "fabric of continually shifting sites and boundaries," to repeat Kirby. By installing a situated perspective, spectators are invited to insert the different tracks and traces into the map of their subjectivity; a cartography of plural time-spaces and multiple viewpoints that enables one to touch upon a sense of direction while one is on the move. *Trail Tracking* opens up a space for minor, subjugated knowledge and engages the spectators into a process of articulating particularity. Politics of location thus points to and accommodates the heterogeneity of embodied, embedded spectators.

Witnessed Presence

Trail Tracking's strategies of thinking subjectivity through space lead to a remarkable piece of performative cartography, dealing with drawing and redrawing maps, taking place about three quarters after the start of the hour-long performance. It is a moment where it is not the spectator—the usual witness—but the performer who gives witness to the presence of the spectator, which makes it a remarkable instance of the becoming-spectator of the performer as well. [13] The spectator is asked to enter a train carriage, put a record on, turn out the lights, and take a seat. In the darkened carriage the spectator listens to a story told by the performer over the phone, which is the recounted story of the childhood route the spectator has provided during his or her maneuvers through the railway station. The performer composes and redraws the map of the spectator's childhood, by using slightly different scale and projection technologies. The story, for instance, is organized by a Google Earth-inspired storytelling technique of zooming in—from the city, to the street, to a front-door, to that particular life related to the front-door—or zooming out. Another storytelling mode is that of enlarging sensory details: "it is winter, the streets are white, the car of the neighbors is white, your doorstep is white" (Groot Nibbelink 2008). The story is told in the present tense, in order to explicitly address the perspective of childhood.

In one of my interviews with Dries Verhoeven, he informed me that most of the spectators were deeply moved by these recounted mappings. When I asked him why, he was hesitant to provide an explanation, as he did not have one, and preferred to reply by demonstration. He then posed some questions about my childhood home and next improvised a story in which he recounted my answers. Strangely enough, I was emotionally moved as well. When Verhoeven mentioned my parents, for instance, it felt like he knew them, while at the same time I knew he did not. Verhoeven: "It just works. To me, the word 'Wim' is just a three letter word, but to you it is the name of your father: an entire life is related to that word" (Groot Nibbelink 2008). When a performer in *Trail Tracking* recounts that the stairs were grey, or that they were cracked, to the performer these are just the words "grey" or "cracked." However, to the spectator they open up a space of intensities: it is a particular grey that evokes certain feelings or memories, related to particular moments of disturbed silence, of sneaking around perhaps, reminiscent of someone who is not supposed to be there, and so on. A word like "grey" thus achieves the qualities of a deictic marker. As mentioned above, in relation to the "You are here" flyer—which is also the motto of the navigable map of course—deictic utterances are empty words until they are appropriated in a particular time and space. *Trail Tracking*'s deictic markers link space, location, and subjectivity, and solicit engagement.

One may argue that these recounted geographies are instances of "freezing mobility" that bring the corporeal archive to rest. I am inclined to think, however, that they are moments in which relational subjectivity materializes, where corporeal matter comes to matter and installs a sense of connectivity. It is somehow comforting, when a stranger bears witnesses to personal experiences, even if they are entirely trivial, or perhaps exactly because they are trivial. It reminds me of the closing lines of *De Avonden* (1947), a classic in Dutch literature, in which Gerard Reve describes a young man who feels

Figure 4.2 Closing scene of *Trail Tracking* by Dries Verhoeven, Utrecht 2005. Courtesy Studio Dries Verhoeven.

existentially estranged from his parents. After ten extremely long days in his parents' house, in which all the nauseating details of this habitual hell are penned down in a diary, the protagonist concludes his diary with relief: "It has been noticed. It has not remained unseen," which also implicates the reader, of course.[14] In *Trail Tracking*, an actual living, breathing person sees and notices. At the end of the performance, the spectator is asked to open the suitcase that was carried along all the time, which happens to contain a pillow. The spectator then is invited to lie on a bed that is mounted on the tracks, to put the phone down and leave it aside, and to rest his head on the pillow. As soon as the spectator lies down, the bed starts moving slowly, as it is drawn over the tracks, out of the railway station (Figure 4.2). While leaving the station, the spectator sees someone waving on a raised platform. This is the first and only eye contact between the performer and the spectator, after an hour-long conversation. The spectator waves back. A wave: it has been witnessed, it did not remain unseen.

The Cartography of Theatre

Trail Tracking's spatial dramaturgy is grounded in the creation of a wide range of maps—maps that operate as assemblages, as they accumulate flows of semiotics, histories, memories, intensities, bearings of real-and-imagined spaces, all of which can be understood as ways of thinking subjectivity through space. *Trail Tracking* creates affective and material relationships with one's own bearings, and provides the spectator with a space for discovering oneself, while on the move. The virtual map plots a route through the railway station, whereas the actualized maps facilitate a process of articulating particularity. The map thus is negotiated in a process of "constant modification where each encounter with the map produces new meanings and engagements with the world" (Dodge et al. 2009, 9).

This chapter investigated performative cartography as a staging strategy. Performative cartography creates theatre spaces on the basis of shifting and collaboratively maintained coordinates; it opens up places and spaces to layered realities; it investigates embodied forms of mobility, addresses the spectator's situatedness, and defines spectatorship as a process of articulating particularity. The multiplicity of cartography substitutes the linear, logocentric structure of dramatic theatre, and offers a model for describing the composition principles of the postdramatic landscape. When theatre becomes a navigational practice, it thrives on the continuous assessment and negotiation of one's bearings, and the creative investigation of one's relationship to place. As an epistemological tool, cartography exposes the performer–spectator–space constellation as being plugged into an open-ended map, which allows for staging connections between various theoretical concepts and models, ranging from feminist theory to haptic architecture, from situated maps to screen-based urban interfaces.

This chapter also mapped the ongoing encounter between the nomadic and the theatre. Through my discussion of politics of location and the focus on embodied, situated spectatorship, this chapter presents a similar argument as the previous chapter, although taking another route. *Trail Tracking*'s situated and embodied cartographies sustain my view that the nomadic is not a form of loose, directionless wandering. Instead, the encounter with the theatre reveals the nomadic as a series of local operations—operations that can be regarded as an ongoing investigation of the relationship between place, location, and subjectivity. These operations are instances of procedural navigation, that is, the creative reading and making of spaces through which one moves and that are created through movement.

Dodge et al. note that performative cartography shows how the world takes shape by how we act upon the world. A map does not simply describe or explain the world; instead, "it describes the world as exposed to our method of questioning" (2009, 12). Performative cartography understands subjects and worlds to be involved in a co-constitutive process in which they simultaneously appear and disappear, which also demonstrates a relational understanding of subjectivity. Such a co-constructive process is at work in the next chapter as well, where I will discuss Ontroerend Goed's *The Smile Off Your Face*. Although based on a rather different staging strategy, *The Smile*, just like *Trail Tracking*, deals with worldmaking processes, showing a world that unfolds through a diffractive reading of scales, from the closest geographies to the wider socio-political spheres, through which both subjects and world emerge in a process of continuous zooming in, and zooming out.

5

Diagrams

Staging Proximity in Ontroerend Goed's
The Smile Off Your Face

A Nomad Does Not Necessarily Move

In this chapter I explore patterns of de- and reterritorialization in one of the closest and most intimate domains of the theatrical encounter, that of sensory perception. I do so by taking *The Smile Off Your Face* by the Flemish company Ontroerend Goed as my theoretical object.[1] Contrary to the other cases in this study, in this performance the mobility of the spectator takes a somewhat different form as the spectators are seated in a wheelchair, blindfolded, with their hands tied. Equally, it could be argued that in this performance movement and mobility are the defining parameters. Whereas a performance like *Call Cutta* targets the conventions of the theatre space on the level of global economy, *The Smile* upsets the notion of territory on the scale of proximity. Instead of extreme separation, the encounter between the performer and the spectator is one of close physical contact, and literally addresses the boundary between both. This performance experiments with sense perception, intimate experience, and imagination, and due to the personal address is quite "moving" in terms of emotional impact. The address to the senses incites, however, even more radical forms of movement, as it mobilizes conventions of spectatorship; it deterritorializes the theatre as *theatron*—a place for looking or watching—and instead reterritorializes the theatre as a *sensorium*, as the theatre space becomes an environment in which all the senses are addressed simultaneously.

In recent years, there seems to be an increase of performances that work with close encounters, one-to-one formats, sensory scenography, immersive theatre, and other forms of intimate performer–audience relationships (Hill and Paris 2014; Machon 2013; Chatzichristodoulou and Zerihan 2012; White 2012). My focus in this chapter does not concern the senses in performance as object of enquiry in itself. In line with the spatial perspective in this book, I rather look at how this particular address to the senses creates *spaces of proximity* and *stages of interiority*. My aim is to elucidate how movements in the realm of the small, the close, and the private unfold towards the infinitely large sphere of subjectivity itself and towards relationships between self and world. In this chapter I introduce the *diagram* as a staging strategy that invites spectators into a fundamentally open process, while at the same time the composition of this process provides the conditions for the spectators' mode of engagement.

In "Diagrams as Piloting Devices in the Philosophy of Gilles Deleuze" (2001), Kenneth Knoespel points out that the Greek *diagramma* refers to the process of marking out something by way of drawing lines, figures, forms, or plans. Remarkably, it also carries a connotation of crossing out, of redrawing or reconfiguration, which indicates the diagram's qualities of transformation, differentiation, and potentiality (147). This expectancy of redrawing points to the double nature of the diagram: the diagram is firstly a stabilizing force, as it gestures towards definition; and secondly, the diagram is open to change, re-articulation and reviewing (148). The open-ended nature of the diagram may explain its frequent use in performative architecture (Spurr 2007; Vidler 2000). As mentioned earlier, performative architecture does not approach designed space as static, fixed, or finished at the moment of construction, but instead is interested in how designed space invites performance and in turn changes in accordance with use (see Chapter 6). On a similar basis, one may think of play, games, laboratories, and other experimental set-ups as organized through diagrams. Diagrams provide the conditions for play and give directions, without prescribing or determining the outcome. Diagrams then are piloting devices, to borrow Knoespel's terminology, as they provide a structure, are directional, and intimate a "horizon of thought," yet they are open to various use and achieve their form only in actualization (Knoespel 2001, 148). Diagrams are "central to a theory of emergence," argues Knoespel (159), which also characterizes my approach to *The Smile*'s diagrammatic design and emergent dramaturgy.

This idea of the diagram as a piloting device is quite relevant, as Deleuze actually employs the diagram to describe the (abstract) forces and power relations at work when material forms or social realities come into existence. Deleuze qualifies the diagram as a cartography that maps the relations between forces, in any social field. These forces or functions only become manifest in the assemblages through which they are actualized (Deleuze 1986/2006a, 32). Therefore, the diagram is an *abstract machine*, an engine or force which allows the actual to emerge from the virtual: "The diagrammatic or abstract machine does not function to represent, even something real, but rather constructs the real that is yet to come" (Deleuze and Guattari 2004, 157). In the essay mentioned above, Knoespel describes how the diagram appears at several moments in Deleuze's work, notably in his studies on Foucault and Leibniz. Deleuze observes, in relation to Foucault's study on Panopticism, how the panoptical prison is not only an optical and spatial arrangement that creates relations of seeing without being seen, but organizes behavior and imposes a particular conduct. As such, the Panopticon must be regarded as the materialization of a certain (societal) function—in this case punishment and control—a function which is distinct, yet inseparable from its concrete manifestation. The Panopticon is a diagram in which this specific function becomes apprehensible; the diagram itself is a "functioning," that cannot be separated yet "must be detached from any specific use" (Deleuze 2006a, 30).

The attempt to describe how abstract forces achieve a specific articulation also reverberates in the folds of the Baroque house, an allegory with which Deleuze investigates principles of infinity and seriality in the work of the Franco-German philosopher Leibniz. The fold is a figuration of the infinite itself. It involves a movement pattern in which multiplicities are folded into each other and unfold upon the other—one may think of inflections of body and mind, of exteriority and interiority, of the public and the private, the small and the large, as always mutually connected, through endless variation (Deleuze 1993/2006b; Bal 2002, 87, 102). The folds of the Baroque engage a specific category of relations—also across various historical periods in time: non-centered relations of co-existence and mutual interference. In the introduction to Deleuze's *The Fold* (1993/2006b), translator and editor Tom Conley suggests that Deleuze's pleats, furlings and foldings are instances of geophilosophy, as they help to express "our experience of a shrinking globe" where "compressions of time and space" have erased clear-cut distinctions between the inside and the outside, the public and the private, or the global and the local (2006b, xvi). He observes that contemporary artists transform Leibniz's "*monadology* into *nomadology*," as they fold these territories into each other and deterritorialize them (2006b, italics in the original).[2] These geophilosophical themes traverse this chapter as well, in which I explore the connection between Deleuzian folds, nomadic theatre, and the tonalities of sensation in *The Smile*, while using the Panopticon and the Baroque house as architectural thinking models for unpacking and fleshing out the diagram.

The diagram, in brief, can be regarded as an engine of composition. In *The Smile*, the focus on the spectator's sensory experience effectuates a thoroughly indeterminate and open situation. Whereas the address to the senses and related spaces of proximity are the pre-given conditions of this performance, the spectator's response to this address each time newly actualizes *The Smile*'s diagram. As such, the performance may be understood as a laboratory, where spectators themselves become a force of composition. I consider the diagram a useful tool for asking what is actually subjected to experimentation in this laboratory, and to which particular "horizons of thought" (Knoespel) these experiments point. There are in fact many horizons that emerge in this chapter, as *The Smile* explores the (im)possibility of intimacy and authenticity in the theatre, cuts across debates about participatory performance, plays with theatrical conventions, and experiments with different tonalities of sensation. *The Smile*'s emergent dramaturgy comprises a twofold movement in which the extremely small is connected to the infinitely large; in which the personal and the intimate reverberate with and within the social and the abstract; in which the scale of proximity unfolds onto the twisting surfaces of advanced capitalism, and vice versa. Deleuze and Guattari remark that a nomad does not necessarily move (2004, 420), and *The Smile* may serve to underline this observation.[3] Even if the spectator is quite restricted, the perspective of nomadic theatre invites us to understand the constellation of performer, spectator, and space as vibrantly mobile.

A Wheelchair's Thresholds

Have I been kissed by a stranger, just now? Was it real, or did I just imagine it? Until this day, I do not know for certain what actually happened, that particular evening in September 2008 when I visited Ontroerend Goed's performance *The Smile Off Your Face*. My uncertainty is caused by the particularities of my situation at that time, as I was blindfolded, with hands tied, seated in a wheelchair, and had been wheeled around the performance space for some time until I lost my orientation. With scarcely time to make up my mind on why I had voluntarily exposed myself to this situation, someone gently touches my hands, opens them, leads my hand to feel his face—some beardlike elements afford at least to establish a sense of gender— while he caresses mine. This all happens with much tenderness and it affects me deeply, somehow. But just before it gets too pleasurable, he pulls lightly at my arms, indicating that I am supposed to leave the wheelchair. I will not, I do not want to, my body says, I cannot see anything, I do not know if I will fall. Indeed, when I stand I do fall, or rather, I stumble clumsily out of the wheelchair. It is amazing how this freedom-confining situation in the chair has become my safety zone in such a short time. The alternation of connection and solitude, of ease and discomfort, will prove to be a recurring element throughout the performance and provokes an increased awareness of my presence, as a spectator, in the work.

This ad hoc attachment to the wheelchair perhaps arises from its resemblance to that *other* chair in the theatre: the seat in the auditorium. That seat situates the spectator as a member of the audience: a group of onlookers, a collective that is often thought to represent the public as part of the social contract of the theatre. To be invited to stand up, to stand out as a single member of the audience and to literally relinquish spectating, can be regarded as a radical inversion of those theatre conventions. The intimacy of this one-to-one encounter produces ambiguous relationships between the private and the public, between looking and other modalities of perception. My passage into the realm of *The Smile* as described above immediately touches upon this ambiguity: instead of a semi-private seat in a darkened auditorium, I stand out and am seen, although this is a private encounter. I am a spectator but I cannot see anything. I am a singular spectator, yet I belong to a group of spectators: I have been waiting together with some of them, in the foyer of a small theatre in The Hague, strikingly called *Paradise*. We have seen each other, slightly nervous or lightheartedly expectant, waiting to enter the theatre, one by one. We have seen people exit the performance space, moved to tears, or confused, or filled with extreme joy. My experience probably could be archived into the Department of Confusion, hovering somewhere between ease and unease, between giving trust and feeling embarrassed. Stepping out of the wheelchair serves as a threshold on which these in-betweens suddenly appear.[4] Several other in-betweens show up too, on that threshold, themes that also characterize today's debate on participatory spectatorship and that will emerge throughout this chapter: the (inter)active versus the passive spectator; freedom of experience versus manipulation and confinement; individualism versus community in the theatre.

Because of the personal address to the spectator, it seems apt to take up a first-person perspective again (similar to Chapter 2), when describing this performance. I do so in order to establish a sense of interiority and provide an impression of the performance's inside. Yet with the figure of the fold in mind, this way of traversing and engendering spaces of proximity also creates openings toward other spatial and theatrical registers. In *The Fold*, Deleuze observes that the fold is always a movement in two directions, which does not divide in parts but creates mutual inflections. The fold is not a "fold in two—since every fold can only be thus—but a 'fold-of-two,' an *entre-deux*, something 'between' in the sense that a difference is being differentiated" (2006b, 11, italics in the original). As the personal impression of *The Smile* indicates, the sensation of the in-between this time exposes a differential relation with the conventions of theatre. Right from the start of the performance these conventions are put to the test, in such a manner that, interestingly, the *inversion* of theatre conventions self-referentially redirects the attention back to the theatrical event itself. The *entre-deux* in this case produces (self) reflexivity, in which particular parameters indicate oppositional directions, yet fold back onto each other in order to arrive at an intensification of traits.

The Smile is full of such twofold movements. This is in fact astutely captured by the object of the wheelchair itself. A chair on wheels, supporting a spectator, carries within itself the idea of mobile spectatorship. The suggested freedom is, however, compromised by that same situation, as the spectator is prevented from moving independently due to the blindfold and tied hands. The physical confinement addresses the corporeality of spectatorship, precisely through the partial incapacitation of the body. The spectator is disabled from seeing or applauding, which indicates that the spectator is apparently supposed to engage differently with this performance. Limitation in this case paradoxically points to an expansion of spectatorship, as *The Smile* foregrounds the sensorial, the experimental, and the playful—which are core components of the nomadic theatre concept as well. These modalities of perception experiment with the spectator's personal experience. I understand "experience" here as the conscious perception of both self and world, and of perceiving this relationship, which induces an engagement with one's capacity to be affected.[5] Whereas this focus on experience suggests a certain freedom—experiences are usually thought to be personal, non-restricted, "owned" by the "experiencer" (Nelson in Bay-Cheng et al. 2010, 45)—the spectator is also manipulated. This manipulation in turn redirects the attention back to the theatre, because if there is one place in the world where audiences are manipulated, and imagination is being tricked *and* triggered, it would be the theatre. In sum, the wheelchair's thresholds evoke an array of magnifying glasses directed toward the theatre itself.

This self-referentiality is quite characteristic of the work of Ontroerend Goed. The Ghent-based company became known in the early 2000s and since then they have provoked their audiences with performance events that foreground the direct encounter between performers and spectators, whether by confronting the spectators through chaos, nudity, meta-theatrical dialogue, one-to-one performances, or larger scale performances set up as energetic, noisy parties. However varied these forms are, this commitment to the live performance is a primary animating principle in the company's work (Ontroerend Goed 2014; Groot Nibbelink 2009a; Smeyers 2004).

Pleats of Proximity

The description of the wheelchair scene above intimates that this chair on wheels is a powerful engine for thinking about movement in the theatre. The chair literally mobilizes spectatorship. Pushing the wheelchair onto the stage "charges" the stage with movement, destabilizes spatial conventions, and produces relations of proximity with the performer, all of which cause the stage to implode. Although the term implosion has strong connotations of destruction and disappearance, I use this word here to indicate that the stage is shattered *from within*, in order to *appear again* differently. In *The Smile*, akin to the other cases in this book, the spectator is put on stage, but instead of the recurring emphasis on the gap between performers and spectators in *No Man's Land*, or *Call Cutta's* distribution of stage and auditorium across the globe, *The Smile* merges the auditorium and the stage by bringing performers and spectators extremely close. To complicate things further: the spectator is put on stage, yet the stage is obscured from view. This re-enforces the questions put by this performance: where is the stage exactly, what is the nature of this stage, what are the basic conditions for a stage to appear? The borders and coordinates of the respective territories have become unclear, which does not mean, however, that the territories have disappeared. Instead of an erasure of the distinction, the auditorium nests within the stage, and the stage captures the auditorium. As argued earlier, the spectator on the stage distorts the stage from the inside (see Chapter 2). This situation resembles the empty center Heiner Goebbels referred to, in his discussion of *Call Cutta* (2007, 123), a staged and simultaneously remarkably undefined sphere, and also alludes to the incommensurability of Lehmann's event/situation. Whether performers and spectators share a distance of 6,000 miles or the same square meter, in both cases the performer no longer occupies the center of the stage. Fundamentally different from Peter Brook's empty space, the performer has left the center; the stage itself has no center; the stage deterritorializes by means of an engine that is the spectator. A spectator who is not mobile per se; just as a nomad does not necessarily move.

Alan Read, in *Theatre, Intimacy and Engagement*, remarks that contemporary performance often refuses to be discussed in dialectical terms of presence or absence. Instead it seems to be involved in processes of "appearing to appear" (2008, 16). The same might be argued for the stage in *The Smile*: caught up in a process of appearing to appear, the focus lies not on what there is to be seen on a stage, but instead on the conditions of appearance itself. In *The Smile,* the stage folds back onto itself to explore its own conditions of appearance and folds out towards the infinite space of the spectator's subjectivity. Already present in the wheelchair's thresholds, but demonstrated in more detail below, the address to the senses deterritorializes the theatre as a seeing-place, and instead engages the spectator in a process of becoming-space. Before the actual encounter with the first performer, the spectator is immersed in a soundscape of noises, chatter, and laughter, and a scenography of indistinctive but pleasant scents. It is agreeably warm as well: space meets body temperature. The theatre space therefore becomes a *sensorium*: the spectator is invited to probe the surrounding environment through all the senses.[6] As various authors in *The Senses in Performance* (2007) indicate, tuning in on the tactile, the auditory, and particularly the olfactoral produces borderless, formless spaces; in other words: smooth space.[7] Compared to *No Man's Land* or *Call Cutta*, which tapped into the smooth space of the urban environment, *The Smile* constructs a smooth stage by the appeal to the senses and close physical contact with a performer.

Due to this particular address, the performance not only takes place on the (in)visible stage shared by both the performer and the spectator, but enters the private space of the spectator. The stage, as a platform for performance, thus becomes a *stage of interiority*. A scent does not stay on the outside, but enters the spectator's olfactory system; the sense of being touched is felt in or below the skin. This interior stage folds the outside onto the inside and vice versa: the address to the senses provokes an increased sensitivity for the surrounding environment, yet the spectator's attention is also drawn inward, orientated towards one's own subjectivity. As I discussed in Chapter 4, subjectivity is a relational process in which both subject and world appear and also disappear. Because the spectator cannot see, the performance highlights another personal space as well, namely that of the imagination. The interior stage thus withdraws from, yet also extends the physical stage on which performers and spectators meet. Directed towards interiority, the stage tends to disappear, but only to re-emerge elsewhere, as it reterritorializes on the body and mind of the spectator. Oriented towards disappearance, the infinitely small resonates with the endlessly large of subjectivity. In *The Smile*, the stage "happens" in the encounter between performer and spectator, nests in the affective spaces evoked by this encounter and by the enveloping environment, folds into interiority, and unfolds toward the spectator's subjectivity. Under these conditions, the stage no longer has a spatial coherence. Put in other words: the stage has been captured by the *event*.

Event/Situation

The folds and reverberations of the stage in *The Smile* allude to Hans-Thies Lehmann's "event/situation," although Lehmann does not restrict this particular subset of postdramatic theatre to one-to-one performances (Lehmann 2006, 104–7). In *Postdramatic Theatre*, he argues that the postdramatic event does not represent reality, but foregrounds the real itself. The event refers to "the execution of acts that are real in the here and now and find their very fulfilment in the very moment they happen, without necessarily leaving any traces of meaning or a cultural monument"

(2006, 104). To a certain extent, the event *does* leave traces, and neither is bereft of meaning, as I hope to demonstrate within the course of this chapter. Coupling it with the term "situation," Lehmann adds a dimension of spatiality and a sense of interiority to the event, by observing that spectators are playfully put into a position from which they are unable to face the perceived but are participating in it—which *The Smile* takes quite literally. Theatre thus is "no longer spectatorial but instead a social situation" which "eludes objective description, because for each individual participant it represents an experience that does not match the experience of others" (106).[8] Although I use a first-person perspective as well, the underlying aim of this chapter is to demonstrate that despite the personal address, we may still investigate how these subjective experiences are staged and designed, and move beyond the mere personal description. In view of *The Smile*, it is worth mentioning that Lehmann also gives testimony to the self-referential qualities of the event/situation. Due to the ephemerality of the event, next to the responsibility of the participants in the event/situation, the vulnerability of the process becomes its primary mode of existence. Theatre then "simultaneously takes a step towards the dissolution of theatre *and* to its amplification" (124, italics in the original). A similar dissolution–amplification axis is active in *The Smile*, where the wheelchair's thresholds and the inversion of theatre conventions redirect the attention back toward the theatre itself.

The event also plays an important role in Deleuze's work, albeit a rather different event than Lehmann's. In *The Logic of Sense* (1969/1990), Deleuze turns to the *paradox*, and more specifically to two stories by Lewis Carroll, to characterize his understanding of the event. He provides a description that reverberates with the inward-outward movements of *The Smile*'s spaces of proximity:

> *Alice* and *Through the Looking-Glass* involve a category of very special things: events, pure events. When I say "Alice becomes larger," I mean that she becomes larger than she was. By the same token, however, she becomes smaller than she is now. Certainly, she is not bigger and smaller at the same time. She is larger now; she was smaller before. But it is at the same moment that one becomes larger than one was and smaller than one becomes. This is the simultaneity of a becoming whose characteristic is to elude the present. Insofar as it eludes the present, becoming does not tolerate the separation or the distinction of the before and after, or of past and future. It pertains to the essence of becoming to move and to pull in both directions at once: Alice does not grow without shrinking, and vice versa. Good sense affirms that in all things there is a

determinable sense or direction [*sens*]; but paradox is the affirmation of both senses or directions at the same time. (Deleuze, quoted in Boundas 1993, 39)

It goes beyond the scope of this study to fully explore Deleuze's understanding of the event, but a few observations are in place, since this will help to grasp the particularities of the (Deleuzian) diagram. The event provides the ground on which the diagram operates—and vice versa, the diagram causes the event to emerge. To Deleuze, the event is pure movement; it never arrives at "the same" but is always in a state of becoming. As indicated in the quote above, the event eludes the present. The event resides in *virtuality*, it belongs to the plane of immanence, to the not-yet-actualized. Yet the event needs to materialize in some way, however abstract or obscure, in order to be known. In *The Fold*, Deleuze remarks that the event needs the intervention of "a sort of screen" which allows the event to move from the virtual realm of "chaotic multiplicity" to the actual, and to emerge as matter (2006b, 86). This "screen" then functions as the abstract machine of the diagram, as it distinguishes the virtual from the actual. Both these modalities of reality are components of the event, as Deleuze and Guattari argue in *What is Philosophy?*, where they describe the event as

> the part that eludes its own actualization in everything that happens. The event is not the state of affairs. It is actualized in a state of affairs, in a body, in a lived, but it has a shadowy and secret part that is continually subtracted from or added to its actualization: in contrast with the state of affairs, it neither begins nor ends but has gained or kept the infinite movement to which it gives consistency. (Deleuze and Guattari 1994, 156)

Deleuze's event functions on the level of onto-epistemology, as life, thought, affects, things, and in particular concepts themselves are events, always involved with change and differentiation (Deleuze and Guattari 1994, 158–61). It is due to these qualities that Deleuze links the event to the theatre. Yet in theatre discourse, the event is regarded not as eluding but as affirming the present, alluding to the "here and now" of the live performance (cf. Lehmann 2006, 104). The event is equally associated with ephemerality and potentiality, yet it must be acknowledged that it has gained a much more solidified form, as the Event itself has become a sort of genre. These two rather different readings of the event, one philosophical and one theatrical, encounter each other somewhere halfway when further investigating *The Smile*. *The Smile* gives "ground" to the fluidity of the event, by subjecting the lived experience to a process of (regulated) experimentation.

Into the Laboratory

The Smile consists of four encounters with different performers on particular spots in the performance space. With an interval of about ten minutes, spectators enter the room by means of the wheelchair and start their personal trajectory. My first encounter is not over yet: after having left the wheelchair, back on my feet again, I am guided around with care until suddenly I am pushed against a wall, rather violently. Without the guiding hands I feel quite lonely—particularly because I had just begun to surrender myself to the situation; I considered whether to stop wondering what would happen next, and rather "see" what actually happens instead. Now I have just been left, or so it seems. To make things worse, a photograph is taken of me—or at least, I hear the sound of a camera clicking—which is quite an intrusive act, as it crosses the borders of privacy. Ontroerend Goed member Alexander Devriendt informed me in an interview that this once led a very angry spectator to leave immediately, because this man associated this particular scene with Abu Graib-like acts of imprisonment (Groot Nibbelink 2009a). My concern here is not whether this association was "just" or not, but on the contrary to understand this reaction as one of many potential readings of this scene. In my memory for instance, this moment is primarily archived as an auditory sensation. Amidst the distant chatter of voices and noises, the camera click stands out as a nearby sound, which increases spatial awareness.

In the same interview, Devriendt explains that the company did not allocate any specific "content" or meaning to this scene, which I regard as indicative of *The Smile*'s diagrammatic design. Ontroerend Goed approaches all the relays on this trajectory as acts of providing the conditions for encounters. Devriendt characterizes *The Smile*'s design as an open-ended scenario, and literally qualifies the rules in play as rules *of* play. In the second encounter, the spectator is gently thrown out of the wheelchair to land onto a bed, next to a female performer. She snuggles up close, places her leg on top of yours and starts to inquire about pleasant and secret memories. Devriendt recounts that spectators respond very differently to this situation: they resist or give in; they share their deepest secrets or treat the encounter as a playful and agreeable experiment.[9] These and other encounters in *The Smile* render this performance into a laboratory of human behavior; a laboratory in which experience and experimentation coincide. In fact, the first entries of the *Oxford English Dictionary* define "experience" precisely in terms of experimentation: the action of putting to the test, to trial in order to make experience of, to fulfil in practice; a tentative procedure, an experiment.[10] *The Smile* traverses the heterogeneity of spectators: each trajectory is a singular laboratory, a personal yet cooperative investigation of the value of distance and closeness in performer–spectator relationships. This really makes *The Smile* an "essay in intimacy," as reviewer Joyce McMillan accurately put it (2008).[11] It is a collaborative essay, in fact, with as many authors as there will have been spectators to the performance.

The conjunction of a set of parameters and an inherently open-ended situation is not only a prerequisite for games, essays, or laboratory experiments; it also characterizes *The Smile*'s diagrammatic design. Both Kenneth Knoespel and Sher Doruff regard the diagram as the becoming-matter of ideas or meaning, for instance as they materialize in sketches, scribbled notes, a preliminary outline of a text, or (re-used) examples or concepts (Knoespel 2001, 146–7; Doruff 2009). Becoming-matter produces an inseparable connection between meaning and form: that what *The Smile* is "about," is actually inseparable from the way the diagram materializes in the lived experience. And yet, the diagram is an abstract machine that in itself has no specific meaning, as Deleuze remarks in *Foucault*: "It is a machine that is almost blind and mute, even though it makes others see and speak" (2006a, 30). In the end, the spectators' personal responses to intimate or intrusive behavior define the (temporary) content of the scene. Experimentation is the substance of this performance, which in turn is formative for, and informed by, lived experience.

Thinking Through the Diagram

As mentioned above, Deleuze and Guattari approach the diagram as an abstract machine, a force that has neither substance nor form, yet plays a "piloting role" in the process of creation, to repeat Knoespel, and "reveals the exercise of a force upon other forces" (Deleuze 2006a, 30). A diagram produces directions that are "fractal in nature," which may evolve toward stratification but finds its true potential in qualitative differentiation (Deleuze and Guattari 1994, 40). The highly unstable and fluid nature of the diagram brings Deleuze to observe that this abstract machine is actually closer to theatre than it is to the factory; it fosters connections and constantly evolves, it is always intersocial and likely to bring about change (Deleuze 2006a, 30). In *The Smile*, experimentation is quite restricted on the level of concrete actions; yet the lived experience opens up a non-limited space of change and variation. Spectators actively participate in drawing and redrawing the lines that form the diagram, which occasionally results in literally drawing the line—as did the spectator with the Abu Graib association. This particular response is not only indicative of the diagram's qualitative differentiality, it also addresses the diagram as a conduit of power and control. Despite their relative muteness, diagrams are not neutral and may serve to enquire how diagrams mediate in the production of meaning and function as relays for the constitution and reconceptualization of knowledge. Diagrams then are *models to think with* or figures to "think through": they "reveal matrices through which meaning is negotiated on an individual and social level" (Knoespel 2001, 146, 149). This particular understanding of the diagram leads to exploring how *The Smile* rearticulates what can be considered as knowledge or meaning within the context of theatre.

Kenneth Knoespel discusses the role of diagrams in the work of Deleuze, mentioning Deleuze's enquiry into Foucault's Panopticism as one of the earliest manifestations, and his study on Leibniz, the fold, and the Baroque house as one of the latest. Both these architectural structures are valuable thinking models to further investigate *The Smile*'s diagram. In *Foucault*, Deleuze discusses the Panopticon as a diagram. The Panopticon is a particular type of prison, conceived by the eighteenth-century social theorist and philosopher Jeremy Bentham, which situates the prisoners' cells around a central observation tower in such a way that the isolated prisoners perceive themselves as always being observed, without being able to see who observes them. The inmates internalize this awareness of being observed, which renders the actual occupation of the observation point in fact redundant. The Panopticon is a diagram because it designs behavior. It involves much more than a prison building itself: it establishes intersocial relationships and functions as a conduit for power, control, and discipline; it organizes patterns of observation and (feelings of) being observed (Foucault 1975/1995, 195–201; Deleuze 2006a, 27–38). Such a relationship is rather literally distinguishable in *The Smile*: most of the time, the spectators are subject to a situation in which they are (or feel) observed by performers without being able to observe themselves—this becoming-spectator of the performer is of course also an inversion of theatre conventions.

On the other end of the spectrum we find the folds of the Baroque house. Although I do not pretend to describe this Leibnizian concept in all its complexity, the Baroque house summons up a relationship between matter and the senses on the one hand, and subjectivity on the other. The Baroque house is an allegory of the fold, and provides Deleuze with a model for understanding the Baroque not in terms of a historical genre, but as a style that exceeds historical periodization (Conley in Deleuze 2006b, xi). Characteristic of this style is the entangled relationship between interiority and exteriority, seen as both distinct and as always enfolded into each other. The Baroque house is a two-story house: the upper floor is a closed space without windows, a place of interiority; the lower floor instead opens up to the world outside and designates exteriority. The upper floor houses the soul, as Leibniz puts it, a term equated with the mind (Deleuze 2006b, 97). On the base level there is the raw matter of the body living in the world; this floor has windows, which refer to the senses (5).

The division between an upper and lower floor may easily evoke a Cartesian dualism between mind and body, as well as a hierarchy of a body subordinated to the mind. However, it is precisely through the figure of the fold that such a dichotomy is prevented. As mentioned above, the fold is a figuration of infinity and endlessness. Any single unit or monad, whether a piece of cloth, a paper, a soul or a subject, can be folded in an infinite number of ways, and as such the fold is always a variety, a manifestation of potentiality. In the Baroque house, both floors are connected to each other through an infinite series of folds. Impressions on the lower floor unfold onto the upper floor to find their individuated articulation. In turn, the upper floor projects itself onto matter in order to be substantial and find a form of expression (Deleuze 2006b, 97–8, 114–16). The sensations and movements on the lower floor resonate in the sounds on the upper floor "as if it were a music salon," and continuously fill up and ripple the folds the soul is made of (4). A soul on the upper floor can never manifest itself directly: there are no windows on this floor. The walls of the upper room are covered with cloths, indicating that the soul itself consists of infinite folds. This interior room, then, does not suggest an essence of the subject, residing in the mind, but instead articulates infinity present within subjectivity, and the body or matter as the equally infinite form in which the soul expresses itself.

To summarize, the Panopticon serves as a reminder that the diagram may be understood as a conduit for power and control, whereas the folds of the Baroque house relate the diagram to the subtle yet complex patterns by which subjectivity becomes "matter." The Baroque house envisages subjects as enfolded within the world and vice versa, with the senses functioning as windows onto the world. Previously, the diagram was introduced as the becoming-matter of ideas or meaning. In what follows, I look closer into this (embodied) matter and explore the laboratory of corporeal spectatorship, first by bringing the Panopticon to the front, and placing the Baroque house at the back of the stage, whereas later I will switch this scene of enquiry the other way round.

The Grid of Capital

The Smile manipulates the spectator, exemplified by simple tokens such as the blindfold and the tied hands, which creates a relationship of dependency with the performer. In order to map the relations between forces in a

Panopticon-sensorium, though, in this section I draw a parallel with another performance, namely *Het Sprookjesbordeel* (The Fairy-Tales Brothel, 2001–5) by the Flemish Toneelhuis, composed by writer-director Peter Verhelst. This performance equally delves into the corporeality of spectatorship, but negotiates the performer–spectator relationship through the most intensive of affects, that of (unfulfilled) desire. Intoxicated by the close physical contact with a performer, the carnal language of Verhelst and in particular the haptic sensations of touching another body and being touched, spectators are seduced into giving up control, to living their personal imagination, and to falling in love with a stranger. The performance uses a small cell in an obscure part of a conventional theatre building, such as a cellar or an elevator shaft, which is transformed into an immersive environment: an agreeable warmth and scents of pleasant aromas and of freshly cut wood invite the single spectator to probe the space through all the senses, and to perceive the skin as a porous membrane between self and world, between body and environment.

Soon after the start of the performance, the spectator lies down on a vibrating bed, blindfolded, and becoming-space shifts toward becoming-body. Another body joins the spectator on the bed, while a voice touches the ears: "Breath in and out the room, the heartbeat of the bed, the warmth." Cherry juice is dropped onto the corners of the mouth. The performers— "masseurs" or "tongue cats" in Verhelstian vocabulary—tease the spectator by asking not to believe them, while in the meantime they announce they are going to undress. The spectator's hands are lead to touch the bare skin of the performer, invited to feel the sentence that is said to be inscribed there: "The definition of a labyrinth: it is not about finding the exit, it is about getting lost" (Dragstra 2005). The spectator is seduced by the synaesthetics of language: words seem to have become edible and tactile, as if they can be tasted and swallowed, they are rubbed into the body's surface and felt just below the skin. *Het Sprookjesbordeel* conjures up erotic fantasies and mutates consciousness: instead of distant reflexivity and control, the spectator is addressed as a fully sensitive body, aroused and ready to give in to desire.

As strongly as the spectators are taken in by this performance, they are repelled from it just as forcefully. After forty minutes the blindfold is lifted, the imagined-beloved performer is gone and instead the spectator faces a second, *other* performer. As if that were not enough to cool off, temperatures fall even lower as the spectator is directed toward a door that opens onto the streets on a remote side of the theatre building—left alone with unfulfilled desire and extremely confused feelings of arousal, shame, desire, or embarrassment. Probably the most unnerving thoughts arrive when everyday consciousness sets in, leading the spectator to wonder how it is possible to feel so intimately connected to a stranger, a stranger who is, above all, a performer. The thrill caused by the uniqueness of this personal experience now suddenly starts to falter, as the spectator comes to the realization of being just one of many, caught up in a theatrical contract, while the performer-beloved has already moved on to serve a new customer. A customer, indeed: the spectator awkwardly resembles a client visiting a brothel. In a parallel to *Call Cutta*, the spectator has been provided with a (theatrical) service, be it with rather different means, as this time the spectator's personal, sensory experience has been hooked up onto a system of consumption.

This junction of experience and consumption brings to mind the experience economy (Pine and Gilmore 2011, 1999), which treats products and services as memorable experiences or *events* that are (seemingly) adjusted to consumers' personal tastes. Ironically, whereas 1960s performance art regarded the elusive and non-repetitive live event as an antidote to consumer culture (Allain and Harvie 2014, 221), the experience economy turns the immateriality of experience into a commodity. Lehmann briefly mentions the commercial event as well, but immediately dismisses it as something altogether different (2006, 104). I prefer to use the connection, however, to expose how diagrams draw relations with other diagrams. In *The Experience Economy: Work is Theatre & Every Business a Stage*, business theorists Joseph Pine and James Gilmore use the theatre as a model for presenting and staging experiences. Performances like *Call Cutta* or *Het Sprookjesbordeel* work the other way round: they address the spectator as a customer. By installing a service relationship between the performer and the spectator, they model the theatre upon formats of capitalism. Similarly to the panoptical diagram of *The Smile*, in *Het Sprookjesbordeel* an impression of individual observation is created, and following the logics of the experience economy, it is suggested that the spectator is personally attended to. There is a fundamental inequality in this distribution of power relations, in which the spectator surrenders and the performer is fully in control. Instead of vision, exploited by the Panopticon, desire is the dominant regime here; desire that is not fulfilled and that capitalizes on lack. The very notion of lack transcodes the spectator's body into a "commodity-body" (Massumi 1992, 129). In other words, in *Het Sprookjesbordeel*, the diagram is (re)written on the grid of capital.

In *A User's Guide to Capitalism and Schizophrenia: Deviations from Deleuze and Guattari* (1992), Brian Massumi observes that the "grid of capital is simple. Its categorical distinctions are two in number: worker/capitalist and commodity/consumer … The categories do not have to be perceived by the body they apply to … in order to be activated. They are automatically in operation in any state of things touched by capital" (128). Wherever an image of capital appears, such as money, stock, wages, or desire, such a commodity relation is likely to be actualized (130, 136). Massumi in fact ascribes a number of diagrammatic principles to capital itself: capital is an abstract machine that operates through (unmediated) desire; it "has images but is imageless as such"; it is capable of transforming bodies or state of things; capital is an *operation* that "can be analyzed as a virtual mode of composition" (131). According to performance scholar Elke van Campenhout, *Het Sprookjesbordeel* perversely de-masques this commodity relation, a relation that usually remains unnoticed as capital's abstract machine tends to obscure consumers' lack of control and the commodification of lack itself (2003). Similar to *Call Cutta*, the service economy is not critiqued from the outside but explored from within, as the spectator is the subject of this (theatrical) service, and challenged to give in to desire.

In another review, Pieter Verstraete remarks that the reiterated use of the words "don't believe me" puts the spectator's sense perception and imagination to the test, to such an extent that it is hardly possible to distinguish between the reality of the illusion, and the lie of the truth (2003). This paradox is also active in *The Smile*, where the spectator is aware of being subjected to a staged situation, yet, simultaneously, the emotions aroused by this situation are often experienced as "real." Here we touch upon an enigmatic relationship between authenticity and the stage—which neither escapes the grid of capital. In their book *Authenticity: What Consumers Really Want* (2007), Pine and Gilmore observe that the experience economy produced a world of pretense and hence created a need for authenticity, a longing for true encounters in which customers are able to interact with or directly relate to the product or service of their choice.[12] *Authenticity* is equally a retailers' handbook, in which Pine and Gilmore offer ways to *stage* authenticity, with the help of an intriguing matrix of fake and real, fake-real and real-fake categories, stating that as long as you clearly admit that what you do or sell is fake, but either true to one's ideology or to what you promise to sell, customers will accept the fake as authentic. Showing explicitly that something is staged is thus the most authentic thing to do (2007, 95–114, 220). Such overt tokens of theatricality interestingly reverberate with current dramaturgical strategies in the theatre, also distinguishable in Signa's *The Ruby Town Oracle* (Chapter 6). Many contemporary artists do not regard fiction and reality as opposites, but as folded into each other, and their work often relies on (examining) intertwined and shifting layers of reality.

Despite the parallels drawn between economical and theatrical events, there are considerable differences as well: Pine and Gilmore advise trading companies to demonstrate self-reflexive awareness, but this is something other than creating (perceptual) awareness on the side of the customers. This is what ultimately distinguishes retailing from the theatre. Performances like

Het Sprookjesbordeel and *The Smile* invest in spectators' self-reflexivity, by exposing the grid of capital itself. Massumi attests that a

> commodity-body is generalized in a way that not only disregards minor deviations from a norm but is basically disinterested in the body's intrinsic qualities and their similarity-difference to those of other bodies. The commodity-body is reduced to a pure equivalence. It is generalized in the sense that any number of other bodies carry the same numerical value, and could be substituted for it, exchanged in its stead. (Massumi 1992, 129)

Het Sprookjesbordeel stages the conditions for this commodity-body to emerge and leaves the spectator-consumer in doubt as to whether the encounter with this particular performer was really unique: "did it matter that it was me, in this performance?". The immediate answer to follow is that perhaps it did *not* matter, not to the performer anyway. The spectator treads upon the uneasiness and discomfort of that awareness, and is provided with the "perverse pleasure" that Claire Bishop assigns to delegated performance in the arts (see Chapter 3), which precisely renders the commodity-relation perceptible.

Distributions of the Sensible

The Panopticon organizes relationships between observation or watching, and being seen or watched, and just like Massumi's commodity-body reduces inmates to numerical values. This abstract machine produces a particular "distribution of the sensible," the term Jacques Rancière uses to describe how the visible or the perceptible obscures the "shadowy and secret parts" (Deleuze and Guattari 1994) that are subtracted from the sensible, and hence are rendered imperceptible. Rancière applies the term as well to theatre, although the *teatron* also substantially differs from the Panopticon (Bleeker 2008a, 166). In *The Emancipated Spectator* (2009), Rancière in fact attributes a certain limitlessness to the act of looking itself, an argument by which he also critiques participatory performance. His study resonates in interesting ways with *The Smile*, while there are strong contradictions as well.

Despite the strategies of confinement, both *Het Sprookjesbordeel* and *The Smile* rely heavily on audience participation. As mentioned in the Introduction, the emergence of immersive and related forms of theatre has issued an extensive debate on participatory performance, where interactive audiences or otherwise engaged spectators are repeatedly described as involved in much more than "simply watching" (Oddey and White 2009, 8). One remarkable voice in this debate is Jacques Rancière's, who in *The Emancipated Spectator* strongly resists participatory theatre. He argues that (conventionally seated) spectators are autonomous, active onlookers, involved in countless heterogeneous performances, who all learn something different from a performance, by means of active interpretation and the translation of this knowledge to others and further fields of knowledge (2009, 11).

Based on this acknowledgment of heterogeneity, the spectators in *The Smile* can equally be considered emancipated spectators. Not because spectators are entirely free to do what they want—the performance is too manipulative to assert that—but because each of them will respond differently to their encounters with performers. It seems rather ironic to speak of tied, blindfolded people as emancipated spectators, yet each encounter in *The Smile*, more so than in *Het Sprookjesbordeel* perhaps, offers a space for spectators' particular ways of perceiving, thinking, and doing; processes influenced by cultural background, social habits, and personal histories. However, *The Smile* is a type of performance that is strongly criticized by Rancière, as it requires physical participation and transcends the separation of stage and auditorium. Rancière states that such a redistribution of places at its best leads to an "enrichment of theatrical performance" and "intellectual adventure" but nevertheless confirms a traditional distribution of the sensible, which is the assumption that communality is the true essence of theatre (2009, 15). He takes Brecht and Artaud as examples, stating that they share this communitarian belief, however different their strategies. Both counter the illusion of mimesis with the idea of a living community, in which activity is linked with communality and looking with passivity. This is what Rancière understands as a particular distribution of the sensible, "an a priori distribution of positions and capacities and incapacities attached to these positions" (12). For Rancière, looking is in itself an active process and people assembled in a theatre do not necessarily form a community. In a theatre, just like in a museum or cinema, people are "plotting their own path"; the only thing that is shared is the power of "equality of intelligence" (17). His argument relocates the spectators in the audience, separated from the stage, equipped with the tool of (aesthetic) distance.

Rancière thus critiques performances that remove the distance between performers and spectators and, through this, abolish the role of performance as a mediating third party in the event (14–16). Although a certain "vanishing act" takes place in *The Smile*, since the performance—as a mediating third— is actually located in the encounter between performer and spectator, the (aesthetic) distance between performers and spectators in my view does not dissolve, simply because they share the same space. The distance just appears elsewhere, namely in the spectator's aesthetic orientation, and in the performance's diagrammatic design. Contrary to Rancière's analysis, the spectator on the stage does not produce communality, but differentiality.

Perhaps distributions are inescapable. Rancière's work is surely an inspiring appeal for acknowledging the heterogeneity and equality of any spectator, but it is meanwhile remarkable that Rancière's distribution of the *sensible* hardly pays attention to *corporeal* intelligence: knowledge that is present in affects and sensations. By mainly referring to spectatorship in terms of interpretation, storytelling, and cognitive processes of translation and knowledge production, Rancière seems caught up into a distribution of the sensible of his own, which borders on logocentrism.[13] *The Smile* questions this distribution, through the explicit address to the senses. In *Visuality in the Theatre*, Maaike Bleeker convincingly argues that each performance functions by way of address, whether hardly perceptible or persistently present, and points to the body as the locus of looking. What Rancière seems to neglect, in my view, and what Bleeker purposefully emphasizes, is precisely this (corporeal) address. This is highly relevant in view of contemporary (postdramatic) theatre and performance, which tend to evoke, to use another observation by Bleeker, "intense experiences that often are not easily explained in terms of signs and referents. Often, this theatre addresses the spectator as a sensible body, rather than a decoding mind" (Bleeker 2005, 109).

As suggested above, the folds of the Baroque house could be a way to account for the spectator as an embodied subject. Arts and performance scholar Sher Doruff proposes to re-articulate the diagram as a *biogram*, in her analysis of translocal music performances (2009). She derives the term from Brian Massumi, but whereas Massumi primarily relates the concept to synaesthetics (Massumi 2002, 187), Doruff regards the biogram as a diagram that is transcoded by lived experience, and geared towards the distribution of affects. The biogram is a conduit that channels and filters embodied sensations, and operates through "the power to affect and the power to be affected" (Doruff 2009, 124). Similar to my argument, she too suggests that lived experience may be understood as expressive content in itself (127). Doruff sees the biogram as an assemblage of compositional forces. Whereas diagrams may pertain to buildings, sketches, or abstract models, when transcoded by lived experience these compositional forces materialize in the acts and responses of participants in the event themselves. In a similar vein, I propose to understand both the performers and the spectators in *The Smile* as compositional forces, although their relationship remains asymmetrical. The biogram is actualized through affective modulations and tonalities of sensation—patterns of expressive content which may lead spectators to inquire into the (im)possibility of intimacy in the theatre, to reflect on their own responses, or, likely, to follow the lived experience folding back onto itself.

A Spectator in the Dark

About halfway through *The Smile* I arrive at the third encounter. A performer describes her dress—"red, with lace"—and then tells me she is dancing in front of me, and that she loves horses. "Would you like to sit on my lap?" she whispers, while she puts some chocolate and pieces of tangerine in my mouth. I hear the rustling of her dress as she stands very close, and when she laughs I know she has moved a few steps away again. The scene borders on the erotic; she teases me by raising my curiosity, which invites me to start "looking" for her. This is a rather curious situation: while this performance questions spectatorship in all sorts of ways, I am actually in a position very well known from conventional theatre: in the dark. However, quite consistently with the other dissolution-amplification axes in this chapter, the darkness in *The Smile* increases the spectator's engagement. In *The Smile* the obstruction of vision foregrounds the act of perception itself, and in particular draws attention to the corporeality of spectatorship.

The Smile addresses the spectator through a variety of senses, as the scene above well indicates. My ears seek to register the location of sounds while I try to establish what I taste; my skin indicates whether the performer is near or far; the proprioceptive memories of stumbling out of the wheelchair inform my wish to remain seated this time; and all the while I try to visualize what I hear. This multiplied address renders the spectator into a sensitive organism or a "web of sensation" as Stephen Di Benedetto puts it, in *The Provocation of the Senses in Contemporary Theatre* (2010). He suggests that the processing of multiple sensory stimuli induces a "sensuous thinking," which is a way of paying attention, a staying alert to how senses act as porous membranes between self and world (167–8). When thinking through the folds of the Baroque house, the senses draw a relation of exteriority with the body's environment, but also reverberate with the mind on the (dark) upper floor.

Taking away sight on the one hand makes way for other modalities of sense perception, and on the other hand reveals looking as a dominant mode of engaging with and thinking about theatre. In *Visuality in the Theatre*, Maaike Bleeker describes the strong conceptual and historical bond between vision, objectivity, rationality, and scientific truth, where looking from a distance is connected to the "modern fable of vision as true and objective, of the possibility of seeing it 'as it is'" (Bleeker 2008a, 5). Drawing on Jonathan Crary and Hal Foster, amongst others, Bleeker points out how this "scopic regime of modernity" produces a disembodied notion of vision, which is also at work in the theatre (2008a, 2–5, 165–7). Bleeker counters the (Cartesian) disembodied eye/I by dissecting the "vision machine" of theatre, demonstrating that bodies/subjects are always involved in what there is to be seen, and that we are "cultured to see" by existing conceptions of visuality (2008a, 7).[14] *The Smile* fits Bleeker's line of reasoning, albeit with different means. Whereas Bleeker exposes the corporeality of spectatorship in conventional set-ups, *The Smile* deterritorializes the theatron by bringing performers and spectators extremely close. Instead a place for seeing, the stage is distributed over the senses, and reterritorializes the sensorium.

The sensorium establishes a (re)distribution of the sensible, though without rejecting vision. *The Smile*'s biogram instead advocates the equality of the senses. In his essay "Seeing nothing, now hear this…" Martin Welton describes a play performed in full darkness, and observes that seeing nothing is still a part of seeing, not a lack of seeing (in Banes and Lepecki 2007, 146–55). Although seeing into darkness differs from wearing a blindfold, my urge to look for the performer equally indicates that the visual cortex is still active. When sight is addressed as but one of the senses, within an "altered sense ratio," as Welton puts it, this "offers an opportunity 'to make sense' of vision afresh, to reclaim the visual in the theatre for the realm of the senses" (in Banes and Lepecki 2007, 152). Such a "visceral visuality" characterizes the proceedings of the third encounter. While teased by the performer, with the taste of sweets still in my mouth, the blindfold is suddenly lifted and with great hilarity I discover a completely different situation in front of me than the one made up in my mind.[15] It is a clash of the senses. With Bleeker's analysis of the "scopic regime" in mind, one may think that vision is again linked to objectivity here, portraying the scene "as it really is." Lifting the blindfold, however, does not follow up on that particular logic. Instead of presenting vision as the agent of true knowledge, the scene invites awareness of how collaborative and disjointed sense mechanisms constitute different types of knowledge and modes of engagement with the world. The scene presents the spectator with a Deleuzian Baroque perspective: "For Leibniz … perspectivism amounts to a relativism, but not the relativism we take for granted. It is not a variation of truth according to the subject, but the condition in which the truth of a variation appears to the subject" (Deleuze 2006b, 20). The term "point of view" does not satisfy here; instead, what counts, quite analogous to Bleeker's analysis of perspective (Chapter 2), is "what remains in point of view, what occupies point of view, and without which point of view would not be. It is necessarily a soul, a subject" (Deleuze 2006b, 24).

Perceiving this clash of the senses might be regarded as an instance of what Brian Massumi names a "thinking-feeling of what happens" (2008). Thinking-feeling is a self-referential process, which involves the "perception *of* the event of perception *in* the perception …. in the immediacy of its occurrence, as it is felt" (2008, 6). Thinking-feeling points to the qualitative dimension of perception, and like the Baroque perspective sees perception as never stable, but instead as always relational, vivid, and processual (5–7).[16] In everyday life, senses tend to function automatically and sensory input therefore, partly as a necessity, is largely ignored. Foregrounding the qualitative dimension of sense perception, however, leads to re-articulating something quite evident yet hardly perceptible in daily life, namely that humans (and animals) are intrinsically connected to the world, through the senses. Sense perception is not (only) a way of gaining knowledge *of* the world, or of the self; rather, we constitute our understanding of both self and world through corporeal perception. From the very first entrance into the sensorium, *The Smile*'s biogram addresses the senses as the primary tools through which we probe the world "outside"; a world that is constituted by the senses and is constitutive of relational subjectivity.

The Dramaturgy of Proximity

Looking at the spatial dramaturgy of *The Smile*, this parkour of close encounters and intimate spaces facilitates a politics of perception, which mobilizes what it means "to make sense" of a performance. Baz Kershaw indirectly gives testimony to such a redistribution of the sensible in his description of Teatro de los Sentidos' *The Labyrinth* (1996), directed by Enrique Vargas. This performance bears similarities with *The Smile*, although it differs significantly in size and scale. Kershaw describes how the absence of sight and the address to all the senses not only reject a hierarchy of the senses, but also subvert the hierarchy of signs (1999, 213). Kershaw goes on to explain how the disruption of perceptual habits, the experience of isolation, and the absence of hierarchical order in *The Labyrinth* simultaneously induce a confirmation of the self as well as provoke an increased sense of social and environmental connectivity. Kershaw understands this twofold awareness as the *ecology* of performance. A similar ecological alertness characterizes my response to *The Smile*'s biogram, as the distribution of affects induced both an increased self-awareness as well as a conscious perception of the world "outside." All in all, perhaps nothing spectacular happens in this performance. Visiting *The Smile* may lead instead to a rediscovery of something quite ordinary, yet precious: the experience of one's presence in the work; the awareness of one's senses and how they (dis)function; the perception of the proximity of human beings; the impression of slowing-down toward the (Deleuzian) speed of lived space. This biogram maps the forces of the imagination as well, as it charts the capacity for otherworld making, through which the world will always appear larger than was thought of before—and smaller than it has become.

A slow, modest attentiveness to the ordinary, that which usually remains unnoticed, is also characteristic of Alan Read's *Theatre, Intimacy and Engagement*. Although Read does not discuss instances of physical intimacy, and mainly focuses on the lives of those who are usually not included in the theatre, his appreciation for the proximity of relations offers a parallax view on the close encounters in *The Smile*. For Read, intimacy is the potential equivalent of engagement, and the theatre a means to investigate the relational capacity of sentient "human animals" (2008, 8). Theatre, then, may contribute to an ethics of association and, drawing on Bruno Latour, a reassembly of the social (Read 2008, 32, 40–4, 68–70).

The Smile equally investigates this relational capacity, by employing the folds and furls of the senses, self, and world to question our mode of engagement with other beings in that world. This also becomes apparent in the closing scene, where the blindfold is lifted for the second time and I look a performer straight in the eye, seeing a performer who weeps. This scene provokes a dense "web of sensations" (Di Benedetto 2010) and is therefore hard to describe. Despite the knowledge that the situation is staged, the intensity of this encounter is that of two close friends saying farewell. While I feel sad and resistant to let go of the eye contact with the performer, I am slowly driven backward, which allows me to see all the various scenes at once, with other spectators involved now, next to spectators' photographs displayed on the wall, all in one room (Figure 5.1). Like in "The Aleph," a story by Jorge Luis Borges, this scene displays the infinitude of a multiplicity.[17] I am a singular spectator in a multitude of other spectators, who have found or will find their own spaces of proximity. They will have (had) similar sensations to mine, or entirely different ones; I am connected to them as we are all writing our part of this kaleidoscopic essay that marks *The Smile*'s emergent dramaturgy.

Zooming out theoretically, I think it is an interesting paradox that a focus on the single, individual spectator eventually investigates the spectator's relational capacities. In this regard, *The Smile* addresses the spectator again, but with a different attentiveness, as a societal being. This potential of connectivity may be a fruitful alternative to Rancière's "problem" with theatre's claim to communality. Collectivity, then, is not a homogeneous

Diagrams

Figure 5.1 Closing scene in Ontroerend Goed's *The Smile Off Your Face*. Courtesy Ontroerend Goed, photo Virginie Schreyen.

community, nor an arbitrary gathering of individuals, but a re-articulation of the social. Instead of communality, this performance explores the potential of connectivity, with the acknowledgement of the heterogeneity of any spectator in the theatre.

A Theatre of Folds

Close friends, saying goodbye—how much can one be tricked? This particular performer and I, we are not friends. It may have been a *semblance* of friendship, the term Massumi uses to indicate how previous experience and knowledge is always enfolded within and reverberates with current experiences and perceptions (2008, 6). My trajectory through *The Smile* produced both an inward- and an outward-oriented attentiveness, a kind of openness one may associate with friendship. Although I know I am being manipulated, at the same time my sense of joy or embarrassment is not fake, and neither is the performer's concentrated attention. Some may argue that *The Smile* comes closer to the Panopticon than to the folds of the Baroque house, but I propose instead that these diagrams are drawn *through* one another. *The Smile* produces a texture of affective modulations, as distance intersects with closeness, limitations give rise to infinite vibrations in the soul, interiority unfolds toward connectivity, and exteriority curls up into the imagination.

Thinking through the diagram exposes the performer and the spectator as asymmetrical yet equal compositional forces in an open-ended event. Diagrams help to investigate the (dynamic) form of the event and to articulate horizons of thought without fixating the event entirely. Diagrams are a way to think through the event but, as Knoespel points out, they are also open to revision and redrawing. Following up on that suggestion, *The Smile* allows for the possibility of rethinking the absolute ephemerality of the event in performance. Instead of the ephemeral, *The Smile* invites a particular attentiveness; instead of foregrounding the real, what is real is subjected to experimentation; instead of the use of signs that refuse to function as signs (Lehmann 2006, 104), this performance enquires into what is meaningful or valuable for the singular spectator. The event does leave traces, as the tonalities of sensation become part of the corporeal archive of both spectators and performers. The event materializes in the corporeality of spectatorship, in the procedurality of perception, and in the relationality of subjectivity, all of which are ways of attaching ourselves to fluidity.

In the introduction to *The Fold*, Tom Conley observes that the fold is an intrinsically mobile concept, especially when related to the senses: "Movement of a concept that has bearing upon a subject's impressions of the physical world does not elevate according to a spiral plan ... but radiates and ramifies everywhere in the geography of experience" (in Deleuze 2006b, xiv). The fold maps patterns of (endless) de- and reterritorialization and, as such, this concept has an exoconsistency with the concept of nomadic theatre. I have foregrounded the ramifications of the fold in order to describe how spaces of proximity deterritorialize the stage, but the folds of theatre radiate within other geographies as well. As a figure of reverberation, the fold may render visible how the theatre itself is subjected to inflection and (self-)reflection, or zigzags across mash-ups of fiction and reality. The fold is equally a figure of temporal modulation and may be put to work to investigate the folds of past and present, of scenography and seriality, of processes and procedures. Such radiations dilate the geographies of experience in Signa's *Ruby Town* in the next chapter, where the concept of nomadic theatre once more bends into another direction and encounters another web of architecture, next to the limits of play.

6

Architextures

The Rhizomatic Gameboards of Signa's The Ruby Town Oracle

Drifting/Dwelling

Let us recall: the majority of theatre performances feature spectators sitting in rows, sitting next to and behind each other. As soon as they enter the auditorium, audience members start to find their seats; they know where to go, they know where the theatre space wants them to be. The performance described in this chapter, however, entices spectators to wander on and over the stage; they hardly know where to go, they are adrift in space. The governing principle is that of a psychogeography: spectators' navigational moves are led by atmosphere and energy bursts; they follow their curiosity or linger on the spot. The performance in case is *Die Erscheinungen der Martha Rubin—The Ruby Town Oracle* (2007–8) by the Danish collective Signa. Contrary to the other cases discussed in this volume, the spectator steps into a drastically fictional world. Drastically, as the performance lasts for nine days nonstop and the performers stay in character for the entire length of the event.[1] Drastically fictional, as *Ruby Town* portrays everyday life in a totally imaginary village. The performance presents an immersive, highly politicized world where the military intervenes in a community of outsiders who worship their common ancestor Martha Rubin.

Ruby Town was situated in a large abandoned industrial hall, in which Signa built a complete settlement with approximately twenty-two houses, caravans, shops, a peepshow and adjoining military quarters. Ruby Town is a poor and shabby village, situated in a Temporary Autonomous Zone, in-between an anonymous North State and a South State, surveilled and controlled by North State military personnel (Figure 6.1). The performers play the inhabitants of this Zone and they do so by truly inhabiting the place: they live in these dwellings during the entire event. This twofold playing and doing, a combination of *acting* and acting, is paralleled on the side of the spectators. Visitors to the performance buy a ticket to enter the village—which grants them access for twelve hours—after which they become visitors of Ruby Town; the "real"

Figure 6.1 A military officer guarding the Temporary Autonomous Zone, in Signa's *Die Erscheinungen der Martha Rubin—The Ruby Town Oracle*. Courtesy Signa, photo Erich Goldmann.

visitors to the performance take up the role of visitors or tourists who dwell around in this fictitious town. In order to enter Ruby Town, every spectator has to pass through a military checkpoint, run by the North State. Upon providing a name and a fingerprint one receives a passport that legitimizes the maximum stay of twelve hours. Next, the spectator is led into a room and required to watch an instruction video that gives off warnings about the rude behavior of the villagers and the advice to stay at a distance for reasons of hygiene. When passing the gate to the village, however, this distance is immediately trespassed by the villagers, who compliment the visitors on their beautiful hair or nice jackets, meanwhile begging for alcohol and cigarettes, in order to surpass the rations set by the military. Trespass and the subversion of borders are recurring themes in this performance; playing with and being at the limits defines the performance's spatial dramaturgy. With "territory" and "deterritorialization" written all over the place, *Ruby Town* is an excellent theoretical object to further explore the concept of nomadic theatre, also because this performance installation uses the aesthetics of dramatic theatre—fictionality, characters, role-playing—to fuel up and transgress the processual, participatory "real" event of a postdramatic performance.

In comparison to the previous chapters, which featured single or isolated spectators, here the spectator is one amongst many. Similar to the other cases, though, this performance accumulatively builds upon singular trajectories, as each visit is a variation on *Ruby Town*, thus exposing the performance's virtuality. The set offers ample opportunities to move around, to step in and out the micro-sceneries of separate houses, to straddle sideways, to stumble upon quarrels, fights, and flirtations in obscure corners. Spectator-visitors are invited for a talk or a drink at the bar—preferably paid for by the visitor—or they may decide to visit Martha Rubin, an ancestral oracle from whom all the villagers are descended. Distributed through this labyrinth, the spectators perceive loose yet strangely connected storylines, dispersed as gossip and rumors. They are courted by performers who are obviously playing roles but meanwhile get genuinely drunk, all of which makes it hard if not impossible to capture the event in its entirety. In this chapter I approach this labyrinthine stage as a *rhizomatic game board*, a playing arena without a center, where open-ended scenarios and becoming-stories emerge alongside the spectators' singular yet interconnected trajectories.

These stories and scenarios are to a large extent embedded in the setting and the set design, next to the spatial relationships that emanate through these, which is why in this chapter, scenography is presented as a vital force of composition. Whereas in the other cases the spectators were primarily guided by performers to find their bearings, this time the designed environment provides the tags and coordinates for movement. *Ruby Town* demonstrates that contemporary scenography does much more than providing a background for action; instead, spatial design is a compositional force which interacts with and orchestrates the embedded movements and events (McKinney and Palmer 2017; McKinney and Butterworth 2009, 4). Scenography implicates the writing of space but is also a writing *with* spaces, which will be a recurring theme in this chapter (cf. Van Kerkhoven 1992). In an interview with Signa and Arthur Köstler, founders of the Signa collective, Signa remarks that the scenography actually functioned as a script, as it defines the actions of the performers (Groot Nibbelink 2009b). A script is often conceived as a blueprint for performance or serves as a work-document when rehearsing a play. In *Ruby Town* the "play text" is deterritorialized and shattered into a multiplicity. The script gets dispersed throughout the site, it reterritorializes on the staged environment and emerges through localized actions. The set no longer serves only the performers, but creates an authoring environment for the spectators as well. Consequently, the stories presented by the performers lose coherence and re-emerge in bits and pieces, becoming part of the *texture* of the event. In fact, the script itself becomes a textural, layered phenomenon.

A texture designates a tissue or a woven fabric. In semiotics and linguistics, the term often serves to support the intertextuality of (performance) texts, as the etymological kinship between text and texture epitomizes the text as the interweaving of signs, codes, and actions (Barthes 1977, 155–64; De Marinis 1987/2003, 119). Without entirely neglecting the semiotic or literary text, I propose that a texture is also a weaving together of spaces. In relation to *Ruby Town*, I will describe this texture as an assemblage of navigational, narrative, affective, and procedural spaces, sliced by shifting frames and perspectives. In order to highlight the inherent spatiality of the term, I put texture in conjunction with (performative) architecture and name this new aggregate *architexture*.[2] An architexture is a particular type of *diagram* (Chapter 5), a fabric of intersecting spaces and perspectives, which reveals the live event as staged through scenography, or, to borrow the words of architect Bernard Tschumi, as "organized and strategized through architecture" (in Turner and Behrndt 2008, 5). While the architexture orients behavior, this layered spatiality is also open to alternative use, to (re)writing, and change. The architextural diagram, then, provides a model for enquiring into how spectators are addressed as co-creators of the event and become part of a process of building performance, a process that bears many similarities with play and games. *Ruby Town*'s architextures not only join texture with architectural thought but also create an exchange between performative architecture and play theory. Subsequently, on *Ruby Town*'s rhizomatic game board, the logic and linearity of "the play" deteriorates and makes room for playfulness as an attitude of engagement.

Borderzones

An architexture is a tissue of interconnected spaces and twisting perspectives, which also characterizes my way of describing *Ruby Town*, as I connect third-person and first-person perspectives to viewpoints derived from interviews, essays, and reviews. Such a "tissued" approach seems appropriate in relation to Signa's rhizomatic game board. In order to dress up this game board, I continue with what looks like a detour but actually is not. As stated above, *Ruby Town* severely compromises the idea of a linear, coherent story. Although there are scraps of stories, the underlying narrative seems that of the lived space itself: the social order in kitchens and bedrooms, pubs, shops, and squares; the everyday life of washing, sleeping, cooking, partying, and quarrelling. Except, all these activities take place in an extraordinary, artificially shaped environment, in a world that is both distinct from and similar to the "real" world; a world that is as multi-layered and open-ended as everyday life, yet simultaneously it is obviously staged. The blurred distinction between reality and representation is perfectly captured by an essay in *Theater der Zeit*, in which Sebastian Kirsch refers to a cartographic fantasy by Jorge Luis Borges and weighs Signa's uncanny world against the Borgesian map (Kirsch 2008). Borges' one-paragraph story is entitled "On exactitude in science" and is fully quoted here:

> … In that Empire, the Art of Cartography attained such Perfection that the map of a single Province occupied the entirety of a City, and the map of the Empire, the entirety of a Province. In time, those Unconscionable Maps no longer satisfied, and the Cartographers Guilds struck a Map of the Empire whose size was that of the Empire, and which coincided point for point with it. The following Generations, who were not so fond of the Study of Cartography as their Forebears had been, saw that that vast Map was Useless, and not without some Pitilessness was it, that they delivered it up to the Inclemencies of Sun and Winters. In the Deserts of the West, still today, there are Tattered Ruins of that Map, inhabited by Animals and Beggars; in all the Land there is no other Relic of the Disciplines of Geography. (Borges 1946/1999, 325)

Borges playfully captures the heart of the cartographic imagination here, as he charts the desire to map the world on a scale of 1:1 and follows this Utopian idea to its extremity and beyond. Kirsch observes that wandering through Ruby Town feels like walking around in such a map of the world. However, Borges exhausts the very idea of the map, as he traces the map's expansion up to the point where the map can no longer exist. Kirsch's comparison therefore directly touches upon questions of representation: while engaged in this performance installation, are we part of the real world, or part of a representation of it? As life in this town is *both* actual and a representation of reality, concerned with both acting and *acting*, this lived space seems to be mapped on a scale of 1:1. Borges' story is not coincidentally paradoxical, and serves to indicate how *Ruby Town* folds reality into representation and unfolds fiction upon reality, an issue that will be addressed further below.

Kirsch made a felicitous comparison in my view, as the Temporary Autonomous Zone that houses Ruby Town is indeed a Borgesian Land of Beggars, situated in an abstract place, somewhere on the outskirts of the civilized world. Borges refers to a generalized "West," and Signa uses similar geographic poetics, so to say, by situating this town in-between a North State and a South State, without providing further details. This abstraction invites to associate the North State with First World politics, including the military apparatus of control. Spectators enter the Autonomous Zone via the North State side, and as the few South-State-born descendants of Martha Rubin are black and presented as poorer and of lower class than the rest of the villagers, connections with Third World circumstances are easily made. *Ruby Town* is also emblematic of First World immigration politics. The Ruby Towners are forced to stay in their village; the "inclusion" of stateless immigrants actually implies the appointment of designated areas to those who have no part, in order to prevent further distribution. *Ruby Town*, however, subtly inverts this distribution of power relations—offering quite a critical perspective on contemporary society and politics—as the apparatus of control obviously fails: members of the military have affairs with villagers; the captain is a cross-dresser; there is smuggling and illegal trading going on; villagers have their own rules and systems of punishment. In the above-mentioned interview, Signa recounts that, in fact, the military are outsiders themselves: being stationed here actually represents degradation or punishment. In turn, the villagers, who are presented as wild, uncivilized, and unruly, are in fact subject to strong social hierarchies. These inversions all subtly refer to the decline of what was once called a First World.

In his review, Sebastian Kirsch points out that navigating through *Ruby Town* feels like walking *within* a map of the world. Although Borges exhausts the map, I follow Kirsch's course for a moment and his suggestion that spectators are positioned on the inside of the map, and inside a closed fictional world. The performers, for instance, constantly negate any inquiries related to life outside the industrial hall; I observed that they seem completely oblivious of buses, timetables, or any other link to present-day Berlin. This (relatively) closed fictional world alludes to the logic of play and is in fact not so different from Johan Huizinga's early characterization of a play-world as a marked off and limited area with a disposition of its own. Play produces a temporary world with a distinct order, duration, and locality; an imaginary world separated from, yet persistent within, the ordinary world (Huizinga 1938/1998, 8–11). The Borgesian map too portrays the "real" and the "as if" as two distinct yet completely coinciding modes of existence. This ambiguity is characteristic of (attempts to define) games and play, as the pretense of play precisely constitutes the play itself and partly produces the pleasure of play (Sutton-Smith 1997/2001). Play has fun as an essential characteristic, yet is also deeply serious, as it requires a total commitment to the rules of play (Salen and Zimmerman 2004). This certainly pertains to Signa's performers, who do not step out of their roles for the entire length of the event.

Due to this commitment to play in all its various aspects, *Ruby Town* in many ways resembles a Role Playing Game (RPG) or Live-Action Role Playing (LARP), games that engage multiple players in either digital or mixed-reality environments, or in the case of LARPs, in live events (Montola 2012).[3] *Ruby Town*, and other projects by Signa as well, such as *Night at the Hospital* (2007), *Salo* (2010), or *Club Inferno* (2013), equally work with fictional characters in an imaginary world. RPGs often make no distinction between performers and spectators. Instead, all the players are involved in collaborative storytelling (Jenkins 2004, 121). Often there are distinctive roles though, identified by functions or (archetypical) characters—game masters, orchestrators, explorers, chasers, magicians, healers—each provided with certain capabilities and storytelling vocabularies. Signa's artistic directors also function as game masters or orchestrators, in a way, as they play influential characters in the village.[4] RPGs may last for several days, or considerably longer periods of time. Next to chasing riches or unravelling plots, participants may also opt to wander around freely and enjoy the (narrative) environment (Benford and Giannachi 2011; Copier in Van den Boomen 2009, 159–71; Montola 2007; Montola and Stenros 2004). Particularly in LARPs, players often make huge efforts to dress up as characters and invent extensive role biographies. Juxtaposed with Signa's spectators, LARP players tend to arrive at the game fully prepared, whereas the visitors to *Ruby Town* are relatively clueless spectators without a character sheet, and due to their double role of spectators/visitors they remain anchored to the layer of reality in which they are spectators of this performance.

Despite these distinctions, the many similarities with play invite a conceptualization of *Ruby Town*'s stage as a *rhizomatic game board*.[5] Spectators literally enter and exit the game board at different times and intervals. For most of the visitors, the performance has already started before they arrived and the event will continue after they leave; they step right into the middle and become part of the event at the very moment of its unfolding. James Corner (1999) uses the game board and the rhizome as models for urban mapping, discussed in Chapter 4. Joined in this chapter, the rhizomatic game board operates through the tension between the rules of a game and the contingent connections of the rhizome. For Corner, the game board orchestrates the conditions through which urban processes may achieve certain (social) ends (1999, 240). In comparison, Signa's rhizomatic game board is far less goal-oriented and may lack any clear outcome at all. Similar to the Go game, performers and spectators arrange themselves within an open space; they are distributed into a sphere without center, where the action turns out to be everywhere.

This smooth stage, however, is strategized through an architextural diagram. As suggested above, the notion of architexture joins text, texture, scenography, and architecture in a multiplicity of interconnected spaces. As such, an architexture shows a remarkable resemblance with computational hypertexts. Surfing the internet by activating hyperlinks has been literally defined as an act of writing space (Bolter 2001, 1991). In an early work on hypertexts, media theorist Jay David Bolter attests that users create "sentences" by activating the hyperlinks that connect disparate elements in the (digital) network. This is a writing *with* places, a (playful) strolling around, in which the reader moves from one element to the other (Bolter 1991, 25, 57–60). A hypertextual network is an endless, fundamentally unstable and restless network—prototype of the rhizome—in which the same building blocks participate in several paths. Dependent on particular trajectories they can achieve a special significance, or become conceptually active as critical, explanatory, or subversive elements (24, 75).[6] Writing with spaces thus exposes a dialogical relationship between (spatial) design and use. In the following sections I explore several (analogue) modes of writing with spaces. I describe three architextural layers that are important building blocks of *Ruby Town*'s rhizomatic network: *narrative architecture* (Jenkins 2004), involving environmental storytelling and becoming-stories; *evocative spaces*, which target the affective modulations of intertextual space; and *procedural passageways*, where game-inspired procedural rhetoric (Bogost 2007) meets process-based architecture. These textures are separated in description but mutually entangled in the lived spaces of *Ruby Town*. Each offers a shift in perspective, while their intersections build up toward the over-all architexture of this performance, despite the lack of a center.

Narrative Architecture and Environmental Storytelling

Strolling through *Ruby Town* is an encounter with Borges' "Tattered Ruins" in all sorts of ways. Ruby Town is built from scrap, wrecks, and garbage. Houses and caravans are primitive and electricity is sparse. The shelves in the shops verge on being empty, the few products on display seem to have since long surpassed their "best before" date. The same could be said of the interiors, the costumes, the bar, or the beauty parlor. In reality circumstances were equally harsh: performers had barely enough to eat, as the rations were set by the military. They had to do all the cooking and washing themselves, without modern equipment to hand. Signa's work often has this aesthetics of bleakness, and enquires into the darker sides of life by subjecting performers to the same conditions as the portrayed characters or situations (Burckhardt and Behrendt 2008). *Ruby Town* is not a performance that is fully rehearsed; it is partly the unpredictability of the non-rehearsed that qualifies *Ruby Town* as a postdramatic event. Nevertheless, there was repetition involved, except this concerned the intensive rehearsal of the villagers' histories in *advance* to the event. These invented pasts are extremely complex stories in which individual biographies, including those of the disappeared and the deceased, create rhizomatic connections. These biographies surface in the set design: in the partition of go and no-go areas, as well as in the material archives to be found in every habitat. In the above mentioned interview, Signa Köstler recounts:

We wanted to give people the idea, in a subtle way, that there is a lot to find out. Actually you had to be many hours or preferably days in Ruby Town to find out all the stories, because in every drawer you could find letters, and photographs, there were things everywhere. The people from Ruby Town who were smuggling had their routines; the military would do their rounds and confiscate things. If you really took the time to listen you could have heard all sorts of stories that were talked around behind houses. There were secrets all the time, on all kinds of levels. (Groot Nibbelink 2009b)[7]

Wandering through Ruby Town actually feels like walking in a living archive, where the settlements and military quarters become information spaces or memory palaces.[8] This way of distributing narrative information onto the performance environment can be regarded as a form of *environmental storytelling*, a concept introduced by game theorist Henry Jenkins, in "Game Design as Narrative Architecture" (2004). He uses this spatial concept in order to find a middle ground in what is known as the ludologist–narrativist debate in game studies.[9] Inspired by Michel de Certeau and Henri Lefebvre, he posits spatial stories next to gameplay and narrativity, and proposes seeing game designers less as storytellers but more as narrative architects. For Jenkins, a game designer is primarily concerned with the creation of narrative universes, level design, and interactive maps that chart the geographic finesses of these imaginary worlds. Similar to cartographers, game designers are engaged in worldmaking processes, which is why they often find their resources in fantasy and science fiction novels (Jenkins 2004, 122). Environmental storytelling involves the creation of (fictional) environments in which stories or narrative elements are infused into physical or digital gamespace. Stories emerge as a result of players' activities and explorative moves, while the space provides a vocabulary for possible actions and sets the parameters for involvement.

"Spatial stories are not badly constructed stories; rather, they are stories which respond to alternative aesthetic principles," states Jenkins (124). Environmental storytelling requires a different conception of plot: instead of linearity and causality, the organization of the plot entails the development of a geography, in which story fragments are episodically structured or emerge as localized incidents (125). Jenkins' account is remarkably close to postdramatic architecture, as his analysis of geography reverberates with Lehmann's view on the landscape stage (Lehmann 1997). Despite Jenkins' call on a different aesthetics, he still seems to rely on dramatic plot elements such as conflict, battle, betrayal, or secrets awaiting discovery, and mentions melodrama as a resource for game design. Even though Jenkins does include games without (successful) end, the rule-oriented nature of many games still tend to adhere to principles of *logos* and *telos*. This dramatic bend also defines the narrative universes of Punchdrunk, which to some extent affiliate with Signa's work. Punchdrunk's immersive performances, however, are often based on existing plays and (hence) the company puts more emphasis on narrative coherence, also illustrated by the fact that the actors repeat storylines by playing on a loop. Audiences are partly addressed as voyeurs, exemplified by Punchdrunk's hallmark of providing spectators with (neutral) masks.[10]

In comparison to Punchdrunk, *Ruby Town* is not based on repetition; the characters' pasts are fully rehearsed but what happens in the here and now is not. In *Ruby Town*, the stories always evolve, they never return to the same. They are dispersed through space and fractured in time, and emerge as *becoming-stories*. Becoming-stories are marked by their continuous variation; they exceed the repetition-of-sameness. These stories are told, modified, retold by spectators, mutated by gossip, seen from different angles; they blend in with actual occurrences in the village and produce a dense web, or texture, that no one can oversee, not even the artistic directors. In *Ruby Town* there are also battles, betrayals, and secrets awaiting discovery, yet there is no final resolution or teleological plot-development.[11] The best illustration of this is perhaps the regular lack of excitement. The simultaneity of action suggests a dynamic, pluralistic whirlwind of things occurring. Instead, often there was very little action. Next to excitement, I also experienced boredom—similar to real life. Some spectators left rather quickly, when finding the majority of performers asleep at the time of entrance, with a cynical comment: "Nothing going on here." Sleeping performers resist the imperative of action known from the dramatic theatre, and interrupt the idea of progress. Slowness and duration are essential to Signa's "eventness."

Next to Lehmann's landscape aesthetics, Jenkins' account strongly resonates with concepts and practices in the field of performative architecture. Architectural theorist Anthony Vidler, for instance, remarks that architectural space is increasingly seen as being charged with information, activated by bodies, operated through movement, open to various interpretations, unpredictability, cross-cuttings, rhythm, and temporality (Vidler 2000). Performative architecture provides a rich discourse that helps to construct *Ruby Town*'s architextures—without wanting to claim that Signa's scenography exactly behaves like the liquid or fluid architecture that has emerged in line with the increasing interest in the performance of buildings.[12] Understood as a particular kind of thought, however, the discourse provides a theoretical climate for a further unpacking of architextural practices.

Architectural Performances

In "Architecture's Unscripted Performance," architecture theorist David Leatherbarrow remarks that we do not so much enter rooms, instead rooms "happen to us" (in Kolarevic and Malkawi 2005, 10). Rooms can depress or delight us; they serve or fail to meet expectations, the exact experience and function each time depending on the particular operations taking place in accordance with that room. Buildings are not static objects, but performances and, as such, always in a state of becoming. Their latent potential is actualized through particular encounters—encounters of rooms and users, of buildings and weather, of built environments and time (Kolarevic and Malkawi 2005, 16–18). Architecture, then, is intimately tied to performance. On the one hand, buildings "do" something to us and are being "done to," on the other hand architecture is aligned with the variability, unpredictability, and non-repeatability that characterizes the act and actuality of performance.

Leatherbarrow's account fits a broader pattern in architectural discourse, in which the "eventness" of architecture precedes and intertwines with the turn toward performative architecture in the last decades of the twentieth century (Salter 2010, 81–112). Represented in the work of, for instance, Bernard Tschumi, Peter Eisenman, Rem Koolhaas, and more recently Lars Spuybroek/NOX Architecture, performative architecture entails a shift away from modernist approaches to architecture, where space is understood in terms of quantity, geometry, fixed form, or as an encompassing framework or container for action, toward dynamic conceptions of space as activated by bodies, evolving in time, created in movement, and responding to use (Hannah and Khan 2008; Spurr 2007). Architect Bernard Tschumi, for instance, locates architecture at the intersection of space, movement, and events, and primarily sees architecture as a mode of thought. Much more than knowledge of form, it is a form of knowledge in itself (Tschumi 1996). Performative architecture thus is interested in how space is produced through performance, how designed space invites movement and is created in accordance with use, how architectural programs structure events, how they may construct or contest social relationships, and are appropriated for alternative use in turn (Filmer and Rufford 2018; Salter 2010; Spurr 2007).

The shift toward performative architecture and the rapid development of digital design technologies explains the increasing use of diagrams in architectural design and discourse. Architectural diagrams start to equal choreographic notation systems, in a way, as they connect spatial relations to (corporeal) movement, and are open to various interpretations and use. As reading or using them activates them, diagrams are *generative* instead of representational devices (Vidler 2000, 3–6). In *Performative Architecture:*

Design Strategies for Living Bodies (2007), Samantha Spurr describes a range of diagrams, including non-digital drawings. She focuses on the mutual relationship between bodies and spaces, discussing spatial events in which bodily movement creatively produces and transforms spaces, while architecture in turn acts upon people. In particular, her comparison of Tschumi's *The Manhattan Transcripts* with the *Masques* series of architect John Hejduk are striking examples of architextural thought, or spatial hypertexts. A short description serves to render both projects productive as thinking models for *Ruby Town*'s architextures.

Tschumi's *Transcripts* (1976–81) is a series of books comprising drawings, pictures, architectural sketches, and movement diagrams, which envisions late-twentieth-century urbanism by means of disjunctive and changing spatial perspectives. The chapters, with titles such as The Street, The Park, The Fall or The Block, are each structured as cinematographic narratives. They contain sequences of urban scraps, seen from different angles. One is taken into the interior of buildings, or posited in-between passengers on the street, or jolted into witnessing space as if falling from great height. These frames and perspectives also operate in the context and contingency of their interrelationships. The books invite one to randomly scroll the pages, and as such they form a spatial hypertext—a trans-script—with erratic structures and singular connections between various viewpoints. The *Transcripts* resist overview or coherent perspective; instead they allow for multiple uses and invite the viewers to produce their own urban score (Spurr 2007, 179–92; Migayrou 2014).

Writing with spaces is also key to John Hejduk's *Masques*, a series of (book) projects each with a collection of drawings and texts, successively named after particular European cities. Whereas Tschumi extensively draws on the cinematographic, Hejduk's strategies lean toward the theatrical. The *Masques* portray free-standing, ephemeral structures, accompanied by precise lists of materials, additional tools, and enigmatic descriptions of characters and their moods, memories, and actions. "Retired General's Place," for instance, part of *The Lancaster/Hanover Masque* (1992) is a wooden tower on wheels, equipped with "navy binoculars, telescope, periscope, opera glasses, earphones, sonar technology, removable ladder, fishing chair, army cot and telephone" and describes a general driving around Berlin in a black Mercedes, dreaming of past achievements while listening to the sound of snow on a winter's day (in Spurr 2007, 156). Hejduk playfully addresses the text as integral to architectural drawing, but instead of a complementary relationship between text and object, he creates surrealist collages that coalesce play, fantasy, intertextuality, and the carnivalesque, self-reflexively exploring the limits of architecture (Hays 1996, 7–21). Spurr states that

Hejduk's drawings are deceivingly simple and transparent, but on closer inspection, one is drawn into the subsurface level and discovers other worlds hidden below the surface of architecture. This is the pleasure generated by the (hyper)text, where newly associated elements subvert the order of ideas on the surface level of the text (Bolter 1991, 22; Barthes 1975). With an eye to Tschumi's *Transcripts*, Spurr describes the *Masques* as follows:

> In the Transcripts perspective becomes multiplied and montaged ... In Hejduk's Masques perspective is something one travels through. The Masque is read in movement from one event and structure to another ... the spaces unfold as one moves through them. There are site plans showing the layout of structures, lists of structures and characters, rough sketches. They are almost incomprehensible when read individually but in accumulation they build up the performance. There is no finished, single performance—and one is forced to give up on the idea of finding it. As one begins to randomly look at different structures or pick out character names, one realizes that the performance is already underway in one's reading of it. The drawing is not the Masque, it is the script for the Masque. (Spurr 2007, 166-7)

These observations characterize *Ruby Town*'s rhizomatic game board as well, which equally provides a script for a performance that is already on its way. The performance installation resists single perspective, and builds worlds through the accumulation of spatial stories and experiences. *Ruby Town* is similarly a masque where spaces unfold as one moves through them, constantly hinting at other realities and possibilities below the surface of appearance.

Tschumi's and Hejduk's diagrams are spatial hypertexts that reveal the necessity of performance: they need to be "done" in order to be actualized and, in turn, they provide a script for performance. These architectural performances suggest that an architexture may be understood as an assemblage of intersecting frames and perspectives (Tschumi); of perspectives one *moves through* (Hejduk); of spaces that are constituted in performance, created by the actions of those who look, scroll, stroll, play, and imagine.

Evocative Spaces

Henry Jenkins distinguishes several modes of environmental storytelling, one of which pertains to the creation of *evocative spaces*: intertextual gamespaces that are based on existing stories, films, or genres and render the source active within the adaptation (2004, 123–4). I use his term here not strictly in the same sense, as *Ruby Town* does not rely on such pre-existing source materials. In line with Tschumi and Hejduk, I focus on the spatiality of intertextuality itself, as yet another architexture, and especially the affective modulations that are generated and evoked by those spatial scripts. As a second entry into Signa's maze, I thus draw on the interconnections of texture, tissue, intertextuality, and the haptic and stereographic qualities of the text. Although in current discourse the poststructural work-as-text paradigm is hardly in use anymore, and has been replaced by the diagrams of performative architecture, I prefer to temporarily excavate intertextuality again, as it opens a door to how spaces happen to us (Leatherbarrow), crawl under subsurface level (Hejduk, Bolter) and in fact point to the lived space of intertextuality. In her introduction to Tschumi's three essays on "Architecture and Limits" (1980–1), which also rely on intertextual thought, Kate Nesbitt provides a concise description of intertextuality, based on that by Julia Kristeva and Roland Barthes, as "a web or network of relations between the components of a sign, or between an individual work and the works which precede or surround it, on which it relies for meaning" (Nesbitt 1996, 163). Tschumi drew on Roland Barthes, amongst others, and if one looks at Barthes' essay "From Work to Text," a short piece on intertextuality, it occurs to me that Barthes actually practices a kind of psychogeography. He describes a becoming-space of the phenomenological body. To give ground to this observation, I have selected a rather lengthy quote:

> The Text is plural …The plural of the Text depends, that is, not on the ambiguity of its contents but on what might be called the *stereographic plurality* of its weave of signifiers (etymologically, the text is a tissue, a woven fabric). The reader of the Text may be compared to someone at a loose end … what he perceives is multiple, irreducible, coming from a disconnected, heterogeneous variety of substances and perspectives: lights, colours, vegetation, heat, air, slender explosions of noises, scant cries of birds, children's voices from over on the other side, passages, gestures, clothes of inhabitants near or far away. All these *incidents* are half-identifiable: they come from codes which are known but their combination is unique, founds the stroll in a difference repeatable only as difference. So the Text: it can be it only in its difference (which does not mean its individuality). (Barthes 1977, 159, italics in the original)

Barthes' account may as well have been a description of the sensations evoked by strolling through Signa's passages. At least, such affective modulations mark my personal experience. While I wander around, my sight lingers on the houses' interiors; laughter and shouting drift out through the windows, standing out against a buzzing choir of close and distant voices, mingling with the scent of the aged wallpapers. I move along past the graphic design of pre-Fordist products in bathroom cabinets and on store shelves; I smell traces of stress or boredom as the ashtrays spill over in the military quarters. Moving through Ruby Town instills an accumulation of evocative spaces; it is an encounter with a "half-identifiable" world in which somehow recognizable elements are connected in unfamiliar ways. This Situationist, psychogeographical looking-glass also alerts us to the pleasure of (intertextual) strolling. Roland Barthes describes this pleasure as the seam between a conformist and a subversive way of writing or reading, in *The Pleasure of the Text* (1975). Barthes locates this pleasure in-between two *edges* in a text, one that creates order or structure, and one that deviates from or defies the logic of coherence; their collision creates interstices and produces bliss.

Barthes is well known for highlighting the role of the reader (rather than the author). In a similar vein, Tschumi's *Transcripts* and Hejduk's *Masques* require performance in order to be actualized. They derive their significance from the accumulation of visited sites and frames. A texture thus has a temporal dimension as well, as the past is rendered active in the present. Such a spatio-temporal texture is also addressed by performance theorist Marvin Carlson, in *The Haunted Stage* (2001), who argues that when we perceive spaces in the theatre, we remember other spaces through them. Spaces, as well as texts, bodies, and objects, are always infused by a sense that these have been seen before. These (uncanny) impressions haunt or ghost the theatre. More than any other art, theatre is always concerned with repetition and recycling—this pertains in particular to the body of the actor—and returns past perceptions and experiences (1–17). Ghosting surpasses "sameness," as these memories are produced in the present, contingent to new contexts of recollection, adjusted and modified as they "move through" different productions and new "imaginary configurations" (3–4).

Ruby Town surely offers such sites of remembrance, in a rather remarkable way. Apart from the occasional caravans, through which one may remember fairgrounds, Roma camps, countless sad camping sites, or zones of urban disobedience, the majority of houses in Ruby Town are literally recycled from floors, walls, curtains, and interiors of existing houses, taken from an abandoned coal miners' village—a ghost village—taken apart, and rebuilt again. Ruby Town is also literally ghosted, by way of the figure of Martha Rubin, an oracle from whom all the villagers are descended. Ruby Town comes with a myth of origin that reports the long and adventurous life of Martha Rubin, who suddenly disappeared after a last sighting in Constanta,

Figure 6.2 Signa Köstler, as the oracle Martha Rubin, in Signa's *Die Erscheinungen der Martha Rubin—The Ruby Town Oracle*. Courtesy Signa, photo Erich Goldmann.

Romania, in 1913. She had been stuck in limbo, so the story goes. It is only recently that she gained living form again, and returned to Ruby Town, in order to foretell the future. However, she keeps disappearing from time to time; visitors to Martha Rubin's sanctuary then will find her sound asleep, or run into an empty bed (Figure 6.2).[13] Martha's awakenings are often the start of celebrations and festive rituals; coming "from the past," Martha initiates events in the present.

There are additional ways of seeing spaces (moving) through other spaces. The combination of quarters and in-between walking areas, for instance, also recycle the medieval staging practice of *loci* and *platea*. The *loci* were a number of designated areas, elevated platforms, or simple mansions that identified allegorical situations or characters, grouped around an open place or *platea*. Essential to the medieval stage, and to Signa's game board as well, is the simultaneity of play. Medieval loci presented juxtaposed allegories such as heaven and hell, or houses of saints and heathens, robbers and merchants (Tydeman 1978, 57–61). With a little goodwill, *Ruby Town*'s loci of the tourist shop, the bar, the beauty parlor, or the peepshow might equally be seen as allegories for contemporary consumer and entertainment culture, flavored by capitalism, cosmetics, and pornography, whereas the (border)zone in its totality enacts the society of control (Figure 6.3).

Architextures

Figure 6.3 Peepshow scene in *Die Erscheinungen der Martha Rubin – The Ruby Town Oracle* by Signa. Courtesy Signa, photo Erich Goldmann.

To imagine the *Masques* is to inhabit them, argues Spurr. With an eye to Gaston Bachelard's *The Poetics of Space* (1958/1994), this imagination deepens when drawings are revisited, when one is enticed to curl up in corners, to follow the secrets of stairways, to enjoy the pleasure of the attic. Architecture thus starts to equate memory, in the sense that both are instances of "layered experience, built up in time" (Spurr 2007, 159).[14] Like Hejduk's *Masques*, Signa's world hugely expands below or behind the surface. One would need days to discover the stories and secrets of this world, to see through the cracks in the mask of friendliness and discover, in fact, a "rotten world" beneath, to quote Signa's Arthur Köstler, a world full of discrimination, violence, and betrayal. And yet there are always other possibilities and entry points. In this spatial hypertext, the spectators' differential trajectories are diverging accumulations of lived spaces and affective modulations. Strolling through *Ruby Town* is like living in (spatial) writing. Spectators build the world of performance by visiting spaces through other spaces, thus countering Signa's signature with their own paths.

Procedural Passageways

Signa's rhizomatic game board raises the question of whether visitors to *Ruby Town* are perhaps better conceived of as players, instead of as spectators.

Entirely replacing the one term with the other is not totally satisfying in my view. Instead, I propose that playfulness is a mode of spectating. Next to Jenkins' account, game studies offers another type of "narrative" architecture, which is *procedural rhetoric*. A short inquiry into this concept prepares a third way of cutting across *Ruby Town*'s labyrinth. Videogames critic and designer Ian Bogost coins this term, in *Persuasive Games* (2007), and defines procedural rhetoric as the practice of conveying ideas and arguments through rule-driven and behavior-organizing processes (Bogost 2007, 29). Bogost acknowledges yet counters the negative connotations surrounding both "procedures" and "rhetoric." Procedures are often seen as static, confining, simplistic, or as vehicles of bureaucracy or ideology, yet Bogost argues that procedures found the logics that structure all processes, including complex and dialectic ones. Rhetoric sometimes equals pretentious, "empty" rhetoric, or is dismissed as a one-way argument used to compel or influence others. For Bogost, rhetoric is above all expressive, a way of meaning-making through processual arguments, and as such he also speaks of procedural representation (3–21).

Although Bogost primarily focuses on videogames, procedural rhetoric is not the exclusive domain of computational processes; any medium can express certain ideas via the organization and inscription of processes (2007, 46). Indeed, procedural rhetoric is also discernible in process-driven performances such as *Ruby Town*, and is no stranger to the scripts and scenarios of performative architecture. In fact, Bogost's procedurality can be seen as performative architecture itself, as the game's structure authors and builds processual, participatory environments.[15] *Ruby Town* is probably less straightforward than the persuasive games mentioned by Bogost, yet his proposition that the organization and structure of processes are in themselves meaningful and expressive is quite relevant.[16] Procedural rhetoric implies that certain ideas are conveyed by the logics that structure processes, by the rules that delineate behavior and define the parameters for decision making. Together these elements mount a procedural argument and advance certain claims or propositions. Through testing, trial and error, and manipulation of the procedural environment, the player erects a space of possibilities, based on "the myriad configurations the player might construct to see the ways the processes inscribed in the system work" (2007, 42). These processes *generate* representation through player participation, "rather than authoring the representation itself" (5). Procedural representation investigates processes by means of other processes, the enactment of which may either support or challenge the understanding of those processes. This facilitates a "dialectical interrogation of process-based claims about how real-world processes do, could, or should work" (57). Continuing the comparison with (performative) architecture, and revisiting Bernard Tschumi, it can be argued that procedural processes, just like architecture, "combine the representation of space and the space of representation" (Tschumi 1996, 111; see also Chapter 4). Put in other words, procedural rhetoric is well suited to examine how micro-cosmoses of play-worlds simultaneously think and act out the macro-cosmoses of society at large.

Playing at the Limits

With Bogost's observations in mind, *Ruby Town* can certainly be understood as a procedural environment, since it portrays a world driven by rules, limitations, and borders. Rules and choice-making processes are the distinctive features of games and play (Salen and Zimmerman 2004). As soon as one enters *Ruby Town* one is confronted with procedures, rule-based instructions *and* the subversion of those imposed laws, as both Ruby Towners and military personnel make these rules elastic. Performers are abiding by yet another set of rules, which is the agreement to stay in character for the entire length of the event. As to the spectators, they are particularly enticed to make choices: they have to decide whether they will trespass borders or enter the peepshow, how they will behave in this world, whether they stay at a distance, or get fully engaged. Some spectators felt challenged in becoming completely involved: performance footage shows visitors carrying out a Shiatsu-massage on one of the performers and some spectators decided to stay overnight. Signa Köstler aptly describes the relation between rules, instructions, and decision-making processes, and their rhetoric:

> We told the performers: get someone into the fiction but don't cling on too long. If you see this person is fine and you have given some information on where to go now, like "meet my uncle in the restaurant" or "if you need this you should go to Leo," then send them on. This also gives the audience the very important possibility to actually make choices on their own. I really don't like this idea of theatre as a kindergarten where the performer holds your hand all the time and tells you what to do. I think part of the art experience is to show people that the things you experience in life in general are totally dependent on what you decide ... It is very much an artistic goal of ours, to reach some kind of reflection or awareness that everything is a choice within a constructed frame. (Groot Nibbelink 2009b)

The rhizomatic game board of *Ruby Town* is a possibility space. One is not obliged but definitely gets more out of this world when prepared to experiment with the situation at hand. *Ruby Town* addresses playfulness as a mode of spectating, understood here as a willingness to test and explore unexpected situations. This does not necessarily involve "grand adventures" but may as well pertain to modest experiments, as a personal experience demonstrates. Quite soon after my entrance to Ruby Town, I was invited into the beauty parlor where I had my nails done. I left the varnish on for three days after the event. Even though I never wear nail varnish, I did not want to clean it off. For one reason, I liked the idea of carrying a material trace of the performance, as a way of literally staying in touch with this captivating event. Secondly, I suddenly became fond of the idea of being someone who *does* wear nail varnish. To be more precise, I did not seriously contemplate on the pros and cons of nail varnish—nor did I venture into the impossible exercise of identifying "a nail varnish type of person"—but I relished the freedom to considerate it as one of the things I *could* do. I delighted in the *playing with the idea* itself. There is joy in the option to behave other than one is used to doing; in the awareness of things being potentially different than one thinks they are. This possibility space opens up a line of flight, a field of potentiality. In a very modest and trivial way, this nail varnish event instills an expansion of limits, a becoming-other: a spectator in touch with the virtual—a becoming-spectator. *Ruby Town* also houses becoming-performers, as this nine-day nonstop event brings performers, and some spectators as well, to a liminal state, at the edge of exhaustion and beyond; tiredness causes out of the ordinary behavior and dilates the surface of everyday life.

Ruby Town is constituted through play, yet is also deeply serious. On a larger scale, rules and choice-making processes disclose harsh social and political circumstances, reminiscent of refugee camps and asylum politics, alluding to rules that organize patterns of inclusion and exclusion and exhibit questionable laws and punishments. Throughout, there is a continuous subversion of those rules—smuggling, trading, secrecies— that is also characteristic of games and play. Thus, the major procedural rhetoric on *Ruby Town*'s rhizomatic game board seems to be that of gameplay, rule-sets and decision-making itself. This rhetoric asks how one chooses to deal with rules and restrictions, and explores the limit of limits. This critical approach to rules, edges, borders, and limits defines the performance's spatial dramaturgy. In creating this rhizomatic game board, *Ruby Town* exposes a particular understanding of play that is very close to the nomadic: Signa offers a space to play *with* the rules, a laboratory where limits are trialed and tested, where borderzones are subjected to experimentation, and where the test results show that one cannot escape the society of control, as manipulation is deeply embedded in the curls and corners of lived space.

Next to societal rules, *Ruby Town* plays with the rules of theatre. This post/dramatic performance challenges horizons of expectation. Recalling the "Nothing going on here" of disappointed spectators, who probably expected a neatly constructed story and ditto tension span, Signa clearly refuses to adhere to the conventions of dramatic theatre. Paradoxically the collective achieves this by absorbing (most of) the spectators into a fictional world and drawing on the suspension of disbelief, a suspension that in turn is driven to the extreme. In Signa's world, the dramatic theatre is a war machine within the postdramatic theatre—or the other way round—spreading infections and contaminations with every move. In the slipstream of these observations, Tschumi's essays "Architecture and Limits" (1980-1) come into view. In line with Derrida's take on architecture, Tschumi argues that deconstruction is not concerned with the destruction of architecture but explores the limits of architecture, in order to investigate what exactly defines or delineates architecture. Limits are architecture's ontological and epistemological base, argues Tschumi: architecture cannot exist without limits, and simultaneously the design projects situated at the limits of architecture—"disturbing, disconcerting elements at the edge of production, hinting at other definitions and interpretations"—provide the ground from which existing conditions can be interrogated (in Nesbitt 1996, 152). *Ruby Town* similarly is situated at the edge of theatre, and hints at other definitions and interpretations. Both the artistic directors of Signa remark that they never conceived of this work as theatre and subtly add that they are not very fond of theatre either. *Ruby Town* may as easily be qualified as either an art installation, a game, performative architecture, a LARP, a memory palace, lived space strategized through scenography, or all of this: an architexture.

The Entirety of the Map

Ruby Town's play with limits paves the way for a re-entrance of Borges and his intriguing story of a map of the world on a scale of 1:1. His paradox triggers the type of questions that can only be answered by negation: how can such a map exist? In what kind of space could this map reside? How would one deal with depicting a world that constantly changes—while at the same time one is *in* that world? Borges' exhaustion of the map is like a Moebius-strip, in which the world as an object to be mapped is both on the inside and on the outside of the world in which the object is being mapped. This figuration of the fold (Chapter 5) also invites enquiry into how *Ruby Town* relates to and represents the world "outside." After visiting *Ruby Town*, this outside world may strike one as even more unreal or constructed than the life in the village. And when on the inside of this installation, one is to a certain extent still on the outside. It is strange to share a vodka with someone who is totally in character, while you are not; you are still that visitor to *Ruby Town*—and yet, on a scale of 1:1, visitor to Ruby Town. Signa Köstler sums it up neatly:

> Actually the question of fiction and reality has become irrelevant to me, because in these performances we reach a point where the difference really doesn't exist anymore. If I can speak for myself, there are a lot of moments with the other performers or with members of the audience that are real experiences to me, as well as to the audience and to the other actors. What is going on between us: I cannot say that is not real. The same goes for life itself. The facts of life, the writing of history, the bible, everything is a construction; there is no clear distinction between fiction and reality. (Groot Nibbelink 2009b)

This implosion of the reality/fiction axis is also discernible in other cases in this study, where lived space is tethered to deliberately constructed situations. Staging these situations is a means through which these modes—or folds—of reality are displayed and interrogated. Moebius-izing fiction and reality exposes Soja's both/and also paradigm of real-and-imagined spaces (1996), discussed in Chapter 3, yet also marks the mixed or augmented reality games that emerged in the advent of digital culture (Benford and Giannachi 2011; Lavender in Bay-Cheng et al. 2010). Although thoroughly pre-digital in its surface aesthetics, *Ruby Town* surely tunes in with this digital paradigm.

Both Signa's *Ruby Town* and Borges' map raise the question of whether a play-world should be conceived of as a *closed* magic circle, that is, an autonomous, free zone whose subversive or fun potential lies exactly in its independence from outer reality, or whether play should be seen as a social and cultural practice, distinct from yet constitutive of or embedded in this culture.[17] It is beyond the scope of this study to draw out the nuances of this debate, nor do I intend to choose sides. Instead, raising this question is a means to ask how *Ruby Town* tackles the play-versus-reality relationship. Ruby Town is a distinctively closed off world, yet with Bogost's procedural rhetoric in mind, one cannot ignore seeing how play-world procedures continuously parallel real-world processes. In his essay "Simulacra and Simulations" (1981/1998), Jean Baudrillard takes Borges' story as an allegory of the simulacrum, or rather as a first stage toward simulation: the phase where the real becomes a rotten carcass, on its way to disappearance. Whereas a representation still is based on the real, as the sign is suggested to be the equivalent of the real, the simulacrum has no relation to any reality whatsoever, as there is no longer a real to refer to. Signs of the real have replaced the real itself; they become emptied-out objects—surfaces without depths (Baudrillard 1981/1998, 166-7). In that sense, Borges' is a "useless" fable for Baudrillard (166), as it still draws on the (im)possibility of depicting a real world, even at the very edge of exhaustion—without the option of reality this edge cannot exist. In this 1980s essay, Baudrillard names Disneyworld, the Watergate scandal, and capitalism as examples of increasingly expansive simulations, not because they are phantasmagoria, but because they serve to conceal that the world outside is equally infantile, scandalous, or amorally monstrous as the staged hyperreality itself (171-4). In *The Return of the Real* (1996), art theorist Hal Foster counters Baudrillard's analysis by describing how 1990s art and theory brings subjectivity and material bodies to the forefront, next to the social sites where art and society are produced, aptly captured in his observation that "certainly the subjects related to these objects have not disappeared" (144). A similar analysis supports this study, where lived space, embodied spectatorship, and situated knowledge are consequently put in relation with how a spectator as a subject is addressed and positioned.

Play, experimentation, and procedural rhetoric are equivalent to the formulation and testing of hypotheses. As a theoretical object, *Ruby Town* invites a hypothesis as well, since the implosion of the fiction/reality axis seems to open the door for a "return of the fiction," to go along with Hal Foster's "return of the real." Moving away from Baudrillard's world of simulacra, the works considered in this study do not regard fictional constructions as replacements of reality, but rather as *also* constitutive of reality. They are part of *lived* reality. Contrary to Baudrillard's examples and analysis, *Ruby Town*'s procedural rhetoric continuously points to real-world constructions and simulacra, not to arrive at a "truth" but to examine the implications of living in such a world. One of those implications is connected to choice making, in the full awareness of acting out these choices within constructed and manipulative frames. However fictional these frames may be, the choices one makes are real and have real effects.

The self-referential character of the works discussed in this book also point to the procedural rhetoric of staging itself, both in and outside the theatre. These works direct our attention to *how* something is staged, to how someone is addressed and responds to this address, to the strategies by which something is made imperceptible or brought to the light. *Ruby Town*, perhaps more than any of the other case studies, places the *imagination* next to staging, by orchestrating a fantasized world. Imagination is of course also at the heart of play. To highlight the value of imagination is perhaps far from astonishing within a context of play and game studies, or the "ludic turn" in society (Raessens 2010, 22–4). However, as I have sought to make the twin concept of play productive for the theatre again, this aspect of play perhaps deserves some closer attention, as it productively shifts the attention from re-presentation to creation, to *inventing* ways in which we might engage with a fluid and contradictory world.

Tissue, Traces, Tracks

A nomad follows customary paths, observe Deleuze and Guattari (2004, 19), and traces its own tracks (Braidotti 2004, 61). In a similar vein I end with locating some traces in the web of architextures that formed this chapter's spatial tissue. This chapter discussed architextures, but achieved some architextural qualities in itself as well, despite the linear disguise of the written page. The chapter has become a restless labyrinth, where connections fight for supremacy and endings can easily be exchanged for beginnings. This spatial hypertext is a weaving together of spaces, stemming from different disciplinary backgrounds. This way, play and game theories come to function as a kind of postdramatic performance theory, which also puts forward a process-based proposition, namely that play theory *is* postdramatic theory—a proposition also made by Lehmann albeit articulated somewhat differently (2007).[18] Linking both play-concepts and Signa's *Ruby Town* to performative architecture served to show how ambulatory performers and spectators write, produce, and appropriate space, while at the same time these spaces script their behavior. Through this "dialectical interrogation" (Bogost 2007), performers and spectators are positioned as both users and producers of space. This pertains not only to Signa's rhizomatic game board but as well to other playgrounds, installations, ambulatory performances, or walking trajectories. As such, the cases in this book are all involved with performing architecture: performers and spectators produce spaces as they move through them. These spaces expose the theatre as a diagram of layered realities, as an assemblage of various meanings and intensities, built up in time, composed in play, embodied and lived, and fueled by situated knowledge.

Additionally, the concept of architextures sheds a light on my way of dealing with the questions, topics, and cases addressed in this book as a whole. Similarly to architexture's intersecting spaces and shifting perspectives, I discussed practices and theories from different angles and on different scales: performance descriptions alternated between first-person and third-person perspectives—terms also frequently used in games; dramaturgical frameworks provided viewpoints for theoretical reflection, and vice versa;

and theatre and performance theory dialogically encountered concepts derived from philosophy, cartography, or architecture. Lefebvre's lived space opened up both affective spaces and social territories; the scale of proximity proved to be as large as present-day social reality. As an architexture, this book is a writing *with* spaces.

The concept of architexture helps to demonstrate that nomadic theatre does not stick to particular domains; it knows no boundaries, it questions territories by cutting across them—and of course always arrives back at the limits, as there is no deterritorialization without territory. Architexture points to the limits of the concept of nomadic theatre, limits that, to follow Tschumi, do not destroy but instead point to a concept's ontological and epistemological base, and are thresholds to the virtual. Concluding, this book in general, and this chapter in particular, has a procedural rhetoric of its own: it demonstrates nomadic theatre, it "does" nomadology.

7

Distributed Performance
Epilogue

Pop-up Stores

Once upon a time I nearly stumbled over the legs of a man lying on the street in the center of Utrecht, his body elegantly draped halfway across the pavement and the road. It appeared that I had unknowingly stepped into a one-minute choreography, called "Resting," part of the rich assortment of moves that were on the menu at Matsune's and Subal's *Store*.[1] Passers-by and visitors to this performance shop could purchase a micro-choreography for one or two euros, including "Half-Resting" for half of the price—which involved leaning gently against a doorpost. Also available were the slightly more expensive "Copies"—Madonna copy, Buddha copy, and other canonized gestures—and occasionally a customer received a take-away gift. Many clients stayed in order to see what their co-customers would acquire, and as such they collaboratively composed *Store*'s choreography. Around that same time I learnt about Hannah Hurtzig's *Blackmarket of Useful Knowledge and Non-Knowledge*, which employs the format of the (black) market to put specialists of all thinkable areas—ranging from beekeeping and robotics to palliative care—in contact with a client, each on one side of a table, in order to impart knowledge. The *Blackmarket* is a mobile academy that moves from city to city. It draws on local, situated knowledge, and employs experts from diverse areas and all social classes to question the boundaries of knowledge.[2]

Both these initiatives playfully appropriate an exchange format that is deeply ingrained within capitalism—the store, the market—and put this concept-form to work in another area, that of dance and theatre.[3] They appropriate consumption and use it for another purpose. Demonstrative of a nomadic attitude, they escape the grid of capital and open a space for something else, something that flows through and underneath the codes of consumption. In this act, they also expose the limits of capital, because, as Brian Massumi notes in his still relevant *A User's Guide to Capitalism and Schizophrenia* (1992), capitalism can displace its own limits but will always be trapped within its own system: "For although capitalism has turned quantum in its mode of operation, it has done so in the service of quantity: consumption and accumulation are, have been, and will always [be] its reason for being" (Massumi 1992, 138).[4] Both *Store* and the *Blackmarket* create alternative spaces of representation; they use choreography for joyful, light-hearted but committed collaboration, and inquire into what we think is expertise. They both reterritorialize the market by re-purposing its format: these events amount to the consumption of a collective choreography, and to the accumulation of (non)knowledge.

Inherent to the concept of nomadic theatre is the possibility to invert these shells of thought. Instead of reterritorializing the market, it may also be argued that these performances deterritorialize consumption, as they expose the limits of capital and disturb its territory. Both these patterns expose performance's capacity to distribute itself onto the smooth space of capitalism. In the following pages, I will use these examples alongside the cases and theoretical concepts discussed in this book, to show how performance distributes itself towards other realms of practice and expertise. With the concept of nomadic theatre at hand, I describe how emanating patterns of de- and reterritorialization dilate or disturb a number of territories, both inside and outside the theatre. I reflect on how these patterns move back and forth between theory and practice, and how this assists in understanding theatre and performance as forms of material thinking.

Trajectories of the Stage

As I have argued and demonstrated, the concept of nomadic theatre installs connections between heterogeneous fields, creating relationships between theory and practice, between various spatial disciplines, or between theatre and society. The concept allows for the reading of practice through theory, and vice versa. In this study I have employed this concept to investigate how movement and mobility effect and implicate the theatre, how this addresses and positions the spectators in performance, how mobility is staged, and subsequently, how such movements can best be described. In order to do so I followed the whereabouts of the *stage*, and the many ways in which the stage is subjected to acts of de- and reterritorialization. I focused on the stage because this platform for performance unites performers, spectators, and (theatre) spaces, however transparent or imperceptible this stage may appear to be. I showed how contemporary theatre practice distributes the stage into an open, smooth space, as the stage nests within urban space or global space, curls up in the realm of the senses, cuts across the grid of capital, or captures the territory of play. This highly coded theatrical entity is shattered to pieces, and is displaced, twisted, and multiplied. Subsequently, the stage re-emerges as a path, trail, or rhizomatic game board; it appears in the (dis)guise of a store or brothel, and proliferates through differential-synchronous trajectories or flexible platforms of co-presence.

The stage becomes a smooth space, and what remains instead is a flexible threefold constellation of performers, spectators, and spaces. The stage then achieves the speed of minute particles or atoms, "with the possibility of springing up at any point" (Deleuze and Guattari 2004, 421). The stage also ascertains qualities of modularity—hallmark of the digital—as this constellation can be arranged, combined, and configured in an infinite number of ways (Manovich 2001). The flexibility of the triadic constellation on the one hand exposes the conventional stage–auditorium division as only the striated version of the performer–spectator relationship, self-reflexively reminding us of other possible configurations within the theatre: it points to the virtuality of the stage. On the other hand, this modularity allows the stage to be distributed over every possible realm of society, giving witness to the performative turn in society (Kattenbelt 2010), where staging, showing, performance, and display—the stage turned into a verb, a process, a speech-act—not only dominates political or social arenas, but crawls into every corner of everyday life.

In *Theatre, Intimacy and Engagement*, Alan Read critically remarks that theatre and society should not be seen as one-and-the-same. Instead he emphasizes that these are distinct spheres or modalities of reality. He sees theatre and society as two distinct surfaces upon which, however, associative bonds can be perceived. As mentioned in the Introduction, Read describes these as "the crossing and re-crossing of intensities across and between these surfaces" (2008, 37). I agree with Read on this, but would like to add that these crossings sometimes follow patterns of de- and reterritorialization, as theatre and society capture each other's codes and insert these codes into other domains. The practices discussed in this book above all capture the codes of contemporary mobility, as they use the tools of navigation, way-finding and cartography, of co-presence, connectivity, and locality as dramaturgical strategy. These strategies are in my view also exponents of life in a digital, participatory, and neoliberal culture. To single out the spectator and address the spectators' heterogeneity may be regarded as an appropriation of the participatory politics of neoliberalism, which advocates individualism and supposedly free choice (cf. Bishop 2012, 13–14). The performances do not represent these strategies, but use them to organize the performance event. They are part of a wider family of artistic work that operates through individual response, heterogeneity, and user-generated content, but compromises free choice by (exposing the frames of) manipulation and by borrowing the rule-set of a game. Theatre thus captures the codes of digital culture, and is deterritorialized by the participatory and playful components of that culture in turn. Participation nests within the theatre and emerges as one-to-one performance; playfulness provides it with opportunities for experimentation; neoliberalism delivers the grids of capital on which some of these works are based.

In turn, the theatre reterritorializes on participation and playfulness by employing the heterogeneity of audiences and an experimental approach to spectatorship for the investigation of social connectivity—both inside and outside the theatre. Possibly as a response to the excesses of individualism and the elusive abstractness of globalization, theatre emerges as a series of local operations and instills a specific branch of performance ecology: theatre performances tune in with the (social) environment and install a sensuous thinking, an attentiveness to the interconnectedness of subjects and worlds. As such, the theatre joins forces with the revaluation of place and location in current spatial and mobility theories—not to arrive at a new dualism once more, but to investigate embodied relationships with the places and spaces through which we move and that we create through movement. This also reflects back to Read's investigation of intimacy and engagement, which is a plea for the relational capacity of human animals, inspired by Bruno Latour's ethics of association. Both Read's and Latour's reassembly of the social tune in with the "politics of belonging" called for by the publicist and ecologist George Monbiot, who sees solidarity, collaboration, and also locality as antidotes to an exhausted and atomized neoliberal society (Monbiot 2017).[5]

Folds of Spectating

Patterns of deterritorialization and reterritorialization also disturb and dilate the theatre from the inside. As part of the turn from the dramatic to the postdramatic, Lehmann observes a shift from internal to external communication: instead of a focus on an illusionary world on the stage, presented as a closed continuum and established through characters' dialogue, the emphasis shifts towards the exchange between stage and audience, and concentrates on the here and now of the live performance event. Many practices discussed in this study take this external communication to the extreme, to such an extent that it becomes a form of *internal* communication once more, as the one-to-one encounters of performers and spectators often establish the theatre event through dialogue or nonverbal forms of conversation, something which can also be seen at work in Hurtzig's *Blackmarket*. This is why in all the chapters an image of interiority emerges, which places the spectator at the "inside" of performance: inside the performance installation (Chapters 2 and 6); at the "indoors" of the phantasmagoria and the secret theatre (Chapter 3); enveloped by acoustic and haptic spaces (Chapters 3 and 4); connected to interior stages (Chapter 4); and inside the (Borgesian) map and within the world of play (Chapters 3 and 6). This interiority is in my view not a strategy of taking the eyes off the world outside, but instead a means to enquire into the spectator's engagement with that outside world. Hannah Hurtzig connects the *Blackmarket* to a phantasmagoria as well, an arena where the learner is intoxicated by knowledge, although always maintaining the doubt. Simultaneously, by radically opening up the notion of expertise—similar to Rimini Protokoll's experts of the daily life—the *Blackmarket* intervenes in social space and in hierarchies of knowledge. For instance, the *Blackmarket* no. 11 in Liverpool in 2008, entitled "On Waste: The Disappearance and Come Back of Things and Values," opened up a range of ways we might consider (and appreciate) waste by inviting, amongst others, a dumpster diver, a vector-biologist, a bin man, and a guerilla gardener.

Relations between interiority and exteriority also materialize in subtler ways. In Chapters 2 and 4 I have mentioned how performance installations and haptic spaces collapse the distinction between object and subject, and how map-making and sensory perception expose subjectivity as always relational and as an act of "worldmaking." Subjectivity, then, is a process in which, to re-quote Bleeker, both "subjects and worlds appear and also disappear" (2008b, 163). In Chapter 5, I discussed the concept of the fold to elucidate this twofold movement. I used the figure of the fold to point at the self-reflexivity of *The Smile Off Your Face*, exposing the feedback loop that is actually at work in all the discussed performances. All these works can be pinpointed on the dissolution–amplification axis that Lehmann holds as characteristic of the event/situation. The focus on interiority amplifies a quality of theatre that does not always rise to the surface, but never ceases to exist, namely the fact that spectators are at all times at the inside of performance; they are always participants in the work. This observation installs another feedback loop, then, as I seem to have arrived back at Jacques Rancière's emancipated spectator. Over the years, I have been engaged in countless discussions where my interlocutor in one variety or another repeated Rancière's argument, namely that the conventional seat in the auditorium provides a rich enough experience in itself, or rather delivers even more intellectual adventure than when the audience is being asked to participate. They condemned the manipulative nature of these works, or questioned their relative non-repeatability, as the address to personal experience often draws on the parameters of surprise. Even though I am not always a fan of participatory performance myself, when caught up in those discussions about the pros and cons of participatory theatre, I cannot help but think of a reply that is inspired by Stephen Di Benedetto: when was the spectator ever embraced?[6] In line with my discussion of *Het Sprookjesbordeel* in Chapter 5, Di Benedetto argues that the "mass proliferation of somatically obsessed images has denigrated the body to a consumer object to be bought and sold, rather than embraced and touched" (in Banes and Lepecki 2007, 128). He quotes Kristine Stiles, who critically remarks that aesthetic distance and autonomy are "Enlightenment notions" and even "dangerous fictions" that have "little to do with the actual conditions upon and in which real human beings live and artists produce art" (Banes and Lepecki 2007, 127). The works discussed in this book precisely address those lived conditions. They provoke a redistribution of the sensible by challenging perceptual habits, by expanding our notion of spectatorship, or by exposing the entanglement of arts and markets. Claire Bishop's "delegated performance," discussed in Chapter 3, points as well to contemporary artworld conditions and so does Matsune & Subal's *Store*. Although seemingly light and playful, *Store* simultaneously exposes how artists need to become their own brand in the art-market and at international festivals in order to survive (cf. Bishop 2012, 12). *Store* took place in an empty department store in one of Utrecht's shopping streets. Matsune and Subal use the format of the pop-up store, but simultaneously allude to the necessity of popping-up at international dance and performance festivals. Their work needs to be sold, and the best way to do that nowadays is to bring the work close to the audience.

Di Benedetto's remarks indirectly call for widening our understanding of spectatorship, and this book seeks to contribute to such an expansion. Through the concept of nomadic theatre, I regard spectators as compositional forces, who enter into composition with performers and space, and get involved in processes of becoming-performer and becoming-space. These processes cumulatively build up toward the *becoming-spectator of the spectator*, in which spectators enter into composition with their own spectatorship, and explore the relationship between self and world. Such a process is instigated by the appeal to an embedded, embodied spectator who is confronted with problems of referentiality (Chapter 2) or is offered a parallax view (Chapter 3), who follows the paths of situated knowledge (Chapter 4), is jolted into thinking-feeling (Chapter 5), or is taken by play (Chapter 6). The becoming-spectator appears at the point where horizons of expectation are challenged, where perceptual systems become laboratories, where the spectator encounters the potentiality of the always-otherwise, discovers new limitations, and touches upon the virtual. These compositional elements invite self-reflexivity, and time and again fold and unfold upon the intimate connection between self and world, as intensities that cross each other's surface.

Lived Space and Diffractive Reading

The spectator is but one part of a threefold constellation. The present discussion equally gives rise to arguments in favor of the becoming-performer of the performer. My approach to this constellation has been a bit off-balance, bending towards spectators and spaces, as they are the (relatively) new players on the stage. The performer, however, appears alongside in many new roles and disguises: as tour guide, as voyeur, as an outsourced voice, as a game master, or orchestrator. These patterns of de- and reterritorialization similarly prompt a focus on (the becoming-space of) space. Instigated by the discourse on performative cartography and performative architecture, I discussed how (theatre) space emerges as a product of performance itself. The theatre space materializes in a series of local operations or as a procedural space; it emanates from collaboratively maintained coordinates and happens in the encounter of performers and spectators.

The becoming-space of space points to the differential qualities of *lived space*—lived space that in turn is a vital category of *social space*, as spatial experience is always linked to social practice. In Chapter 3 I introduced Henri Lefebvre's approach to these terms, as I find his spatial analysis extremely helpful to get "something through," in the encounter of the nomadic and the theatre. Or rather, Lefebvre's linking of lived space, social space, and spaces of representation exposes what happens in this encounter, as the theatre always deals with these spaces, while the nomadic puts them into a state of continuous variation. Whereas Deleuze points to the radical openness of these spaces, Lefebvre addresses their socio-political attachments. Lefebvre's account can perhaps be regarded as an instance of "meeting the universe halfway," a phrase (and book title) of feminist theorist Karen Barad (2007) that is connected to her methodology of diffractive reading, the affirmative reading of texts through one another. Such an affirmative approach is also present in this study, be it that both "text" and "reading" are infused by a "spatialized consciousness" (Fuchs and Chaudhuri 2004, 4). In Chapter 6, I introduced the concept of architextures, as a diagrammatic texture of interconnected spaces, frames, and perspectives. I used the concept to facilitate the writing of and with (lived) spaces and with perspectives that one moves through. Architextures take Barad's diffractive methodology to the domain of spatial thought and practice. Barad describes her methodology as

> a method of diffractively reading insights through one another, building new insights, attentively and carefully reading for differences that matter in their fine details, together with the recognition that there intrinsic to this analysis is an ethics that is not predicated on

externality but rather entanglement. Diffractive readings bring inventive provocations; they are good to think with. They are respectful, detailed, ethical engagements. (Barad quoted in Dolphijn and Van der Tuin 2012, 50)

Lefebvre's lived space, now read architextural-diffractively, helps to see how Deleuze and Guattari's nomadology is an assemblage of local operations and of "situated cartographies" (Braidotti). Being a vital component of social space, lived space encourages a focus on the social and environmental connectivity that the theatre works discussed here allude to, despite, or rather by way of, singling out the isolated spectator. Lived space is definitely something other than a "myspace" or an "iSpace" and moves beyond individual experience. Such a social space is put on the agenda in Blast Theory's *Rider Spoke*, which explores intimate ways of urban engagement, discussed in Chapter 3; in Rimini Protokoll's *Call Cutta*, which looks at the backstage of call-center work; in the trajectories of a migrant's life in Dries Verhoeven's *No Man's Land*; in the many ways the experts and clients in Liverpool's *Blackmarket* might relate to waste. Lefebvre's analysis of perceived, conceived, and lived space not only builds insights in relation to the cases and theories explored in this book. His triad could also inspire a methodology of "spatial thinking" (Soja 1996), which transcends dualism and surpasses binary oppositions—a way of thinking that is also close to Barad's, as I will explain below.

Of particular relevance for the theatre is Lefebvre's coupling of lived space with a space of representation. This junction reverberates in a remark by Bernard Tschumi, mentioned in Chapter 4. Tschumi describes the affects generated by a fur-lined wall and other sensations of passage, linking spaces of movement to the space of the senses and the space of society, to the "dances and gestures that combine the representation of space and the space of representation" (Tschumi 1996, 111). Such "fur lines" are present in every chapter; they surface in the evocative memory palaces in Signa's world, in *The Smile*'s sensorium, in the personal geographies of *Trail Tracking*, in the uncanny misguides of *Call Cutta*, or in the joint rhythms of *No Man's Land*. All of these examples generate affective modulations by drawing on spectators' embodied archives, situated knowledge, and cultural baggage. These spaces of representation allow for the *appropriation* of representation; they provide opportunities for discovering how corporeal and sensory matter comes to matter, in relation to a specific context of articulation. Nomadic theatre specifically explores and addresses *the conditions of emergence* of such representational spaces.

Staging Connections

The concept of nomadic theatre functions as a searchlight. This concept exposes the theatre as a space of layered realities, as assemblages of various meanings and intensities, built up in time, composed in play, embodied and lived, and fueled by situated knowledge. In order for this searchlight to work properly, I made use of a range of spatial disciplines, such as urban theory, geography, cartography, scenography, architecture, and geophilosophy. This web of disciplinary climates exposes the working of the concept of nomadic theatre as an act of association, a "provisionary staging of connections" that is equally an act of "keeping things in play," to borrow the words of Alan Read (2008, 38). These encounters further demonstrate how performance is distributed over these spatial domains, as all these disciplines profess an understanding of places and spaces as produced and performed, as lived and practiced. All these areas are expressive of a spatialized consciousness, and implicitly prove that interdisciplinarity is intrinsic to spatial analysis.

There is much to be gained by this approach, yet there are also limitations of course. First, it can be argued that each of the previous chapters justifies a full study, to really unpack the potential of the incorporated climate. It is, however, precisely in the wildness of connections and encounters that the potential of the concept of the nomadic can rise to the surface. This wildness is part of the method itself, and alludes to how Deleuze and Guattari equate the nomad with the vague and the vagabond (2004, 405), to how Spurr qualifies Hejduk's *Masques* as engaged with the visceral "messiness" of architecture (2007, 162), or to the mash-up logic of Hurtzig's *Blackmarket*. The latter collects all kinds of knowing, ranging from academic research to household experience, from embodied knowledge to speculative theory.[7] This study is equally an amalgam of theories, and does not shy from occasional vagueness.

This aggregate, when seen as a parallax practice of the *Blackmarket*, is always a mixture of knowledge and non-knowledge, which leads to a second limitation of interdisciplinary research. This research is interdisciplinary, but this necessarily involves a limited representation of the disciplines involved. Inspired by Elisabeth Grosz's *Architecture from the Outside* (2001), I deliberately stayed "on the outside," maintaining the perspective of a theatre and performance scholar. I explored how the various concepts, practices, and theories encountered in these newly traversed fields can be put to work in the theatre, instead of pretending to give a complete representation of the borrowed field in question (cf. Turner 2015). Subsequently, scholars from other disciplines may find some inspiration in this study to do the same.

Procedural Dramaturgy/When Attitude Becomes Form

Performances that address the spectator's unique experience or individual trajectory seem to present the observer-critic with a problem. Because how to write about these performances, whether in an academic journal or in a newspaper, without solely relying on personal experience or without "giving it away" to future spectators? How to avoid spoilers? It is peculiar that we never regard a review of a new version of *Hamlet* or any other repertoire piece as a spoiler, yet this issue easily rises to the surface in cases like the ones in this book. Immersive, ambulatory, and participatory works thus present us with an epistemological dilemma. This particular "problem" suggests that experience is apparently a private and personal affair, which, in line with Claire Bishop's analysis of participatory art, instigates a focus on emotional achievements or ethical aspects—was it a good experience; is it morally justified to be subjected to this situation? Bishop instead argues that relational or participatory works can and should be evaluated according to artistic or aesthetic criteria (2012, 2004). In a similar line of thought I focused on staging strategies rather than participatory experiences. These performances are still designed and created by artists, despite the focus on spectatorial experience. These compositions can be aesthetically reviewed.

Bishop's arguments are grounded in a critical assessment of, amongst others, Nicolas Bourriaud's take on relational art. One of her objections pertains to the latter's equation of structure and subject matter. For Bourriaud, relational art produces relations; relational art is the (social) form, and these social relations also are the content of the artwork. Bishop argues that such a standpoint severs the work from artistic intentionality and neglects the artwork's imbrication with a broader context (Bishop 2004, 62–5). I am inclined to argue, however, that structure can be the subject matter after all, and that this is precisely the location of dramaturgy: the meaning and significance of a performance resides in the way it is structured. This is not an extremely remarkable standpoint in view of theatre, and this is perhaps where art and performance scholarship slightly differ. Theatre is a master supplier of meaningful structure, since every play heavily relies on it. The performances discussed in this book, though, do not bank on solid plot structures or conventional narrative mechanics. Instead, they work with procedural spaces and constructed situations. In many of the cases discussed, spectators have been asked to act: to walk, to find their way, to maintain contact with a performer, to share coordinates, to move along, to enter a space, and so on. These procedural spaces and constructed situations operate through a specific logic of organization. Reminiscent of Deleuze and Guattari's comparison of Go with chess, or of nomadic versus State science, it is in particular this *logic* of organization that gains significance. Each performance is grounded in a logic of doing that undergirds the work and points to a work's horizon of meaning. The content thus reterritorializes on the (processual) structure, and attitude becomes form.[8] Attitude, manifested in a particular logic of organization, materializes in the structure of performance.

This intersection of organizational logic and the content matter of a performance is what I define as *procedural dramaturgy*. In daily life, we tend to regard procedures as confining vehicles of bureaucracy or ideology. Through Deleuze, we may look at this understanding as the striated version of the procedural. I fully agree with videogames critic Ian Bogost who, in *Persuasive Games* (2007), argues that all (social) processes are founded by procedures, whether simple or complex ones. In Chapter 6, I introduced Ian Bogost's procedural rhetoric, referring to the practice of conveying ideas and arguments through rule-driven and behavior-organizing processes (Bogost 2007, 29). Procedures or operations invite one to regard structures as forms—procedural forms, forms produced in relational processes. Instead of rhetoric, I prefer the term "dramaturgy," to explain how the triangular relationship between the composition, structure, or organization of processes, the modes of audience address, and the artistic and socio-cultural context produce meaning and experience.

As Bogost notes, procedures themselves can be expressive; the procedure is the argument. Many cases in this book rely on (aspects of) procedural dramaturgy, where the content arrives at us through the form. Rimini Protokoll's *Call Cutta*, for instance, uses the format of call-center work to assess outsourced performance. Dries Verhoeven's *Trail Tracking* both uses and thematizes the triple logic of geomedia i.e., the intersection of "pervasive present, embedded pasts, and evolving futures" (Verhoeff 2012). In Signa's *Ruby Town*, rule-play and boundary crossings both organize the performance and can be read as a strong political critique on our dealings with outsiders, immigration politics, bureaucracy, and the society of control. In all these examples, the organizational formats both structure the performance and also become content-matter.

Procedures are often said to limit action or to narrow down choices and behavior, but, in principle, they facilitate action. Procedures thus can be understood as the design of possible actions; they create the conditions of engagement, through which meaningful situations and experiences can emerge. Procedural dramaturgy, as an architecture of potentiality, is concerned with the composition of open-ended processes without predefining the outcome.

Procedural dramaturgy thrives on the entanglement of doing and meaning-making, of acting and experiencing, of content and form. This reliance on embodied, performative processes and the rejection of dualisms makes way for the suggestion that procedural dramaturgy is a mode of *material thinking*. The use of the term "materiality," in this context, is indebted to the discourse on new materialism, a cultural theory that strongly rejects the dichotomies that shaped modernist thinking, and consequently examines the intricate interactions between culture and nature, matter and meaning, body and mind, or the human and the non-human (Dolphijn and Van der Tuin 2012; Braidotti 2011a; Bennett 2010). New materialism perfectly captures the qualities of procedural dramaturgy in my view:

> New materialism wants to do justice to the "material-semiotic," or "material-discursive" character of all events ... In terms of artworks, for instance, a new materialist perspective would be interested in finding out how the form of content (the material condition of the artwork) and the form of expression (the sensations as they come about) are being produced in one another, how series of statements are actualized, and how pleats of matter are realized in the real. (Dolphijn and Van der Tuin 2012, 90–1)

Moving beyond cultural materialism (Fortier 2002), "new" materialism strongly critiques anthropocentrism, opting instead for non-hierarchical, relational epistemological models and methodologies. This relationality and resistance to hierarchical thinking is key to the concept of nomadic theatre as well. Nomadic theatre, with hindsight, can be recognized as a new materialist concept.

Thinking Through Practice

In this book, I presented nomadic theatre as an analytical concept, reading quite literal examples of mobile performers, spectators, and spaces as encounters between the theatre and the (Deleuzian) nomadic. I showed how these encounters prompt the mobilization of theory, invite a cutting across disciplinary borders, and instill movements back and forth between theory and practice. In these encounters, contemporary theatre practices become active agents in a discursive event, as they invite theory to become as mobile and flexible as the phenomena they describe. The concept of nomadic theatre thus enables a (transversal) methodology of thinking through practice. Thinking through practice acknowledges the theoretical agency of performance and regards practice itself as a form of embodied thought. As an epistemological tool, thinking through practices seeks to reveal how theorizing takes on "flesh," how it can materialize in staged situations and in procedural processes, and how it instigates (nomadic) non-hierarchical movement between different fields of knowledge. Quite in line with the new materialist agenda, such an approach entails that a theatre performance or artistic practice is not a "passive" object that is subjected to analysis by a reviewer or scholar, but instead is regarded as an expression of thought: a material manifestation of thinking.

As mentioned in the Introduction, it is this "thinking through practice" through which I relate to Deleuze and Guattari's work. My focus is not so much on their work, but on *how* they work; how they use practices and practice theory. Deleuze and Guattari regularly use concepts that resurface throughout different publications; concepts such as the "body without organs," the rhizome, micro-politics, minor literature, and, less frequently, the nomadic. When working with such concepts, one sooner or later is confronted with the question of whether Deleuze and Guattari use these words metaphorically. As discussed in Chapter 2, I think they do not work with metaphors. Metaphors do not exist in a Deleuzian universe, because this presumes a representational logic that installs a hierarchical divide between a first and a follow-up, a source and a copy. Instead, I would like to argue, they think through practice. They build their arguments by attending to the immanent logic of the organization of practices. In doing so, they reveal that specific ways of doing things can be conceived of as expressions of thought. Such a logic of organization became apparent in their discussion of the Go game, which in turn served as a thinking model for a threefold constellation of performers, spectators, and spaces. A similar thinking through practice defines their analysis of twelfth-century Gothic architecture, which is equally an argument for (re)valuing specialist, qualified, and collaborative labor (as opposed to monocultural, template-driven behavior), and for favoring a performative rather than a representational mode of thinking.

Thinking through practice also has an impact on performance analysis. It means that theories are not applied to performances, nor are practices examples added to a theory. To regard these manifestations as fundamentally equal to theory—equal, not similar—implies that ideas or thoughts can express themselves through many different forms and shapes. Theory and practice, then, could be said to relate diffractively, to return once more to Karen Barad. In *Meeting the Universe Half-way: Quantum Physics and the Entanglement of Matter and Meaning* (2007), Barad distinguishes between diffraction and reflection. Diffraction is, just like reflection, an optical phenomenon, but whereas reflection is based on a separation of the object and its reflection, diffraction resides in relationality. In physics, diffraction entails the bending and spreading of waves upon encountering an object, their exact manifestation depending each time on the specific conditions of the encounter (such as (changes in) temperature, light intensity, or surface texture). Water waves or electromagnetic waves "are not things per se, rather they are disturbances (which cannot be localised to a point) that propagate in a medium" (Barad 2007, 76). Barad examines such patterns of interference not only in relation to (quantum) physics but primarily in relation to theory, across a variety of scientific disciplines, ranging from physics-philosophy to post-structural and feminist theory. For Barad, these interferences, or intra-actions, point at the entanglement of fields of knowledge, and expose the intrinsic relationality of meaning and matter.

My proposition is that we can also read theories and (performance) *practices* through one another, which could expose how practices propagate within theoretical fields and vice versa, and operate as nomadic forces of deterritorialization. In his intriguing book *The Sympathy of Things: Ruskin and the Ecology of Design* (2011), architect Lars Spuybroek provides an astute example of such a diffractive reading of practice, when discussing the resonance between Gothic architecture—especially as theorized by John Ruskin and Wilhelm Worringer—and the digital. For Spuybroek, Gothic cathedrals are made not of stones but of computational structures of ribs (Spuybroek 2011, 68). A very useful thinking-through-practice that serves his argument is his comparison of architectural ribs to twigs in a bird's nest. The twigs themselves are breakable, but through their interlocking and intertwining, they become acts that together produce an overall stability. This stability is not a form of rest, but a working, a force (66). Spuybroek observes that the nest is obviously an example of design—hence of material thinking—but "surely we cannot assign these qualities to the bird and proclaim it the designer. There is intelligence in the making of the nest, and there is design, but these occur between things, not behind or above them. That is exactly why it is computable" (67). Through a range of examples, Spuybroek demonstrates that the Gothic, just like the digital, is produced out of the relations and entanglements of disparate elements, elements that can be combined in an infinite number of ways. That is why changeability is a key characteristic, and closely connected to this is savageness, a term frequently used by Ruskin. Ruskin, rather like Deleuze and Guattari's analysis of the Gothic, firmly rejects the original-copy model of standardization, and favors the savageness of expert labor in Gothic architecture, cherishing the small mutations and deviations from design that come with skill and craftmanship, which are also the germs of innovation and change (14).

Through Spuybroek (and Ruskin), we may become aware of a nomadic vitalism, a vitalism that is at the heart of any generative device or process, and which fuels the concept of nomadic theatre as well. Nomadic theatre functions as an engine or machine, enabling the researcher to cut across various domains, to question boundaries between theory and practice, to move back and forth between micro- and macro-levels of expertise, to deterritorialize disciplinary territories, and reterritorialize them through mutations and change. All these observations once more affirm the intrinsic performativity of the concept: it demonstrates nomadic theatre, and does nomadology.

Thresholds of the Imagination

A nomad follows customary paths. Therefore I will end at the beginning, and return to Deleuze's essay "Nomad Thought." In this essay, Deleuze describes the effects, or rather the affects, of reading Nietzsche. For Deleuze, the energy and force in Nietzsche's work demonstrates that philosophy is creativity of thought. However, how to describe energy, or force? In relation to the *Blackmarket*, Hannah Hurtzig defines non-knowledge in three ways, pertaining to either the things you don't know yet, the things that you have forgotten, or the things that you are aware of but that are *inexpressible* to you.[9] Similarly, reading Nietzsche produces a sensation, according to Deleuze, an intensity, a becoming aware of something that eludes description; something that escapes the code of recognition. Deleuze compares this sensation with looking at a pretty painting:

> What is ... a beautiful painting or a beautiful drawing? There's a frame ... But whatever is in the frame, at what point does it become beautiful? At the moment one knows and feels that the movement, that the line which is framed comes from elsewhere, that it does not begin within the limits of the frame. It began above or next to the frame, and the line traverses the frame. As in Godard's film, you paint the painting *with* the wall. (Deleuze 2004b, 255)

Drawing the painting with the frame perhaps evokes associations with Jacques Derrida's essay "Parergon," in *La vérité en peinture* (1979), yet Deleuze strikes a slightly different chord, in my view. Derrida enquires into the frame itself, the frame that limits, defines, and constitutes the painting, yet also is limitless. Analogous to Tschumi's architectural limits (Chapter 6), the frame is the painting's ontological and epistemological base *and* a threshold to other definitions.[10] Deleuze, on the other hand, relates the outside to the inside and vice versa, not to advocate dualism, as may be clear by now, but in order to "traverse and pass through them" (Dolphijn and Van der Tuin 2012, 127). Second, Deleuze emphasizes the *sensation* of movement. He describes the sensation of something that comes from the outside; something that is decidedly present, but does not have words (yet), precisely because it defers from the already-known, the already-existent.

So instead of actually describing Nietzsche's aphorisms, Deleuze seeks to capture their *force*, the force of an event. Events are intensities, they produce affects, and lines of flight. Put in non-Deleuzian words: events materialize in the perception of something that happens and spring up from this encounter; something that forces us to think, or to feel, or both. Events materialize in sensation, and then something else happens: it widens our horizon—horizons of thought, of feeling, of expectation. The widening of the horizon itself is an event, as it produces the sensation of "widening" itself; it is a portal to an infinity of "widenings" and opens up to potentiality. Such events rearrange existing conceptions of what can be known, imagined, thought, or done: they are true redistributions of the sensible (Rancière), no matter how minute.

If we would take such events through a spatialized consciousness, we sooner or later encounter Borges, this master of thinking the outside on the inside. Borges always works at the limits; he exhausts his subjects, such as the cartographer's map (Chapter 4). When following Baudrillard's analysis of this map, we might think of this map, and Borges's stories in general, as the exhaustion of representation (Chapter 6). However, I prefer to see the limits of the imperceptible as thresholds of the imagination. Borges stories are like Moebius strips, as they produce sensations that force us to think. Brian Massumi observes that the Moebius strip is one of those two-dimensional figures "whose folding and twisting on themselves create three-dimensional effects. The 'effects' are real but not part of the formal definition of the figure. They are in the figure as it is really experienced, adding another quality to it, precisely in the way it stands out from its formal limits" (Massumi 2002, 185).

Nomadic theatre cannot do without limits, as I argued in Chapter 6. Limits play a very serious role in many lived spaces. And yet, limits may also serve to maintain that tiny space that any social machinery needs in order to function properly (Lehmann): limits that are thresholds of the imagination, that hint at other definitions and experiences; limits that function as safeguards of qualitative difference. Perhaps we see in Borges the exhaustion of representation. Except, we appear to be no longer in a deconstructionist, poststructural, postmodern universe. We are perhaps in an ecological universe, in which we use embodied, situated, and playful connections in order to attach ourselves to fluidity. We attach ourselves through our perception as we move through this fluid world, a world that is created by our movements. While traversing this universe, we slide in and out of imaginary states, not as the equivalent of shopping (Fuchs 1996, 134) but precisely to move beyond a neoliberal capitalist ideology, to search for attentiveness, to train and maintain our capacity to think and feel differently, to embrace the (in)exactitude of difference, to move in all directions, in all sorts of thinkable and unthinkable ways.

Notes

Chapter 1

1. Matt Adams (Blast Theory) uses the term "Hertzian space" to refer to the hybrid spaces that are created by digital locative media or cell phones, where users simultaneously inhabit "nearby and remote locations, physical and digital spaces" (in De Souza e Silva and Sutko 2009, 72).
2. Mobile audiences are not a new phenomenon. Throughout the twentieth century, there have been many attempts to mobilize the spectator, notably by the historical avant-garde (Bishop 2012; Fischer-Lichte 1997; Kennedy 2009) and in the 1960s rise of Events, Happenings, environmental theatre, and performative installations (Berghaus 2005; Bishop 2005; Carlson 2004). An even wider historical scope shows that the present convention of the separation between stage and darkened auditorium only reached its full form with Wagner in the late nineteenth century, and was preceded by pageants, street theatre, fairs, and medieval practices in which the performer–audience distinction was not that strict.
3. See also Klich (2017), Wilkie (2015a), Ferdman (2013), Birch and Tompkins (2012), Benford and Giannachi (2011), Whybrow (2010), Oddey (2007).
4. Border and migration issues are certainly not exclusively European themes, see for instance Hopkins and Solga (2015, 1–15). For an extensive discussion of the mobility turn in the social sciences, see Wilkie (2015a, 3–8).
5. Earlier versions of this work date back to even before 2006. The work toured primarily between 2006 and 2012 but is still on the company's repertoire. See also Chapter 5.
6. See for instance Raessens (2005) and Bogost (2007, 40–4). Verhoeff offers a counter-argument, i.e., a performative and relational approach to interactivity (2012, 113).
7. Postdramatic theatre is often characterized by what it is not: non-illusionary, non-representational, related to the absence (or death) of characters, and so forth (cf. Fuchs 1996).
8. Fischer-Lichte's approach remains somewhat dualistic: in the performative event, the spectator transforms *into* an actor, the performer no longer represents but presents, the conventional signifier makes room for the material signified, and so on (2008, 11–17).
9. See also Garcin-Marrou (2011) for a short overview of Deleuze and Guattari's writings on theatre, including excerpts of six short plays or "chaosmic sketches" by Guattari.
10. In his *Cinema* cahiers, Deleuze introduces the "movement-image" to argue that cinema does not represent movement, but instead creates affects of

movement: blocks of sensation that produce a direct relationship with the real (Ils Huygens in Romein et al. 2009, 314–15).
11 Deleuze refers as well to Kafka and (elsewhere) to Beckett, writers that "get something through" by writing in a language foreign to their native language, and constitute a minor literature (cf. Elden 2006, 49).
12 This breaking down of boundaries also marks the societal changes and emancipatory movements related to the students' and workers' protests in the May 1968 events (Conley 2003; Cull 2009, 12–14).
13 The full title of the nomadology chapter in *A Thousand Plateaus* is "1227: Treatise on Nomadology—The War Machine." Cf. De Kesel (2006), O'Sullivan (2006).
14 The concept of affirmativity is discussed by, amongst others, Dolphijn and Van der Tuin in connection with new materialist theory (2012, 126–32); by Bal, in relation to critical intimacy (2002, 289–90); and by Brian Massumi as an alternative to critical thinking (2002, 12–13). For a radical approach to affirmativity in politics and theory, see Braidotti (2011a, 267–98).
15 See also the "constructed situations" of the Situationists movement, discussed in Chapter 3.
16 This triadic approach to dramaturgy has been developed in the context of theatre, dance, and performance studies course modules at Utrecht University.
17 I am alluding here to, respectively, Barthes' *The Pleasure of the Text* (1973/1975) and "The Death of the Author" (in Barthes 1977, 142–8).
18 Personal conversation with David Micklem, March 2011. See also http://playgroundprojects.bac.org.uk. Ironically, a huge fire destroyed large parts of the building in March 2015. BAC launched a large fundraising campaign and rebuilt the Grand Hall and other parts, celebrating the recovery with a "Phoenix season" in 2018. See www.bac.org.uk/phoenixrising, accessed March 27, 2018.

Chapter 2

1 The quote is derived from Kafka's *The Great Wall of China*, and preceded by a quote from Nietzsche's *The Genealogy of Morals*, with a similar taste of strangeness, although slightly more disturbing, and (mis)used for various political purposes: "They show up like destiny, without cause or reason, without consideration or pretext, there they are with the speed of lightning, too terrible, too sudden, too conquering, too *other* even to be an object of hatred" (Deleuze 2004b, 256, italics in the original; cf. De Kesel 2006).
2 Since its premiere in Utrecht in 2008, *No Man's Land* has been restaged in various European cities, each time slightly adapted to the particular political-cultural context. I discuss the 2008 performance in Utrecht. For credits, pictures, video and press documentation see www.driesverhoeven.com.

3 The aria is "Dido's Lament," from Purcell's *Dido and Aeneas*, in which she asks Aeneas to remember her while he leaves her. A strange choice for a start of a performance perhaps, but as *No Man's Land*'s dramaturgy is based on patterns of inversion and reversal, the song becomes semiotically active at the end of the performance, where spectators are left behind by the migrant–performers who disappear into town.
4 In the plateau "1440: The Smooth and the Striated," Deleuze and Guattari remark that the sea is the smooth space par excellence, as one cannot capture the sea but only occupy it temporarily. Simultaneously, the sea is the space most fundamentally subjected to striation, as it has been counted, named, and measured, organized by meridians and parallels, longitudes, and latitudes, pruned by radars and submarines, or claimed as territorial water (2004, 529–30).
5 See van Eikels (2011) for an insightful discussion of the concept of synchronicity in relation to the idea of a *dispersed* collectivity in (participatory) performance.
6 The notion of the porous membrane is also addressed in game theory, in order to reconfigure and open up the metaphor of the "closed" magic circle (Copier in van den Boomen et al. 2009, 165–6).
7 In choosing these words I also have Umberto Eco's use of the term "ostentation" in mind, in connection with the remark by phenomenologist Bert States, that on the stage, objects or living entities are "uplifted to the view" that triggers an other-than-daily perceptual consciousness (in Carlson 2004, 36–7).
8 I heard the Dutch version of this text. For the sake of readability I use the English transcription here. Courtesy to Dries Verhoeven for this transcription.
9 Go is a board game in which simple black and white pieces are moved over a grid of vertical and horizontal lines. The pieces are placed on the cross-points of these lines and displaced and arranged in order to encircle or shatter the territory of the adversary.
10 For Deleuze and Guattari, the migrant moves from one point to another, although this second point may be "uncertain, unforeseen or not well localized … The nomad goes from point to point only as a consequence and as a factual necessity; in principle, points for him are relays on a trajectory" (2004, 419).
11 As my dealing with the *concept* of nomadic theatre is based on both Deleuze and Mieke Bal, I should mention that Bal conceptualizes the metaphor altogether differently. She connects the metaphor to (performative) acts of moving or carrying across something; this act of "metaphoring" always involves interactive and retro-active processes of translation and transformation (Bal 2002, 62–7).
12 This text is slightly adapted in each city, in connection with the local context and to the performers participating in the performance.

13 Since I witnessed the Dutch version of this performance, the examples refer to the Netherlands.
14 In Bene's work, the strategy of continuous variation manifests itself amongst others in character representation, as the actors destabilize the characters in *Richard III* by using a variety of acting styles.
15 Based on various reviews and reports from students with whom I visited the Utrecht 2013 performance.
16 Pearson and Shanks similarly connect the assemblage to (postdramatic) dramaturgy (2001, 24–7) and to the process of "ordering or patterning" the different elements into a performance structure (in Turner and Behrndt 2008, 31–2).

Chapter 3

1 See for credits, pictures, and press documentation www.rimini-protokoll. de/website/en/project/call-cutta.
2 This observation is shared in other works that allude to the spatial turn in performance, see for instance Turner (2015), Birch and Tompkins (2012), Whybrow (2010), or various contributions to *Theatre Journal* 67 (4) (December 2015) and *Performance Research: On Scenography* 18 (3) (June 2013). For a critical discussion from the viewpoint of feminist theory, see Levin (2014).
3 The term was coined by James J. Gibson, and discussed in his *The Ecological Approach to Visual Perception* (1979). These affordances are the performatives of designed environment, so to say; a path invites walking, for instance, a (sunny) beach encourages sunbathing, digital touch screens facilitate haptic interfacing and so on (Urry 2007, 50–1).
4 After the ambulatory version of 2005, Rimini Protokoll made a box version, with stationary spectators. *Call Cutta in a Box* had a large international tour, mainly between 2006 and 2012.
5 Goebbels draws on Gernot Boehme's theory of acoustic atmospheres (Boehme 2007, 122).
6 Susan Bennett subtly points out that a history of female flâneuses would reveal an entirely different story, in which prostitutes' and women's lack of access to solitary wandering would enter the stage (2008, 79).
7 Flânerie, marveling at technological inventions or luxury goods; daydreaming; looking at nature or landscape paintings in dioramas and panoramas; these were all strategies of shielding oneself from the negative side-effects of industrial innovation: physically dangerous labor and the sense of alienation (Benjamin 1935/1968, 82; Buck-Morss 1992).
8 Next to the compression of space and time, related qualifications are *Liquid Times* (Bauman 2007), floating worlds (Gergen 2003), and non-places (Augé 1992/1995), which all in different ways refer to an infinite, indistinct flow of people, goods, and information that produces an alienating abstraction.

9 In *Tantalisingly Close* (2012), Imar de Vries argues that mobile phones are also used, developed, and commercially exploited within the *myths* of connectivity, social fluidity, and instant access to omnipresent information.
10 The example does not go without irony of course, after 9/11, and is also indicative of the changeability of place (cf. Cresswell 2002, 24–5).
11 This latter category, *spaces of representation*, has also been translated as *representational space* (Lefebvre 1991, Elden 2004). I prefer Soja's translation (1996), as it more explicitly addresses the potentiality of the term.
12 Despite his non-dualistic approach, Lefebvre tends to connect the theatre to the nonverbal, and the corporeal to the pre-intellectual. Although some of Lefebvre's idea seem more actual than ever, his view on theatre requires an update, to which this study seeks to contribute.
13 Next to Deleuze and Lefebvre, I rely in particular on Stuart Elden here, who studied both authors, see Elden (2006, 2004) and Elden's introduction to Lefebvre (2004).
14 Part of the description is based on Groot Nibbelink and Merx in Bay-Cheng et al. (2010, 218–29). For an extended discussion see also Farman (2012, 103–12). For pictures, video and press documents, see www.blasttheory.co.uk/projects/rider-spoke.
15 Wolf-Dieter Ernst (2009) provides a more detailed discussion of this script.
16 Constant Nieuwenhuys' *New Babylon* provides perhaps the best example of SI's unitary urbanism, much inspired by Huizinga's *Homo Ludens* (1938/1998) and other play theories (Wigley 1998, 26–31, 55–7).
17 Bishop shortly refers to Rimini Protokoll's *Experten des Alltags* (Bishop 2012, 250n8).
18 Not only are the performers involved in outsourced labor, but spectators as well. See for a discussion of the "working audience" Karen Zaiontz's essay "Ambulatory Audiences and Animated Sites: Staging the Spectator in Site-Specific Performance," in Birch and Tompkins (2012), 167–81.
19 Read refers to a performance by Forced Entertainment that investigates silence, not by putting silence against noise but by marking differences between types of silence, or, put differently, between this silence and *this* silence (2008, 17).
20 See also Alan Read, for whom politics is the term "that best describes that interruption of the sensible" (2008, 177).

Chapter 4

1 The flyer announced a local community dance project. Dries Verhoeven also made a performance with the same title (*U bevindt zich hier*, 2006). This similarity is entirely coincidental.
2 Original title: *Sporenonderzoek*, produced by Dries Verhoeven/Huis aan de Werf Utrecht, 2005. For credits, pictures, and press documentation see www.driesverhoeven.com.

3 Verhoeff's "screenspace" thus suggests a radical alternative to the more common notion of the screen as display (2012, 65, 150).
4 See also de Certeau's view on theatre as setting up a field for action, an act of making space for operations (1984, 123).
5 The distortion is further enhanced by situating the vertical center of the map about 50 degrees north of the equator, which increases the northern hemisphere at the cost of the southern hemisphere. The distortions lead to a depiction of Greenland as larger than China (Monmonier 1995, 18); Alaska and Brazil appear a similar size, although Alaska is actually five times smaller than Brazil (Wood 1992, 57).
6 Next to Deleuze and Guattari's view on maps as performance, the turn toward a performative or "post-representational" cartography has been inspired by, amongst others, Bruno Latour's actor-network theory, and Henri Lefebvre's spatial analysis (Dodge et al. 2009, 10–20).
7 See Pearson and Shanks for the difference between reconstruction and (re) constitution (2001, 45–9).
8 Cf. Susan Foster's account of *Call Cutta* (2008). Verhoeven's rehearsal notes too refer to GPS systems. The performers "practiced GPS" by training to navigate each other correctly from point A to B.
9 The virtual here is not the same as in the term "virtual reality," where the virtual (usually) designates an opposition with daily reality (Farman 2012, 35–55; Grosz 2001, 78–9).
10 Examples are the virtual gallery *ARtotheque* and Julian Oliver's *The Artvertizer*, which layers artworks over commercial billboards and screens (Verhoeff 2012, 107–8, 159).
11 See the contributions by Martin Welton and Jennifer Fisher respectively, in Banes and Lepecki (2007, 146–55, 166–78).
12 See Gianna Bouchard, "Haptic Visuality: The Dissective View in Performance" (in Oddey and White 2009, 163–76). Bouchard and also Deleuze and Guattari refer to theories of the nineteenth-century art historian Alois Riegl.
13 The section's title refers to a research project by Dutch designer Caroline Nevejan, on how digital interfaces may induce a sense of proximity or reciprocity across large geographical distances.
14 "Het is gezien. Het is niet onopgemerkt gebleven," my translation.

Chapter 5

1 *The Smile Off Your Face* premiered in 2003, achieved its more or less final form after about three years, toured intensively until 2012, and is still on the company's repertoire. For credits, pictures and press documentation, see http://ontroerendgoed.be/projecten/the-smile-off-your-face.

2 Monadology refers to Leibniz's use of the term "monad." A monad designates an undivided unit, a singularity or "oneness," which is nevertheless a multiplicity because it can be folded in infinite ways (Deleuze 2006b, 25).
3 Deleuze and Guattari qualify movement in this specific context as extensive i.e., going from point to point. On the contrary, speed—not to be confused with fastness—is intensive, and may even involve slowness or immobility. Speed constitutes a body of parts or particles, whose atoms "*occupy or fill a smooth space in the manner of a vortex*, with the possibility of springing up at any point" (2004, 420–1, italics in the original).
4 The threshold is a figuration of the fold, just as labyrinths, curvilinear forms, reverberations, or temporal modulations (Conley in Deleuze 2006b, ix–xx; Deleuze 2006b, 3). In *Deleuze and the Fold*, editors Van Tuinen and McDonell remark that for Deleuze, the limits of material sensation are "thresholds of consciousness" that fold "the outside on the inside" (2010, 11–12).
5 See also the *English Oxford Dictionary* online, Oxford University Press 2013, entry no. 4.
6 In *The Senses in Performance* (Banes and Lepecki 2007), the term "sensorium" alternately is used to indicate a subject's sensory perception system ("the senses") and to indicate spaces or environments that purposefully address the senses in perception. I use the latter understanding of the term.
7 See in particular the introduction by the editors Sally Banes and André Lepecki, and the contributions by Mary Fleischer, Martin Welton, and Jennifer Fisher.
8 Lehmann also refers to the constructed situations of the Situationists (2006, 106), and to the event's predecessors in 1960s performance art, Events and Happenings (Banes and Lepecki 2007, 104; Berghaus 2005).
9 When performed in a remote village in Morocco, some people shared never-told secrets, whereas in other geographic areas spectators were inclined to answer in less serious and more playful ways.
10 *Oxford English Dictionary,* Oxford University Press, 2013.
11 Intimacy is quite a contested concept, when put in conjunction with theatre, as the personal, private, and confidential are often seen as contradictory to the staged, the social and the public "nature" of theatre. In my view, spectators can still experience a performance such as *The Smile* as very intimate, even if they are well aware of this experience being staged. See Groot Nibbelink (2012a).
12 The irony is of course that the authors themselves substantially contributed to the experience economy to come into existence, thus preparing the market and creating a niche for a marketing book on authenticity.
13 Rancière's account in fact strongly resonates with Erika Fischer-Lichte's essay "Disovering the Spectator" (1997), where she values the (postmodern) spectator as a "master of semiosis," free to interpret and associate at will (57).

Next to this similarity, Rancière equates the theatre with (reading) a book, and compares spectatorial activity with "the gaze focused on an image" (2009, 22).
14 In addition, in *Theatre in the Dark: Shadow, Gloom and Blackout in Contemporary Theatre*, Welton usefully observes that using darkness in the theatre regains extra value in view of the current ubiquity of light and related demands of visibility, clarity, and transparency in today's public culture and society (Alston and Welton 2017, 245).
15 It has to be admitted that reporting on performances that strongly rely on individual experience increases the risk of spoilers, so I won't spoil this one.
16 Massumi primary relates thinking-feeling to visuality. When looking at objects or paintings, for instance, we do not only designate meaning or functionality, but "think-feel" an object's volume, weightiness, or depth, due to the body's capacity to move (around) and to feel movement (2008, 6).
17 The Aleph is a space that incorporates all thinkable spaces, simultaneously perceived. It is a sphere without a center, with multiple, contrasting perspectives (cf. Soja 1996, 54–6). As in many of his stories, Borges practices a poetics of exhaustion by following a certain idea to its extreme limits, that is, imperceptibility (see Chapter 6). But, as Bachelard shows when writing on miniatures in *The Poetics of Space* (1958/1994, 148–82), the passage towards the imperceptible is precisely the threshold of the imagination.

Chapter 6

1 *Ruby Town* premiered in Cologne (2007), where it was performed in three blocks of respectively 36, 60, and 84 hours. During the festival *Theatertreffen* in Berlin (2008) the play time was extended towards a nine-day nonstop performance. My discussion relates to the Berlin 2008 event. For credits, pictures, and press documentation, see http://signa.dk.
2 Literary theorist Gérard Genette also uses the term "architexture," but in a different sense and context, that of genre theory. For Genette, the architext denotes a network of overarching elements through which a particular work may be allocated to genre(s) (Genette 1979/1992, 1982/1997).
3 Mike Pohjola connects LARPs to Hakim Bey's concept of the Temporary Autonomous Zone (TAZ) (in Montola and Stenros 2004, 81). For Bey, TAZ equates ontological anarchy, also inspired by Deleuze's and Guattari's nomadology (Bey 1985/1991). *Ruby Town*'s TAZ reverberates with this concept as well.
4 Signa Köstler performs the role of Martha Rubin, Arthur Köstler plays the mayor of Ruby Town, and costume and set designer Thomas Bo Nilsson is the military captain.
5 I use the terms "play" and "game" rather indiscriminately, following game theorist Joost Raessens, who sees play as the overarching category and games as the formalized parts of play (2010, 11–13; cf. Salen and Zimmerman 2004).

6 Opinions differ on whether a hypertext creates either an increase or decrease of coherence. Lev Manovich, for instance, stresses the contingency of connections, whereas Ian Bogost points to the hypertext's argumentative, correlative potential (Bogost 2007, 26).
7 All interview quotes in this chapter are derived from the same interview, see Groot Nibbelink (2009b). Signa Sørensen later changed her name into Signa Köstler.
8 For a comparison between *Ruby Town* and the memory theatre of Renaissance architect Camillo, see Groot Nibbelink (2012b). Camillo's memory theatre has also been used as a metaphor for the internet. See Matussek (2001) and Bleeker and Allsopp (2012).
9 Ludologists see games and their mechanics as radically distinct from pre-existing (narrative) media, whereas narrativists tend to regard games as (transmedial) storytelling media (Jenkins 2004, 118–21; Biggin 2017, 158–60).
10 Interestingly Punchdrunk uses the mask both to stage the *gaze* of the audience as well as to address them as performers. For an elaborate discussion, see Gareth White, "Odd Anonymous Needs: Punchdrunk's Masked Spectators" (in Oddey and White 2009, 219–29). For a thorough discussion of Punchdrunk, also with attention to the game elements in their work, see Biggin (2017).
11 There is a clear and seriously final end to the performance, as *Ruby Town* 2008 closed with a collective suicide, but the event is not structured according to principles of *telos* or *logos*.
12 Examples are *Blur Building* by Diller and Scofidio or the *D-Tower* and the *H20 Pavillon* by Lars Spuybroek/NOX Architecture (Spurr 2007, 250–78). For similar reasons I do not discuss Kim Novak's "liquid architecture" (in Verhoeff 2012, 110) or the mobile huts, shelters, or houses that are often seen as "nomadic architecture."
13 During these disappearances, Signa Köstler performed another role— probably that of a gypsy, at the bottom of Ruby Town's social hierarchy. See Groot Nibbelink (2009b).
14 K. Michael Hays uses Bakhtin's chronotope to qualify this lived temporality in Hejduk's work. A chronotope designates the "distinctive temporal and spatial features within a work, the phenomenal 'feel' of the world *produced by the work*," where (quoting Bakhtin) "time, as it were, thickens, takes on flesh, becomes artistically visible; likewise, space becomes charged and responsive to the movements of time, plot, and history" (Hays 1996, 10).
15 In a similar line of reasoning, but with a focus on interactive audiences, Gareth White discusses procedural authorship, derived from Laura Mulvey's *Hamlet on the Holodeck* on interactive narratives (White 2013, 29–32).
16 Among Bogost's many examples are critical games like *The McDonald's Videogame* (2006) and *Darfur is Dying* (2006).
17 Lehmann places Gadamer and Schiller in the first camp, and prefers the second (Lehmann 2007, 54). Many game scholars plead for a non-dualist

approach to the magic circle, or seek to move beyond it (Raessens 2010; Copier in van den Boomen et al. 2009, 164–8). See also Montola for a concise overview of the game studies debate; Montola proposes to replace the circle with the notion of the contract (2012, 48–55).

18 Lehmann focuses on play elements such as the intrigue, the double-play of the play-within-the-play, and the conflict as (competitive) *agôn*.

Chapter 7

1 *Store* (2005–12), by Michikazu Matsune and David Subal, seen at Springdance festival in Utrecht, 2007.
2 Original title: *Schwarzmarket für nützliches Wissen und nicht-Wissen*. For credits, pictures, video, and press documentation see www.mobileacademy-berlin.com/index.html.
3 In the short video *From Sketch*#5, Hurtzig explicitly uses theatre terms and concepts to explain the *Blackmarket* formula, describing it as a communicative act of performing knowledge, and as a *theatrical* act including text, performers, listeners/spectators, a space or agora, stage directions and a script (ZIA/Arte Creative, May 2011).
4 In a similar vein, Deleuze speaks of the schizophrenic, a small difference that operates between levels of repetition but beneath consumption (1968/2004b, 365).
5 See www.monbiot.com for a large collection of essays and information supporting these arguments.
6 This remark calls forth the work of (the late) Adrian Howells, who literally embraces and carefully touches spectators in highly esteemed one-to-one performances like *The Pleasure of Being: Washing, Feeding, Holding* (2011) and *Foot Washing for the Sole* (2008). See also Howells (2012) and essays by Josephine Machon (in Frieze 2016, 29–42) and Helen Iball (in Birch and Tompkins 2012, 201–15).
7 Apart from this, the *Blackmarket* is open to bribery. Subtly hinted at by Hurtzig in *From Sketch*, the form of the lecture, the lecturer–client relationship and the (financial) logistics all are open to play.
8 The phrase "attitude becomes form" alludes to the widely acclaimed exhibition *Live in Your Head: When Attitudes Become Form (Works - Concepts - Processes - Situations - Information)*, curated by Harald Szeeman (Kunsthalle Bern, Switzerland, 1969), in which the non-hierarchical presentation of (artistic) processes and *situations* radically changed the idea of exhibitions as a display of art objects.
9 *From Sketch*#5: Hannah Hurtzig.
10 Based on Van den Braembussche (2007, 310–21). Derrida focuses on the frame: there is framing but there is no (fixed) frame (Derrida and Owens 1979, 39). See also O'Sullivan on deconstruction vs. Deleuzian theory (2006, 12–15).

Bibliography

Allain, Paul, and Jen Harvie, eds. 2014. *The Routledge Companion to Theatre and Performance*. Second edition. Hoboken: Taylor and Francis.

Alston, Adam. 2016. *Beyond Immersive Theatre: Aesthetics, Politics and Productive Participation*. Basingstoke: Palgrave Macmillan.

Alston, Adam, and Martin Welton. 2017. *Theatre in the Dark: Shadow, Gloom and Blackout in Contemporary Theatre*. London: Bloomsbury Methuen Drama.

Aronson, Arnold. 2005. *Looking into the Abyss: Essays on Scenography*. Ann Arbor: The University of Michigan Press.

Augé, Marc. [1992] 1995. *Non-Places: Introduction to an Anthropology of Supermodernity*. Translated by John Howe. London: Verso.

Babbage, Frances. 2004. *Augusto Boal*. London and New York: Routledge.

Bachelard, Gaston. [1958] 1994. *The Poetics of Space*. Translated by Maria Jolas. Boston: Beacon Press.

Bal, Mieke. 2002. *Travelling Concepts in the Humanities: A Rough Guide*. Toronto: Toronto University Press.

Balme, Christopher B. 2008. *The Cambridge Introduction to Theatre Studies*. Cambridge: Cambridge University Press.

Banes, Sally, and André Lepecki. 2007. *The Senses in Performance*. New York: Routledge.

Barad, Karen. 2007. *Meeting the Universe Half-way: Quantum Physics and the Entanglement of Matter and Meaning*. Durham and London: Duke University Press.

Barthes, Roland. [1973] 1975. *The Pleasure of the Text*. Translated by Richard Miller. New York: Hill and Wang.

Barthes, Roland. 1977. "From Work to Text." In *Music, Image, Text*, edited and translated by Stephen Heath, 155–64. London: Fontana Press.

Bastajian, Tina. 2008. "Some Musings on Iterations and Encounters—Re: CALL CUTTA(s)." *Artnodes* 8 [article online]. DOI: http://dx.doi.org/10.7238/a.v0i8.772.

Baudrillard, Jean. [1981] 1998. "Simulacra and Simulations." In *Selected Writings*, edited by Mark Poster, 166–84. Stanford: Stanford University Press.

Bauman, Zygmunt. 2007. *Liquid Times: Living in an Age of Uncertainty*. Cambridge: Polity Press.

Bay-Cheng, Sarah, Chiel Kattenbelt, Andy Lavender, and Robin Nelson, eds. 2010. *Mapping Intermediality in Performance*. Amsterdam: Amsterdam University Press.

Benford, Steve, and Gabriella Giannachi. 2011. *Performing Mixed Reality*. Cambridge MA: MIT Press.
Benjamin, Walter. [1935] 1968. "Paris, Capital of the Nineteenth Century." *New Left Review* 48 (March–April): 77–88.
Benjamin, Walter. [1982] 1999. "The Flâneur." In *The Arcades Project*, translated by Howard Eiland and Kevin McLaughlin, 416–55. Cambridge MA: Harvard University Press.
Bennett, Jane. 2010. *Vibrant Matter: A Political Ecology of Things*. Durham/London: Duke University Press.
Bennett, Susan. 2008. "Universal Experience: The City as Tourist Stage." In *The Cambridge Companion to Performance Studies*, edited by Tracy C. Davies, 76–90. Cambridge: Cambridge University Press.
Berghaus, Günther. 2005. *Avant-Garde Performance: Live Events and Electronic Technologies*. Basingstoke: Palgrave MacMillan.
Bey, Hakim. [1985] 1991. *T. A. Z. The Temporary Autonomous Zone, Ontological Anarchy, Poetic Terrorism*. New York: Autonomedia. http://hermetic.com/bey/taz_cont.html.
Biggin, Rose. 2017. *Immersive Theatre and Audience Experience: Space, Game and Story in the Work of Punchdrunk*. Basingstoke: Palgrave Macmillan.
Birch, Anna, and Joanne Tompkins, eds. 2012. *Performing Site-Specific Theatre: Politics, Place, Practice*. Basingstoke: Palgrave Macmillan.
Bishop, Claire. 2004. "Antagonism and Relational Aesthetics." *October* 110 (Fall): 51–79.
Bishop, Claire. 2005. *Installation Art: A Critical History*. London: Tate Publishing.
Bishop, Claire, ed. 2006a. *Participation: Documents of Contemporary Art*. London/Cambridge MA: Whitechapel Gallery/MIT Press.
Bishop, Claire. 2006b. "The Social Turn: Collaboration and its Discontents." *Artforum* (February): 178–83.
Bishop, Claire. 2012. *Artificial Hells: Participatory Art and the Politics of Spectatorship*. London: Verso.
Bleeker, Maaike. 2005. "See Me, Feel Me, Think Me: The Body of Semiotics." In *Theater Topics 1: Multicultureel Drama?*, edited by Maaike Bleeker, Lucia van Heteren, Chiel Kattenbelt, and Kees Vuyk, 109–10. Amsterdam: Amsterdam University Press.
Bleeker, Maaike. 2008a. *Visuality in the Theatre: The Locus of Looking*. Basingstoke: Palgrave MacMillan.
Bleeker, Maaike. 2008b. "Martin, Massumi and the Matrix." In *Anatomy Live: Performance and the Operating Theatre*, edited by Maaike Bleeker, 151–64. Amsterdam: Amsterdam University Press.
Bleeker, Maaike. 2008c. "Passages in Post-Modern Theory: Mapping the Apparatus." *Parallax* 14 (1): 55–67.
Bleeker, Maaike, Lucia van Heteren, Chiel Kattenbelt, and Rob van der Zalm, eds. 2009. *Theater Topics 4: Concepten en objecten*. Amsterdam: Amsterdam University Press.

Bleeker, Maaike, and Ric Alsopp, eds. 2012. "On Technology & Memory." *Performance Research: A Journal of the Performing Arts* 17 (3).
Bogost, Ian. 2007. *Persuasive Games: The Expressive Power of Videogames*. Cambridge MA: MIT Press.
Bogue, Ronald. 1997. "Art and Territory." *South Atlantic Quarterly* 96 (3): 465–82.
Bogue, Ronald. 2004. "Apology for Nomadology." *Interventions* 6 (2): 169–79.
Bolter, Jay David. 1991. *Writing Space: The Computer, Hypertext, and the History of Writing*. Hillsdale NJ: Lawrence Erlbaum Associates.
Bolter, Jay David. 2001. *Writing Space: Computers, Hypertext, and the Remediation of Print*. Mahwah NJ: Lawrence Erlbaum Associates.
Boomen, Marianne van den, Sybille Lammes, Ann-Sophie Lehmann, Joost Raessens, and Mirko Tobias Schäfer, eds. 2009. *Digital Material: Tracing New Media in Everyday Life and Technology*. Amsterdam: Amsterdam University Press.
Borges, Jorge Luis. [1946] 1999. "On Exactitude in Science." In *Collected Fictions*, translated by Andrew Hurley, 325. New York: Viking.
Borges, Jorge Luis. [1949] 2003. "The Aleph." In *De Aleph en andere verhalen*, translated by Barber van de Pol, 412–31. Amsterdam: De Bezige Bij.
Boundas, Constantin V., ed. 1993. *The Deleuze Reader*. New York: Columbia University Press.
Bourriaud, Nicolas. [1998] 2002. *Relational Aesthetics*. Translated by Simon Pleasance and Fronza Woods. Dijon: Les presses du réel.
Braembussche, Antoon van den. 2007. *Denken over kunst. Een inleiding in de kunstfilosofie*. Fourth, revised edition. Bussum: Coutinho.
Braidotti, Rosi. 2004. *Op doorreis. Nomadisch denken in de 21e eeuw*. Introduced and edited by Kristof van Rossem. Amsterdam: Boom.
Braidotti, Rosi. 2011a. *Nomadic Subjects: Embodiment and Sexual Difference in Contemporary Feminist Theory*. Second edition. New York: Columbia University Press.
Braidotti, Rosi. 2011b. *Nomadic Theory: The Portable Rosi Braidotti*. New York: Columbia University Press.
Buck-Morss, Susan. 1992. "Aesthetics and Anaesthetics: Walter Benjamin's Artwork Essay Reconsidered." *October* 62 (Autumn): 3–41.
Burckhardt, Barbara, and Eva Behrendt. 2008. "Brave Old World." *Theater Heute* (May 2008). http://signa.dk/theater-heute-2008. Accessed April 18, 2018.
Campbell, Tony. 1987. "Portolan Charts from the Late Thirteenth Century to 1500." In *The History of Cartography*, volume one, edited by J.B. Harley and David Woodward, 371–463. Chicago: University of Chicago Press.
Campenhout, Elke van. 2003. "De intieme ervaring." *Etcetera* 89: 14–15.
Carlson, Marvin. 2001. *The Haunted Stage: The Theatre as a Memory Machine*. Ann Arbor: The University of Michigan Press.
Carlson, Marvin. 2004. *Performance: A Critical Introduction*. Second edition. New York: Routledge.

Casey, Edward S. 1998. *The Fate of Place: A Philosophical History*. Berkeley: University of California Press.
Certeau, Michel de. 1984. *The Practice of Everyday Life*. Translated by Steven Rendall. Berkeley: University of California Press.
Chapple, Freda, and Chiel Kattenbelt, eds. 2006. *Intermediality in Theatre and Performance*. Amsterdam: Rodopi.
Chatzichristodoulou, Maria, and Rachel Zerihan, eds. 2012. *Intimacy: Across Visceral and Digital Performance*. Basingstoke: Palgrave Macmillan.
Collins, Jane, and Andrew Nisbet, eds. 2010. *Theatre and Performance Design: A Reader in Scenography*. London: Routledge.
Conley, Tom. 2003. "A Writing of Space: On French Critical Theory in 1973 and Its Aftermath." *diacritics* 33 (3/4): 189–203.
Corner, James. 1999. "The Agency of Mapping: Speculation, Critique and Invention." In *Mappings*, edited by Denis Cosgrove, 213–52. London: Reaktion Books.
Crampton, Jeremy. 2010. *Mapping: A Critical Introduction to Cartography and GIS*. Chichester: Wiley-Blackwell.
Cresswell, Tim. 2002. "Introduction: Theorizing Place." In *Mobilizing Place, Placing Mobility: The Politics of Representation in a Globalized World*, edited by Ginette Verstraete and Tim Cresswell, 11–32. Amsterdam: Rodopi.
Cresswell, Tim, and Peter Merriman, eds. 2011. *Geographies of Mobilities: Practices, Spaces, Subjects*. Farnham: Ashgate Publishing.
Cull, Laura, ed. 2009. *Deleuze and Performance*. Edinburgh: Edinburgh University Press.
Culler, Jonathan. 2000. "Philosophy and Literature: The Fortunes of the Performative." *Poetics Today* 21 (3): 503–19.
Cvejic, Bojana. 2015. *Choreographing Problems: Expressive Concepts in Contemporary Dance and Performance*. Basingstoke: Palgrave Macmillan.
De Kesel, Marc. 2006. "Ze komen zonder noodlot, zonder motief, zonder ratio. 'Nomadisme' in Deleuze en in het deleuzisme." *De Witte Raaf* 119: 1–4.
De Marinis, Marco. [1987] 2003. "Dramaturgy of the Spectator." In *Performance*, edited by Philip Auslander, 219–35. London: Routledge.
De Souza E Silva, Adriana, and Daniel M. Sutko, eds. 2009. *Digital Cityscapes: Merging Digital and Urban Playspaces*. New York: Peter Lang Publishing.
Debord, Guy. [1967] 2005. *Society of the Spectacle*. Translated by Ken Knabb. London: Rebel Press.
Deck, Jan, and Angelika Sieburg, eds. 2008. *Paradoxien des Zuschauens: Die Rolle des Publikums im zeitgenössischen Theater*. Bielefeld: Transcript Verlag.
Deleuze, Gilles. [1979] 1997. "One Less Manifesto." In *Mimesis, Masochism and Mime: The Politics of Theatricality in Contemporary French Thought*, edited by Timothy Murray, 239–58. Ann Arbor: The University of Michigan Press.
Deleuze, Gilles. [1968] 2004a. *Difference and Repetition*. Translated by Paul Patton. London: Continuum.

Deleuze, Gilles. [1973] 2004b. "Nomadic Thought." In *Desert Islands and Other Texts 1953–1974*, edited by David Lapoujade and translated by Michael Taormina, 252–61. Paris: Semiotext(e).

Deleuze, Gilles. [1986] 2006a. *Foucault*. Translated and edited by Seán Hand. London: Continuum.

Deleuze, Gilles. [1993] 2006b. *The Fold: Leibniz and the Baroque*. Translated and introduced by Tom Conley. London: Continuum.

Deleuze, Gilles, and Félix Guattari. 1994. *What is Philosophy?* Translated by Hugh Tomlinson and Graham Burchill. London: Verso.

Deleuze Gilles, and Félix Guattari. [1980] 2004. *A Thousand Plateaus: Capitalism and Schizophrenia*. Translated and introduced by Brian Massumi. London: Continuum.

Derrida, Jacques, and Craig Owens. 1979. "The Parergon." *October* 9 (Summer): 3–41.

Di Benedetto, Stephen. 2010. *The Provocation of the Senses in Contemporary Theatre*. London: Routledge.

Dodge, Martin, Chris Perkins, and Rob Kitchin, eds. 2009. *Rethinking Maps: New Frontiers in Cartographic Theory*. London: Routledge.

Doherty, Claire, ed. 2009. *Situation*. Whitechapel Documents of Contemporary Arts. Cambridge and London: MIT Press.

Dolphijn, Rick, and Iris van der Tuin. 2012. *New Materialism: Interviews & Cartographies*. Ann Arbor: The University of Michigan Library/Open Humanities Press/MPublishing.

Doruff, Sher. 2009. "The Tendency to 'Trans-': The Political Aesthetics of the Biogrammatic Zone." In *Interfaces of Performance*, edited by Maria Chatzichristodoulou, Janis Jefferies, and Rachel Zerihan, 121–40. Farnham: Ashgate.

Dragstra, Andrea. 2005. *Theater op je bloot vel*. MA Thesis, University of Amsterdam.

Dreysse, Miriam, and Florian Malzacher, eds. 2008. *Experts of the Everyday: The Theatre of Rimini Protokoll*. Berlin: Alexander Verlag.

Dutt, Anjan. 2005. *Call Cutta*, documentary film, DVD.

Eikels, Kai van. 2011. "What Parts of Us Can Do with Parts of Each Other (and When): Some Parts of This Text." *Performance Research: A Journal of the Performing Arts* 16 (3): 2–11.

Elden, Stuart. 2004. *Understanding Henri Lefebvre: Theory and the Possible*. London: Continuum.

Elden, Stuart. 2006. "The State of Territory under Globalization: Empire and the Politics of Reterritorialization." In *Methaphoricity and the Politics of Mobility*, edited by Maria Margaroni and Effie Yiannopoulou, 47–66. Amsterdam: Rodopi.

Ernst, Wolf-Dieter. 2009. "Interactivity." In *Theater Topics 4: Concepten en objecten*, edited by Maaike Bleeker et al., 15–25. Amsterdam: Amsterdam University Press.

Farman, Jason. 2012. *Mobile Interface Theory: Embodied Space and Locative Media*. London: Routledge.
Farman, Jason. 2014. *The Mobile Story. Narrative Practices with Locative Technologies*. London: Routledge.
Feldman, Nick. 2008. "The Art of Displacement: Parkour in the Physical and the Abstract." *The Daily* (University of Washington), February 21.
Ferdman, Bertie. 2013. "A New Yourney Through Other Spaces: Contemporary Performance beyond 'Site-Specific'." *Theater* 43 (2): 5–25.
Filmer, Andrew, and Juliet Rufford, eds. 2018. *Performing Architectures: Projects, Practices, Pedagogies*. London: Bloomsbury.
Fischer-Lichte, Erika. 1997. "Discovering the Spectator: Changes to the Paradigm of Theatre in the Twentieth Century." In *The Show and the Gaze of Theater: A European Perspective*, by Erika Fischer-Lichte, 41–60. Iowa: University of Iowa Press.
Fischer-Lichte, Erika. [2004] 2008. *The Transformative Power of Performance: A New Aesthetics*. Translated by Saskya Iris Jain. London: Routledge.
Fischer-Lichte, Erika, and Benjamin Wihstutz, eds. 2013. *Performance and the Politics of Space: Theatre and Topology*. London: Routledge.
Fortier, Mark. 2002. *Theory/Theatre: An Introduction*. Second edition. London: Routledge.
Foster, Hal. 1996. *The Return of the Real: The Avant-garde at the End of the Century*. Cambridge MA: MIT Press.
Foster, Susan Leigh. 2008. "'Where Are You Now?': Locating the Body in Contemporary Performance." In *Anatomy Live: Performance and the Operating Theatre*, edited by Maaike Bleeker, 169–79. Amsterdam: Amsterdam University Press.
Foucault, Michel. [1975] 1995. "Panopticism." In *Discipline & Punish: The Birth of a Prison*, translated by Alan Sheridan, 195–228. New York: Vintage Books.
Foucault, Michel, and Jay Miskowiec. 1986. "Of Other Spaces." *diacritics* 16 (1): 22–7.
Freshwater, Helen. 2009. *Theatre & Audiences*. Basingstoke: Palgrave Macmillan.
Frieze, James, ed. 2016. *Reframing Immersive Theatre: The Politics and Pragmatics of Participatory Performance*. Basingstoke: Palgrave Macmillan.
Fuchs, Elinor. 1996. *The Death of Character: Perspectives on Theatre after Modernism*. Bloomington: Indiana University Press.
Fuchs, Elinor, and Una Chaudhuri, eds. 2002. *Land/Scape/Theater*. Ann Arbor: The University of Michigan Press.
Fuggle, Sophie. 2008. "Discourses of Subversion: The Ethics and Aesthetics of Capoeira and Parkour." *Dance Research: The Journal of the Society for Dance Research* 26 (2): 204–22.
Gallagher, Kathleen, and Barry Freeman, eds. 2016. *In Defence of Theatre: Aesthetic Practices and Social Interventions*. Toronto: Toronto University Press.

Garcin-Marrou, Flore. 2011. "Gilles Deleuze, Félix Guattari and Theatre: Or, Philosophy and its 'Other'." *Trahir 2* (August). www.revuetrahir.net/2011-2/trahir-garcin-marrou-theatre.pdf.

Genette, Gérard. [1979] 1992. *The Architext: An Introduction*. Translated by Jane E. Lewin. Berkeley: University of California Press.

Genette, Gérard. [1982] 1997. *Palimpsests: Literature in the Second Degree*. Translated by Channa Newman and Claude Doubinsky. Lincoln: University of Nebraska Press.

Gergen, Kenneth J. 2003. "Self and Community in the New Floating Worlds." In *Mobile Democracy: Essays on Society, Self, and Politics*, edited by K. Nyiri, 103–14. Vienna: Passagen Verlag.

Goebbels, Heiner. 2007. "Was wir nicht sehen, zieht uns an: Vier thesen zum Call Cutta." In *Rimini Protokoll. Experten des Alltags: Das Theater von Rimini Protokoll*, edited by Miriam Dreysse and Florian Malzacher, 118–27. Berlin: Alexander Verlag.

Groot Nibbelink, Liesbeth. 2007. "Voor een schilderij hoef je niet te applaudisseren. In gesprek met Dries Verhoeven." *Dramaturgy Database*, Utrecht University, available through https://dramaturgydatabase.hum.uu.nl.

Groot Nibbelink, Liesbeth. 2008. "Performing Stories. Over het maakproces van Sporenonderzoek." *Dramaturgy Database*, Utrecht University, available through https://dramaturgydatabase.hum.uu.nl.

Groot Nibbelink, Liesbeth. 2009a. "Masseurs van de fantasie. Over Ontroerend Goed en het maakproces van The Smile Off Your Face." *Dramaturgy Database*, Utrecht University, available through https://dramaturgydatabase.hum.uu.nl.

Groot Nibbelink, Liesbeth. 2009b. "Staged Intimacy: Signa's The Ruby Town Oracle." *Dramaturgy Database*, Utrecht University, available through https://dramaturgydatabase.hum.uu.nl.

Groot Nibbelink, Liesbeth. 2012a. "Radical Intimacy: Ontroerend Goed meets The Emancipated Spectator." *Contemporary Theatre Review* 22 (3): 412–20.

Groot Nibbelink, Liesbeth. 2012b. "The Signa Store: Nomadic Manoeuvres in Ruby Town." *Performance Research: A Journal of the Performing Arts* 17 (3): 63–7.

Grosz, Elizabeth. 2001. *Architecture from the Outside: Essays on Virtual and Real Space*. Cambridge MA: MIT Press.

Groys, Boris. 2008. "A Genealogy of Participatory Art." In *The Art of Participation: 1950 to Now*, edited by Rudolf Frieling and Boris Groys, 18–31. New York/London: San Francisco Museum of Modern Art/Thames & Hudson.

Hannah, Dorita, and Omar Khan, eds. 2008. Themed Issue on Performance/Architecture. *JAE: Journal of Architectural Education* 61(4).

Hansen-Tangen, Torunn. 2006. "Mobile Phones Take to the Stage." *Ericsson*, website, October 3. www.rimini-protokoll.de/website/en/text/mobile-phones-take-to-the-stage. Accessed April 18, 2018.

Harmon, Katherine. 2004. *You are Here: Personal Geographies and Other Maps of the Imagination*. New York: Princeton Architectural Press.
Hays, Michael K., ed. 1996. *Hejduk's Chronotope*. New York: Princeton Architectural Press.
Hill, Leslie, and Helen Paris, eds. 2006. *Performance and Place*. Basingstoke: Palgrave Macmillan.
Hill, Leslie, and Helen Paris. 2014. *Performing Proximity: Curious Intimacies*. Basingstoke: Palgrave Macmillan.
Hopkins, D.J., and Kim Solga, eds. 2015. *Performance and the Global City*. Basingstoke: Palgrave Macmillan.
Howells, Adrian. 2012. "Foot Washing for the Sole." *Performance Research: A Journal of the Performing Arts* 17 (2): 128–31.
Huizinga, Johan. [1938] 1998. *Homo Ludens*. London: Routledge.
Jenkins, Henry. 2004. "Game Design as Narrative Architecture." In *First Person: New Media as Story, Performance, and Game*, edited by Noah Wardrip-Fruin and Pat Harrigan, 118–30. Cambridge MA: MIT Press.
Kaplan, Caren. 1996. *Questions of Travel: Postmodern Discourses of Displacement*. Durham/London: Duke University Press.
Kaplan, Caren. 2002. "Transporting the Subject: Technologies of Mobility and Location in an Era of Globalization." *PMLA* 177 (1): 32–42.
Kattenbelt, Chiel. 2008. "Intermediality in Theatre and Performance: Definitions, Perceptions and Medial Relationships." *Cultura, Lenguaje y Representación/ Culture, Language & Representation* 6 (La Intermedialidad/Intermediality): 19–29.
Kattenbelt, Chiel. 2010. "Intermediality in Performance and as a Mode of Performativity." In *Mapping Intermediality in Performance*, edited by Sarah Bay-Cheng et al., 29–37. Amsterdam: Amsterdam University Press.
Kennedy, Dennis. 2009. *The Spectator and the Spectacle: Audiences in Modernity and Postmodernity*. Cambridge: Cambridge University Press.
Kerkhoven, Marianne van. 1992. "De geschreven ruimte/The Written Space." *Theaterschrift* 2: 7–33.
Kerkhoven, Marianne van. [1999] 2002. "Van de kleine en de grote dramaturgie." In *Van het kijken en van het schrijven*, 197–203. Leuven: Van Halewyck.
Kershaw, Baz. 1999. *The Radical in Performance: Between Brecht and Baudrillard*. London: Routledge.
Kester, Grant H. 2004. *Conversation Pieces: Community and Communication in Modern Art*. Berkeley: University of California Press.
Kidder, Jeffrey L. 2012. "Parkour, The Affective Appropriation of Urban Space, and the Real/Virtual Dialectic." *City & Community* 11 (3): 229–53.
Kirby, Kathleen M. 1993. "Thinking through the Boundary: The Politics of Location, Subjects, and Space." *Boundary* 2: 173–89.
Kirsch, Sebastian. 2008. "SIGNA oder Der Sinn für die Unwirklichkeit. Die unheimlichen Welten von Signa Sørensen und Arthur Köstler." *Theater der Zeit* 5: 8–11.

Klaver, Elizabeth. 1995. "Spectatorial Theory in the Age of Media Culture." *New Theatre Quarterly* 11 (44): 309–21.

Klich, Rosemary. 2017. "Amplifying Sensory Spaces: The In- and Out-Puts of Headphone Theatre." *Contemporary Theatre Review* 27 (3): 366–78.

Knoespel, Kenneth. 2001. "Diagrams as Piloting Devices in the Philosophy of Gilles Deleuze." *Theorie, Littérature, Enseignement* 19 (Deleuze-chantier): 145–65. Saint-Denis: Presses Universitaires de Vincennes.

Kolarevic, Branco, and Ali Malkawi, eds. 2005. *Performative Architecture: Beyond Instrumentality*. New York: Spon Press.

Lavender, Andy. 2016. *Performance in the Twenty-First Century: Theatres of Engagement*. London and New York: Routledge.

Lefebvre, Henri. [1974] 1991. *The Production of Space*. Translated by Donald Nicholson-Smith. Oxford: Blackwell Publishing.

Lefebvre, Henri. 2004. *Rhythmanalysis: Space, Time and Everyday Life*. Translated by Stuart Elden and Gerald Moore, introduced by Stuart Elden. London: Continuum.

Lehmann, Hans-Thies. 1997. "From Logos to Landscape: Text in Contemporary Dramaturgy." *Performance Research: A Journal of the Performing Arts* 2 (1): 55–60.

Lehmann, Hans-Thies. 2006. *Postdramatic Theatre*. Translated and introduced by Karen Jürs-Munby. London: Routledge.

Lehmann, Hans-Thies. 2007. "Theatre after Theatre: Mirror, Mirror, Fourth Wall!" In *Na(ar) het theater/After Theatre?: Supplements to the International Conference on Postdramatic Theatre*, edited by Marijke Hoogenboom and Alexander Karschnia, 47–55. Amsterdam: Amsterdam School of the Arts.

Lepecki, André. 2006. *Exhausting Dance: Performance and the Politics of Movement*. New York and London: Routledge.

Levin, Laura. 2014. *Performing Ground: Space, Camouflage and the Art of Blending In*. Basingstoke: Palgrave Macmillan.

Lindt, Barbara van. 2008. "Call it Call Cutta in a Box." *Kunstenfestivaldesarts* Brussels. www.rimini-protokoll.de/website/en/text/call-it-call-cutta-in-a-box. Accessed April 18, 2018.

Lister, Martin, Jon Dovey, Seth Giddings, Iain Grant, and Kieran Kelly. 2009. *New Media: A Critical Introduction*. Second edition. London and New York: Routledge.

Machon, Josephine. 2013. *Immersive Theatres: Intimacy and Immediacy in Contemporary Performance*. Basingstoke: Palgrave Macmillan.

MacMillan, Joyce. 2008. "The Smile off Your Face." *The Scotsman*, August 17.

Manovich, Lev. 2001. *The Language of New Media*. Cambridge MA: MIT Press.

Margaroni, Maria, and Effie Yiannopoulou, eds. 2006. *Methaphoricity and the Politics of Mobility*. Amsterdam: Rodopi.

Marzec, Robert P. 2001. "The War Machine and Capitalism: Notes Towards a Nomadology of the Imperceptible." *Rhizomes* 3. www.rhizomes.net/issue3/marzec/UntitledFrameset-14.html.

Massey, Doreen. 1994. *Space, Place, and Gender*. Cambridge: Polity Press.

Massey, Doreen. 2005. *For Space*. London: Sage.
Massumi, Brian. 1992. *A User's Guide to Capitalism and Schizophrenia: Deviations from Deleuze and Guattari*. Cambridge MA: MIT Press.
Massumi, Brian. 2002. *Parables for the Virtual: Movement, Affect, Sensation*. Durham: Duke University Press.
Massumi, Brian. 2008. "The Thinking-Feeling of What Happens: A Semblance of a Conversation." *Inflexions* 1: How is Research-Creation? www.inflexions.org.
Matussek, Peter. 2001. "The Renaissance of the Theater of Memory." *Janus* 8: 4–8. www.peter-matussek.de/Pub/A_38.html.
McAuley, Gay. 1999. *Space in Performance: Making Meaning in the Theatre*. Ann Arbor: The University of Michigan Press.
McAuley, Gay, ed. 2006. *Unstable Ground: Performance and the Politics of Place*. Brussels: P.I.E. Peter Lang.
McDonough, Tom, ed. 2002. *Guy Debord and the Situationist International: Texts and Documents*. Cambridge MA: MIT Press.
McKinney, Joslin, and Philip Butterworth. 2009. *The Cambridge Introduction to Scenography*. Cambridge: Cambridge University Press.
McKinney, Joslin, and Scott Palmer, eds. 2017. *Scenography Expanded: An Introduction to Contemporary Performance Design*. London: Bloomsbury.
Michalzik, Peter. 2006. "On Rimini Protokoll." Translated by Martin Pearce. *Website Goethe Institut*. www.goethe.de/kue/the/pur/rim/enindex.htm. Accessed April 18, 2018.
Migayrou, Frédéric, ed. 2014. *Bernard Tschumi. Architecture: Concept & Notation*. Paris: Éditions du Centre Pompidou.
Monbiot, George. 2017. *Out of the Wreckage: A New Politics for an Age of Crisis*. London: Verso.
Monmonier, Mark. 1995. *Drawing the Line: Tales of Maps and Cartocontroversy*. New York: Henry Holt.
Montola, Markus. 2007. "Tangible Pleasures of Pervasive Role-Playing." In *Situated Play: Proceedings of the Third International Conference of DiGRA*, edited by Akira Baba, 178–85. www.digra.org.
Montola, Markus. 2012. *On the Edge of the Magic Circle: Understanding Pervasive Games and Role-Playing*. PhD Dissertation, Tampere University.
Montola, Markus, and Jaakko Stenros. 2004. *Beyond Role and Play: Tools, Toys and Theory for Harnessing the Imagination*. Helsinki: Ropecon ry.
Nesbitt, Kate, ed. 1996. *Theorizing a New Agenda for Architecture: An Anthology of Architectural Theory 1965–1995*. New York: Princeton Architectural Press.
Oddey, Alison. 2007. *Re-Framing the Theatrical: Interdisciplinary Landscapes for Performance*. Basingstoke: Palgrave MacMillan.
Oddey, Alison, and Christine White, eds. 2009. *Modes of Spectating*. Bristol: intellect.
O'Sullivan, Simon. 2006. *Art Encounters Deleuze and Guattari: Thought Beyond Representation*. Basingstoke: Palgrave Macmillan.

Ontroerend Goed. 2014. *All Work and No Plays: Blueprints for Nine Theatre Performances by Ontroerend Goed*. London: Oberon Books.
Ortuzar, Jimena. 2009. "Parkour or l'art du déplacement: A Kinetic Urban Utopia." *TDR/The Drama Review* 53 (3): 54–66.
Patton, Paul, ed. 1996. *Deleuze: A Critical Reader*. Oxford: Blackwell Publishers.
Patton, Paul. 2010. "Mobile Concepts, Metaphor, and the Problem of Referentiality." In *Deleuzian Concepts: Philosophy, Colonization, Politics*, 19–40. Stanford: Stanford University Press.
Parr, Adrian, ed. 2010. *The Deleuze Dictionary*. Revised edition. Edinburgh: Edinburgh University Press.
Pavis, Patrice. 2003. *Analyzing Performance: Theater, Dance, and Film*. Translated by David Williams. Ann Arbor: The University of Michigan Press.
Pearson, Mike, and Michael Shanks. 2001. *Theatre/Archeology*. London: Routledge.
Pinder, David. 1996. "Subverting Cartography: The Situationists and Maps of the City." *Environment and Planning* A: 405–27.
Pine, Joseph B., and James H. Gilmore. 1999. *The Experience Economy: Work is Theatre & Every Business a Stage*. Boston: Harvard Business School Press.
Pine, Joseph B., and James H. Gilmore. 2007. *Authenticity: What Consumers Really Want*. Boston: Harvard Business School Press.
Pine, Joseph B., and James H. Gilmore. 2011. *The Experience Economy: Work is Theatre & Every Business a Stage*. Second revised edition. Boston: Harvard Business School Press.
Raessens, Joost. 2005. "Computer Games as Participatory Media Culture." In *Handbook of Computer Game Studies*, edited by Joost Raessens and Jeffrey Goldstein, 373–88. Cambridge MA: MIT Press.
Raessens, Joost. 2010. *Homo Ludens 2.0. The Ludic Turn in Media Theory*. Inaugural lecture, Utrecht University.
Rancière, Jacques. [2000] 2004. *The Politics of Aesthetics*. Translated by Gabriel Rockhill. London: Continuum.
Rancière, Jacques. 2009. *The Emancipated Spectator*. London: Verso.
Read, Alan, ed. 2000. *Architecturally Speaking: Practices of Art, Architecture and the Everyday*. London: Routledge.
Read, Alan. 2008. *Theatre, Intimacy and Engagement: The Last Human Venue*. Basingstoke: Palgrave Macmillan.
Ridout, Nicolas. 2006. *Stage Fright, Animals and Other Theatrical Problems*. Cambridge: Cambridge University Press.
Romein, Ed, Marc Schuilenburg, and Sjoerd van Tuinen, eds. 2009. *Deleuze Compendium*. Amsterdam: Boom.
Salen, Katie, and Eric Zimmerman. 2004. *Rules of Play: Game Design Fundamentals*. Cambridge MA: MIT Press.
Salter, Chris. 2010. *Entangled: Technology and the Transformation of Performance*. Cambridge MA: MIT Press.

Smeyers, Bram. 2004. "Theater uit de Hoge Hoed. Over Exsimplicity van Ontroerend Goed." *Rekto:Verso* 6: 36–41.

Soja, Edward. 1996. *Thirdspace: Journeys to Los Angeles and Other Real-and-Imagined Places*. Oxford: Blackwell Publishers.

Spivak, Gayatri Chakravorty. [1988] 1993. "Can the Subaltern Speak?" In *Colonial Discourse and Postcolonial Theatre: A Reader*, edited by Patrick Williams and Laura Chrisman, 66–111. New York: Columbia University Press.

Spurr, Samantha. 2007. *Performative Architecture: Design Strategies for Living Bodies*. PhD Thesis, School of English, Media and Performance Arts, University of New South Wales.

Spuybroek, Lars. 2011. *The Sympathy of Things: Ruskin and the Ecology of Design*. Rotterdam: Spuybroek/V2_Publishing.

States, Bert O. 1992. "The Phenomenological Attitude." In *Critical Theory and Performance*, edited by Janelle G. Reinelt and Joseph G. Roach, 369–79. Ann Arbor: The University of Michigan Press.

Sutton-Smith, Brian. [1997] 2001. *The Ambiguity of Play*. Cambridge MA: Harvard University Press.

Thrift, Nigel. 2008. *Non-Representational Theory: Space, Politics, Affect*. London: Routledge.

Tompkins, Joanne. 2014. *Theatre's Heterotopias: Performance and the Cultural Politics of Space*. Basingstoke: Palgrave Macmillan.

Tschumi, Bernard. 1996. *Architecture and Disjunction*. Cambridge MA: MIT Press.

Tuinen, Sjoerd van, and Niamh McDonell, eds. 2010. *Deleuze and The Fold: A Critical Reader*. Basingstoke: Palgrave Macmillan.

Turner, Cathy. 2015. *Dramaturgy and Architecture: Theatre, Utopia and the Built Environment*. Basingstoke: Palgrave Macmillan.

Turner, Cathy, and Synne K. Behrndt. 2008. *Dramaturgy and Performance*. Basingstoke: Palgrave MacMillan.

Tydeman, William. 1978. *The Theatre in the Middle Ages: Western European Stage Conditions*. Cambridge: Cambridge University Press.

Urry, John. 2007. *Mobilities*. Cambridge: Polity Press.

Verhoeff, Nanna. 2012. *Mobile Screens: The Visual Regime of Navigation*. Amsterdam: Amsterdam University Press.

Verstraete, Pieter. 2003. "Ontvreemde lichamen." *Urbanmag*. September 18.

Vidler, Anthony. 1992. *The Architectural Uncanny: Essays in the Modern Unhomely*. Cambridge MA: MIT Press.

Vidler, Anthony. 2000. "Diagrams of Diagrams: Architectural Abstraction and Modern Representation." *Representations* 72 (Autumn): 1–20.

Vries, Imar de. 2012. *Tantalisingly Close: An Archaeology of Communication Desires in Discourses of Mobile Wireless Media*. Amsterdam: Amsterdam University Press.

Walsh, Fintan. 2014. "Touching, Flirting, Whispering: Performing Intimacy in Public." *TDR: The Drama Review* 58 (4): 56–67.
White, Gareth. 2012. "On Immersive Theatre." *Theatre Research International* 37 (3): 221–35.
White, Gareth. 2013. *Audience Participation in Theatre: Aesthetics of the Invitation*. Basingstoke: Palgrave Macmillan.
Whybrow, Nicolas, ed. 2010. *Performance and the Contemporary City: An Interdisicplinary Reader*. Basingstoke: Palgrave Macmillan.
Wigley, Mark. 1998. *Constant's New Babylon: The Hyper-Architecture of Desire*. Rotterdam: Witte de With/010 Publishers.
Wilkie, Fiona. 2015a. *Performance, Transport and Mobility: Making Passage*. Basingstoke: Palgrave Macmillan.
Wilkie, Fiona. 2015b. "Performance and the Spatial Turn (review)." *Theatre Journal* 67 (4): 735–45.
Wood, Denis. 1992. *The Power of Maps*. London: Routledge/Guilford Press.

Index

absorption 51–3, 90, 161
aesthetic orientation 39–40, 134
affective modulations 18, 134, 139,
    148, 154, 157, 174
affirmativity 20–1, 108, 173, 184
Appadurai, Arjun 63, 71, 72, 76, 184
architecture 1, 3, 5, 9, 18–20, 27–8,
    95–8, 103, 112, 117, 127, 140, 147,
    157, 159, 161, 165, 175, 179, 180–1
  and dramaturgy 21–2, 55, 177
  narrative architecture 148–50, 158
  performative architecture 22, 24,
    70, 116, 144, 150–4, 158, 161,
    164, 173
architextures 27, 144, 147–8, 150,
    152–4, 161, 164–5, 173–4, 190
assemblage 11, 14, 23–4, 31, 51, 56,
    57, 70, 76, 87, 101, 103, 116, 134,
    144, 153, 164, 174, 175
  affirmative assemblage 21
  and dramaturgy 112, 186
attitude. *See* nomadic, attitude
audience address 23
auditorium 1, 8, 12, 33, 35, 37, 39–41,
    44–5, 51, 118–19, 121, 133, 141,
    169, 171, 183

Barthes, Roland 25, 36, 91, 144,
    153–5, 184
becoming 14, 16, 32–3, 92, 96, 98–9,
    108, 123–4, 126, 128, 151
  becoming-performer 57–8, 160,
    172–3
  becoming-space 57, 83–4, 103,
    121, 129, 154, 172–3
  becoming-spectator 57–8, 109,
    127, 160, 172
  becoming-stories 143, 148, 150
Bishop, Claire 8–9, 38, 79–80, 82,
    132, 169, 172, 176, 183, 187

Blast Theory 2, 75–6, 95, 174, 183
Bleeker, Maaike 15, 17, 23, 36, 38,
    48, 50–2, 82, 85, 90, 104, 107,
    132, 134–6, 171, 191
Bogost, Ian 148, 158–9, 162, 164,
    177, 183, 191
Borges, Jorge Luis 138, 145–6, 148,
    161, 162–3, 171, 182, 190
Bourriaud, Nicolas 8, 54, 176
Braidotti, Rosi 107, 108, 164, 174,
    178, 184

Call Cutta 1–2, 6, 11, 26, 59–70,
    72–3, 75, 77–83, 86, 99, 105, 115,
    121, 122, 130–1, 174, 177, 188
  Call Cutta in a Box 26, 186
capitalism 8, 28, 60, 63, 69, 78–9,
    118, 130, 156, 163, 167–8, 182
cartography 3, 18–19, 24, 27, 84, 87,
    90–1, 95–8, 102, 108, 116, 144–5,
    149, 165, 169, 174–5, 182
  performative cartography 26,
    87–9, 92, 99, 104, 106–7, 109,
    112–13, 173, 188
cathedrals (Gothic) 20, 54, 61, 75,
    105, 180
Certeau, Michel de 71, 73, 90, 91,
    105, 106, 149, 188
chess versus Go 20, 44–5, 176
city. *See* urban space
composition 8–9, 70, 108, 112,
    116–17, 131, 134, 140, 143, 172
  and dramaturgy 21–2, 24–5, 177
  entering into composition 33, 57,
    83, 103, 172
  planes of composition 22–3
concept 3–4, 11, 13, 15–21, 24–8, 32,
    36, 47, 74–5, 83, 120, 124, 126,
    140, 142, 150, 165, 167–8, 172,
    175, 178–81, 185

Conley, Tom 18, 75, 117, 127, 140, 184, 189
connectivity 5–6, 23, 32, 43, 54, 67, 76, 83, 86, 110, 137–9, 169–70, 174, 187
constellation (threefold, flexible) 3, 10, 18, 32, 44–5, 169, 173, 179
context 4, 26, 152, 155, 174, 189
    artistic context 21, 23–4, 79, 176, 177
    societal context 5, 23, 56, 60, 67, 177
continuous variation 11–12, 18, 32, 44, 49–50, 56, 150
co-presence 5, 56, 67, 169
Corner, James 88–9, 91, 95–6, 147
cultural transcoding 6, 78

deixis (deictic) 48, 85, 110
delegated performance 79, 82, 132
Deleuze, Gilles 3, 10–16, 19–20, 23, 26–7, 31–3, 35, 44–7, 50, 54–5, 57, 60–1, 75, 81, 87–9, 91, 95, 97, 102, 108, 116–19, 123–4, 126–8, 130, 132, 136–7, 140, 164, 169, 173–7, 179–85, 187–90, 192
dérive 78–9, 95
deterritorialization 2, 8–9, 11–12, 14, 17–18, 25, 27, 31–3, 35, 41, 45, 51, 56, 59, 66–7, 87, 115, 117, 121, 136, 140, 142–3, 165, 168, 170, 180
détournement 78–9
diagram 27, 116–17, 124–8, 130–1, 134, 139–40, 144, 147, 151–4, 164, 173
diffractive reading 113, 173–4, 179–80
displacement 10–11, 17, 25, 41, 46–7, 51, 59, 61–2, 65, 67, 70, 78–9, 81–3, 86, 98, 100–1, 104, 109
distance 5–6, 23, 38, 40, 43, 59, 62, 63, 67–8, 70, 94, 99, 100, 102, 105, 121, 125–6, 133–4, 136, 139, 142, 159, 172, 188
distribution of the sensible 15, 75–6, 132–4, 136–7

DIY 8, 77
dramatic theatre 9, 50, 52, 82, 90, 112, 142, 150, 161
dramaturgy
    and assemblage 112, 186
    and composition 21–2, 24–5, 177
    emergent 18, 23, 55–6, 116, 118, 138
    procedural 177–8
    situational 21, 38
    spatial 4, 21–6

ecology 137, 170
Elden, Stuart 11, 18, 60, 68, 69, 74, 184, 187
embodiment 7, 19, 26–7, 29, 55, 58, 60–1, 70, 72, 76, 81–4, 86, 92, 99, 104–6, 108–9, 112, 128, 134, 163–4, 170, 172, 174–5, 177–8, 182
encounter 25, 31–4, 48–51, 53–7
engagement 5, 7–8, 27, 38, 72, 83, 92, 96–8, 101–2, 110, 116, 120, 135–6, 138, 144, 170–1, 174, 177
environmental storytelling 5, 148–9, 153
event/situation 9, 121–3, 171
evocative space 148, 153, 155

fictionality 27, 142
flâneur 65–6, 186
fold 117, 119, 121–2, 127–8, 131, 134–5, 138–40, 145, 161–2, 171–2, 189
Foster, Susan 63–4, 69, 72–3, 79–82, 105–6, 188
frame 26, 42, 44, 50, 107, 144, 152–3, 155, 159, 163, 170, 173, 181, 192
    theatrical frame 39, 65

games 2–3, 5–7, 27, 29, 32, 65–7, 75–7, 95–6, 116, 126, 146, 148–50, 156, 158, 161–3, 170, 173, 177, 179, 185, 190–2

Index

Go and chess 20, 44–5, 176
 rhizomatic gameboard 143–4,
 147, 153, 157, 159–60, 164, 169
geomedia 91, 99, 101, 106, 177
geophilosophy 117, 175
geotagging 66, 100
globalization 4, 26, 59–61, 67–9, 83,
 170
Go 44–5, 147, 185
 versus chess 20, 44–5, 176
Goebbels, Heiner 1, 63, 65, 69, 72–3,
 78, 81–2, 99, 121, 186
Grosz, Elisabeth 97–8, 175, 188
Guattari, Félix 3, 10–16, 19–20,
 23, 32–3, 35, 44–7, 54–5, 57,
 60–1, 75, 87–8, 91, 95, 102, 116,
 118, 124, 126, 164, 169, 174–6,
 179–80, 183, 185, 188–90

Hejduk, John 152–5, 157, 175, 191
Hertzian space 1, 67, 70, 183
Het Sprookjesbordeel 129–33, 172
Hurtzig, Hannah
 Blackmarket, The 167, 170–1, 175,
 181, 192

installations 62, 164
 installation art 23, 32, 37–8, 41,
 161
 performance installations 2, 27,
 38, 142, 145, 153, 171, 183
interiority 54, 66, 108, 115, 117, 119,
 122–3, 127, 139, 171
intimacy 56, 62, 64, 102, 118–19, 126,
 135, 138, 170, 184, 189

Jenkins, Henry 147, 148, 149–50,
 153, 158, 191

Kaplan, Caren 46, 107, 108
Kirby, Kathleen 83–4, 107–9
Knoespel, Kenneth 116, 118, 126–7,
 140
Köstler, Arthur 142, 143, 156, 157,
 190

Köstler, Signa 142–3, 148, 156–7,
 159, 162, 190–1

LARP (Live-Action Role Playing)
 146–7, 161, 190
layers (layering) 5, 22, 24, 26, 64, 66,
 85–6, 95–7, 100–2, 108–9, 112, 131,
 143–4, 147–8, 157, 164, 175, 188
Lefebvre, Henri 26, 35, 59–61, 68–9,
 71, 73–6, 81, 104, 149, 165, 173–4,
 187, 188
Leibniz, Gottfried Wilhelm 117,
 127–8, 136, 189
limits 27–8, 140, 142, 152, 160–1,
 165, 167–8, 181–2, 189
lived space 18, 21, 26, 35, 59–61,
 68–71, 74–6, 80–3, 88, 92, 138,
 144–5, 148, 154, 157, 160–3, 165,
 173–4, 182
 versus conceived and perceived
 space 60, 74
locality 26, 60, 63, 71–3, 77, 81, 83,
 146, 169–70
logic of organization 176–7, 179

magic circle 66, 162, 185 n.6,
 192 n.17
mapping 66, 87–9, 91–2, 95–7,
 106–8, 110, 128, 138, 140
maps 26, 60, 73, 78–9, 90–2, 94, 98–9,
 102–5, 109, 112, 116, 145–6, 149,
 161–2, 171, 182, 188
 urban maps 88–9, 147
Massumi, Brian 20, 104, 130–2, 134,
 137, 139, 167–8, 182, 184, 190
material thinking 20, 28, 168, 178, 180
meta-philosophy 75, 83
metaphor 25, 46–7, 179, 185, 191
mobile turn 4, 12
mobilities paradigm 5, 29
mobility 2–7, 9, 11–12, 15, 17,
 21, 24–5, 28–9, 46, 62, 67, 73,
 86–7, 95, 101, 108, 110, 112, 115,
 168–70, 183
monads 117, 128, 189

movement 2–5, 9, 10, 12–15, 17, 22–4, 28–9
movement vision 83, 104, 107

navigation 1, 3, 18, 21, 23, 55, 57, 66–7, 72, 79, 83, 97–9, 101, 103, 107, 109, 112, 141, 144, 146, 169, 188
navigational space 26, 70, 86, 96, 100
new materialism 178–9, 184
nomadic
  attitude 167
  nomadology 3–4, 10–11, 13, 15, 44, 46, 54, 75, 117, 165, 174, 181, 184, 190
  versus the sedentary 4, 13, 35, 44
  versus the State 14
nomadic theatre (concept) 3–4, 11–13, 15, 17, 19, 21, 24–8, 32, 35, 75, 83, 140, 142, 165, 168, 172, 175, 178, 180, 185
nomadology 3–4, 10–11, 13, 15, 44, 46, 54, 75, 117, 165, 174, 181, 184, 190
nomad science 55
No Man's Land 6, 25, 31–58, 61, 64, 67, 69–70, 80, 121–2, 174, 184–5

Ontroerend Goed 2, 6, 7, 27, 38, 95, 113, 115, 118, 120, 125, 139, 188
operations 18, 27, 50, 71–2, 74, 96, 105–6, 131, 151
  local operations 19, 26, 60, 70, 84, 89, 99, 112, 170, 173–4, 177, 188
  theatre of operations 89, 91, 95
outsourcing 63, 173
  outsourced labor 26, 59, 77, 80, 187
  outsourced performance 59, 77, 79, 81, 177

Panopticon 117, 127–30, 132, 139
parallax 61–2, 65–6, 69–70, 73, 79–83, 138, 172, 175

parkour 61–2, 64, 69–70, 72, 83, 98, 104, 137
Patton, Paul 13, 35, 46–7
performance installations 2, 27, 38, 142, 145, 153, 171, 183
performative architecture 22, 24, 70, 116, 144, 150–4, 158, 161, 164, 173
performativity 16, 19–20, 181
personal customization 6, 8, 77–8, 81
pervasive games 65–7, 75
phantasmagoria 66, 163, 171
planes of composition 22–3. *See also* dramaturgy
play 18, 20, 27–9, 120, 123, 125, 144–6, 152–3, 158–60, 162–4, 167, 170–2, 182, 187, 190

politics 4–5, 7, 14–15, 23–4, 34, 37, 39, 43, 46, 49–50, 53–6, 60, 64, 68, 70, 72, 74, 81, 88, 91, 113, 141, 145–6, 160, 169–70, 173, 177, 179, 184, 187
  of location 26, 83, 107–9, 112
  of mobility 28–9
  of perception 14–15, 137
postdramatic theatre 9–10, 21–3, 50, 112, 122, 134, 142, 148–9, 161, 164, 170, 183, 186
procedural dramaturgy 177–8
procedural rhetoric 148, 158–60, 162–3, 165, 177
procedural space 144, 173, 176
procedures 78, 140, 158–9, 162, 177
proximity 23, 27, 57, 62, 100, 102–3, 115, 117–20, 123, 140, 165, 188
psychogeography 79, 141, 154
Punchdrunk 28, 150, 191

Rancière, Jacques 7–9, 15, 75–6, 132–4, 138, 171, 182, 189–90
Read, Alan 23, 61, 65, 80–3, 121, 138, 169, 175, 187

representation 9–10, 25–7, 32, 47, 50–2, 73, 75–7, 79–83, 87, 89–92, 99, 105–7, 144–5, 151, 158–9, 162, 179, 182–3, 188
  space of representation 61, 74, 104, 168, 173–4, 187
  versus simulacrum 162
reterritorialization 11–13, 17–18, 24–5, 32–3, 35, 44, 56, 64–7, 80, 99, 101, 115, 122, 136, 140, 143, 168–70, 173, 177, 181
rhizome 32, 87–8, 95, 98, 103, 147–8, 179
  rhizomatic gameboard 143–4, 147, 153, 159–60, 164, 169
rhythmanalysis 34
Rider Spoke 75–7, 83, 95, 174
Rimini Protokoll 1–2, 7, 12, 26, 38, 55, 59, 61, 63–4, 73, 77, 79–82, 171, 174, 177, 186, 187
Ruby Town Oracle, The 27, 45, 66, 95, 131, 140–50, 152–64, 177, 190–1

scenography 18, 40, 65, 115, 121, 140, 143–4, 147, 150, 161, 175
secret theatre 65–6, 171
sensorium 27, 115, 121, 129, 136–7, 174, 189
service
  service economy 131
  theatre service 80
Signa 2, 27, 45, 66, 95, 131, 140–8, 150, 154, 156–7, 160–2, 164, 174, 177
situation
  constructed situations 21, 79, 162, 184, 189
  event/situation 9, 121–3, 171
  situational dramaturgy 21, 38
  situationality 6, 62
  Situationists 78, 95, 106, 184, 189
Smile Off Your Face, The 6, 27, 77, 95, 113, 115–40, 171, 174, 188–9
smooth space 25, 45–7, 56–7, 97, 102–3, 122, 168–9, 185, 189

smooth stage 33, 35, 37, 45, 83, 86, 122, 147
  versus striated space 35, 40, 44–5, 169, 177, 185
Soja, Edward 60, 69, 74–5, 81, 162, 174, 187, 190
space
  acoustic space 65, 100–1, 171, 186
  conceived space 60, 74
  lived space 18, 21, 26, 35, 59–61, 68–71, 74–6, 80–3, 88, 92, 138, 144–5, 148, 154, 157, 160–3, 165, 173–4, 182
  navigational space 26, 70, 86, 96, 100
  perceived space 60, 74
  smooth space 25, 45–7, 56–7, 97, 102–3, 122, 168–9, 185, 189
  space and place 24, 60, 70–1, 95, 102, 109, 170
  striated space 35, 40, 44–5, 169, 177, 185
  urban space 11, 32, 35, 43–5, 59, 65–6, 69, 83, 86, 101, 168
  virtual space 4, 26, 66, 71, 88, 94, 96–9, 112, 116, 124, 131, 143, 160, 165, 169, 172, 188
spatial thinking 69, 174
spatial turn 18, 186
spectatorship 2, 8, 12, 18, 23, 26–7, 32, 36–7, 41, 43, 47, 49, 51, 53, 56–7, 84, 86, 112, 115, 119–20, 128–9, 134–6, 140, 163, 170, 172
stage 1–3, 6–7, 9, 11–12, 25–7, 32–3, 35–45, 51–2, 56–7, 59, 64–7, 80, 86, 95, 120–3, 133–4, 136, 140–1, 147, 149, 168–71, 183, 185
staging 9–12, 18, 22, 24–7, 31, 39–40, 51–2, 56, 59, 65, 80, 82–3, 87–9, 95, 99, 112–13, 116, 130, 156, 162–3, 169, 175–6
Store (Matsune and Subal) 167–9, 172, 192
striated space 35, 40, 44–5, 169, 177, 185

structure(s) of feeling 71, 72, 75, 82
subjectivity 8, 17, 26, 38, 52, 56, 80, 82, 85, 95, 103, 106–10, 112–13, 116, 121–3, 127–8, 137, 140, 163, 171
  nomadic subjectivity 108
synchronicity 5–6, 23, 35, 56, 67, 169, 185

territory 2–3, 8–9, 11–14, 17–18, 24–7, 31–3, 35, 41, 44–5, 51, 56, 59, 64–7, 74, 80, 86, 88–9, 91, 99, 101, 105, 108, 115, 117, 121–2, 136, 140, 142–3, 165, 168–70, 173, 177, 180–1, 185
texture 22, 139, 143–4, 147–8, 150, 154–5, 173
theatrical cubism 12, 41
theatrical frame 39, 65
  and parallax 61–2, 65–6, 69–70, 73, 79–83, 138, 172, 175
theatricality 51–3, 82, 131
thinking-feeling 137, 190

thinking through practice 3, 7, 15, 20, 178–80
thirdspace 69, 74
tonalities of sensation 18, 27, 84, 86, 117–18, 134–5, 140
Trail Tracking 85–113, 174, 177
Tschumi, Bernard 22, 70, 95, 103–4, 144, 151–5, 158–9, 161, 165, 174, 181

unitary urbanism 79, 187
urban space 11, 32, 35, 43–5, 59, 65–6, 69, 83, 86, 101, 168

Verhoeff, Nanna 5, 66, 67, 85–7, 91, 96, 99–101, 105–7, 177, 183, 188, 191
Verhoeven, Dries 2, 6–7, 25–6, 31, 36, 38, 41, 53–4, 61, 86, 93–5, 97, 99, 102–3, 110–12, 174, 177, 185, 187–8
virtuality 4, 26, 66, 71, 88, 96–9, 112, 116, 124, 131, 143, 160, 165, 169, 172, 188

www.ingramcontent.com/pod-product-compliance
Lightning Source LLC
Chambersburg PA
CBHW070316230426
43663CB00011B/2156